YOUR CHILD
IN THE BALANCE

A Norton Professional Book

YOUR CHILD IN THE BALANCE

Solving the Psychiatric Medicine Dilemma

REVISED EDITION

Kevin T. Kalikow, MD

W. W. Norton & Company

New York • London

This book is intended to inform and educate, and it should not be relied upon as an alternative to, or replacement for, appropriate personal medical care. The author and publisher urge readers to consult their own physicians and other health care professionals. Several specific medication names mentioned in this book are fictional and are used by the author for narrative purposes only. Brand names are used only as examples of various kinds of medications and other products and are not intended as endorsements. Patient identities have been fictionalized or disguised, and names and other identifying characteristics have been changed.

Many of the designations used by manufacturers and sellers to distinguish their products are claimed as trademarks. Where those designations appear in this book and the author was aware of a trademark claim, those designations have been printed with initial capital letter.

The author and publisher would like to thank the American Psychiatric Association for permission to use the DSM ADD criteria on pages 40–41.

Copyright © 2012, 2006 by Kevin T. Kalikow, MD

Previous edition published under the title as YOUR CHILD IN THE BALANCE:
An Insider's Guide for Parents to the Psychiatric Medicine Dilemma

For information about permission to reproduce selections from this book, write to
Permissions, W. W. Norton & Company, Inc., 500 Fifth Avenue, New York, NY 10110

For information about special discounts for bulk purchases, please contact
W. W. Norton Special Sales at specialsales@wwnorton.com or 800-233-4830

Manufacturing by Quad Graphics, Fairfield
Book design by Carole Desnoes
Production manager: Leeann Graham

Library of Congress Cataloging-in-Publication Data

Kalikow, Kevin T.
 Your child in the balance : solving the psychiatric
medicine dilemma / Kevin T. Kalikow. — 2nd ed.
     p. cm. — (A Norton professional book)
 Includes bibliographical references and index.
 ISBN 978-0-393-70660-4 (pbk.)
 1. Pediatric psychopharmacology—Popular works. I. Title.
 RJ504.7.K35 2012
 616.8918083—dc23
                                            2011035899

ISBN: 978-0-393-70660-4 (pbk.)

W. W. Norton & Company, Inc., 500 Fifth Avenue, New York, N.Y. 10110
www.wwnorton.com

W. W. Norton & Company Ltd., Castle House, 75/76 Wells Street, London W1T 3QT

1 2 3 4 5 6 7 8 9 0

To Adrian,
whose smile brightens every day

CONTENTS

||||||||||||||||||||||||||||||||||||||||||||||||||||||||||||||||||||||||

ACKNOWLEDGMENTS

|||||||||||||||||||||||||||||||||||||||||||||||||||||||||||||||||||||||||

The mental health of children and adolescents has been recognized only by recent generations and has evolved into a science only by our own. I am deeply grateful to the many clinicians who devote their energies to helping children live fuller, happier lives and to the researchers who do the painstaking work required to make the art of diagnosis and treatment into a science.

I am also indebted to my agent, Danny Baror, for taking this book off the computer screen and into the real world of publishing, and to the team at CDS, including Gilbert Perlman, David Wilk, and Hope Matthiessen who helped with the first edition of this book. Erica Lawrence at Perscus Books and Beth Wright at Trio Bookworks were also invaluable editors of the first edition.

I am ever grateful to those at W. W. Norton who saw the continuing need to communicate the message of Your Child in the Balance and who made the current edition possible. These include Deborah Malmud, Vani Kannan, and Casey Ruble. I am also grateful to Four Winds Hospital for originally asking me to make a presentation on the topic, which resulted in this book.

I further thank the following friends and colleagues for their ideas, enthusiasm, and invaluable comments: Warren Shimmerlik, Ron Emerson, MD, Howard Goldfrach, Vicki Stein Prusnofsky, LCSW, Les Prusnofsky, MD, David Kellogg, Sandra Kellogg, LCSW, Marilyn Emerson, MSW, Sel Shimmerlik, Brian Shimmerlik, Cheryl Goldfrach, Michael Vartabedian, Abe Rychik, Susan Zangler, Mark Banschick, MD, Elisabeth Guthrie, MD, and Bob Seaver, MD, who for years has graciously read and commented on everything I've let him see.

I also thank all my family members, who have been helpful in countless ways—in particular David Beard and Gail Friedman for their comments and encouragement; my sister, Jamie, for her photographic expertise; and my great uncle, the late Yudy Finkelstein, for his unique role in making this book possible. I'm certain he is somewhere in the Great Beyond ordering cartons of books and proudly distributing them to everyone he meets.

I thank my parents, Sylvia and Charles, for giving me the determination to tackle the daunting task of writing a book and the confidence to present this topic in a unique manner.

I am ever thankful to my children, Lauren, Jeff, and Adam, for enduring infinite conversations about medicine in modern life and for their invaluable comments and insights. They have finally convinced me by example that effective criticism does not have to be long-winded.

I especially thank my wife, Adrian, who began editing my writing many years ago when we took freshman English and has been by my side with love and encouragement ever since.

Last, I thank my patients and their parents, who have allowed me to listen to and help them with their deepest and most personal concerns. I hope that, through this book, their experiences help others solve the dilemma of psychiatric medicine.

You're worried about Melissa. She seems sad. She wanders around the house a little lost. The phone doesn't ring for her. She doesn't want to vacation at the beach, and she seems most content alone in her room with the door closed. She was always easily distracted, but now schoolwork just isn't getting done. Her report card is full of "Not working to potential." She's not invited to parties and complains that the other girls in school hate her.

On Sunday night you find her crying in her bedroom. She says she's not going to school tomorrow morning. She says that even Becky, her oldest friend, left her to hang out with the cool kids. You find yourself cursing Becky under your breath. How could she do this to Melissa? Then you remember that you've always liked Becky because she seemed so sensitive, the one girl Melissa could rely on. Maybe it's Melissa.

You're worried about Melissa, and you don't know what to do. Your child is in pain. You need to do something. But what?

PREFACE

||||||||||||||||||||||||||||||||||||||||||||||||||||||||||||||||

Not long ago, researchers reported in the *Journal of the American Medical Association* what was described as an alarming increase in the use of psychiatric medicines to treat preschoolers (Zito, Safer, dosReis, Gardner, Boles, & Lynch, 2000). The research was reported widely by the news media. A local psychiatric hospital, inundated by people's phone calls with questions about the overuse of psychiatric medicines in children, invited me to address the topic in a speech to the public. I hesitated at first. This sounded like an emotionally provocative topic that, if presented scientifically, would end up boring the pants off of almost any audience. Numbers, charts, percentages. I didn't think that people revved up by an inflammatory newspaper report would have the patience for the dull details behind the headline. People would simply line up on one side or the other.

Against my instinct but smelling the challenge, I accepted the invitation. I decided to frame the question of the overuse of psychiatric medicines within the broader question of whether medicines in general are overused or underused in society today. Are pain medicines overused? How do we decide if any medicine is overprescribed?

This is a fascinating philosophical question, the kind of question you could debate for hours in your favorite coffeehouse. It is also a question that begs for deeper attention and understanding. The simple answer is that medicines are overprescribed if more prescriptions are written than should be. So which prescriptions should be written? Put another way, when should we use medicine to change our bodies? Any answer to that question is laden with value judgments that will surely make the fur fly.

But parents are searching for practical answers, not philosophical quagmires, and therefore need to understand how doctors make decisions. Doctors have always relied on the risk-benefit ratio. If the benefits outweigh the risks, the medicine is worth prescribing. We must establish that psychiatric medicines have benefit, and we must learn how to evaluate risks. If you are looking for proof that medicines have benefits and therefore should be used, you will find it in this book. And if you are looking for proof that medicines have side effects and therefore should not be used, you will also find that in this book. The art of prescribing medicine is in learning how to weigh benefits and side effects against each other.

The dramatic headline asking whether psychiatric medicines are overprescribed to children leaves parents afraid of falling victim to the simple answer, "Yes, they are." For parents, this is a provocative question. It is also the wrong question.

The correct question asks, "Is medicine the best choice of treatment for *my* child? And if so, how should it be used with all due care?" This is what parents want to know. This is what parents need to know.

For the longest time, I struggled mightily to decide if this was a philosophical book about the fascinating issues that underlie the alleged overprescription of psychiatric medicines or if it was a practical, commonsense guide for parents who wrestle with the decision to medicate their child. Ultimately, I decided it had to be both. Only if parents understand the philosophical issues will they feel comfortable that their child is not the victim of a dangerous craze to overmedicate children. And only with that same understanding will parents feel free to use modern medicine to control their child's pain or help their child reach his or her potential.

This book will not review the uses and side effects of all medicines. Other books are available to tackle that task (for example, see my book *Kids on Meds*). Rather, using many vignettes, it will reveal the doctor's thought process in deciding whether to medicate.

With its myriad decisions and no crystal ball, parenting is inherently stressful. This book does not remove that stress. No book or person could do that. However, I hope that if parents have a better understanding of what underlies the decision to medicate or not medicate, they will feel that they can act wisely and carefully in their child's best interest.

YOUR CHILD
IN THE BALANCE

||||||||

The "Can Do" Age of Psychiatry

||||||||||||||||||||||||||||||||||||||||||||||||||||||||||||||||||||

Scene From Just About Any Movie Circa Early 1940s

Catherine, an adorable little girl with curly hair spread over the pillow, lies in bed with a brave smile and big, brown, knowing eyes. Tired old Dr. Brown, sitting next to the bed, pats the little girl's hand, then gets up to leave. As he nears the door, Catherine's parents plead, "Doctor, isn't there anything you can do?" Regretfully, Dr. Brown shakes his head slowly from side to side and replies, "I'm sorry, Mr. and Mrs. McCarthy, but there's nothing more we can do." The parents thank Dr. Brown for all his efforts, then bow their heads so that Catherine cannot see the tears welling up in their eyes.

The Age of "Can Do"

"I'm sorry, but there's nothing more we can do." Talk about a line that doesn't fit the new millennium! This sense of futility, which so many generations were trained to endure, today seems as anachronistic as bloodletting. For centuries, the pain of medical powerlessness was a part of life. There was so little to do. Every family experienced mysterious illness they could not comprehend and death they were helpless to prevent.

Today is the "can do" age of science. We confront every adversity enlightened by insights reaped from the latest research and armed with a plan of action utilizing the most advanced technologies. Using the ever-expanding power of pharmacology, we enter the battle expecting to win the day, refusing to cede control to the enemy. No victory is out of reach of the long arm of the modern medical machine. Whether the success story is opening the bronchi of a wheezing asthmatic or halting a rampant infection, Dr. Brown's days of helpless resignation appear to be coming to a close. Although we do not win every battle, we enter expecting to be armed with more than resignation. We can help the patient take charge, and we can do it now.

Helping patients control bodily dysfunction is at the heart of being a physician. But what exactly is dysfunction? As scientific progress allows us more control of a bodily function, our definition of dysfunction changes. We question the boundary between function and dysfunction. For example, using growth hormone to exert control over height leads us to question when shortness is a person's defining characteristic and when it becomes a dysfunction. When should it be controlled?

Defining brain dysfunction is even more uncertain. The complex functions of the brain, our most crucial organ, are only beginning to be understood. The roles of memory, language, and mood, to name a few, are complex. As we learn to control these functions, the debate over where dysfunction begins will intensify. This daunting decision about where we draw the line between function and dysfunction goes to the heart of how we define ourselves and how we define illness.

Enter child psychiatry, which for decades had offered only the talking cure—one remedy for so many diverse illnesses, and one that often took years, offered by doctors who had little else to recommend. Enter child psychiatry, suddenly armed with a barrel full of medicines that actually work. Battling enemies just coming into focus, just being described, we can assure parents, "Yes, there is something we can do."

The possibility that doctors can prescribe psychiatric medicines to control brain function raises the specter of these medicines run amuck. Parents are eager for the relief medicine offers but apprehensive that it will change their child's normal traits or that their child's personality will be altered. Parents want to know that the psychiatric medicine their child is taking is changing a troublesome symptom and that medicine is a necessary intervention.

As physicians, child psychiatrists would like to offer their patients a solution for each of their troubles. Equipped with an ever-increasing cache of medicines, we feel confident that we are able to do just that. But perhaps our confidence outshines our capabilities. Perhaps our pharmacological success seduces us into solving problems that are not yet well defined.

Sometimes we reduce the complex psychological problem to a simple diagnosis whose criteria are still evolving. Sometimes we lose sight of what the patient really wants and needs—someone with whom to talk. Sometimes we get sucked into the need to act, rather than accept what we cannot change. These are the dilemmas of our "can do" age of effective medicines. How do we harness the power of pharmacology? When do we turn it loose? Can we accept its limitations?

This book could have been written about many fields of medicine that grapple with the power of our modern medical tools. As we gain control over bodily function, we are challenged to decide the criteria by which we will take that control. We face the problem in the accepted but sometimes uncomfortable medical practice of prescribing growth hormone to attain height, and we face it in the dubious practice of using steroids to build muscle mass. We will face it more and more often.

The uniqueness of child psychiatry, however, makes it the most provocative field in which to understand the role of medicine in today's world and, in particular, in the life of today's child.

First, child psychiatry studies the complex maladies of the most multiple-functioned, constantly changing, least accessible of human organs: the child's developing brain. And we only started a few short decades ago. We have made progress and can now address more sophisticated questions, but we must confess that we are neophytes. We know more than we ever have but far less than we need. Our small amount of hard data gives us only a modicum of guidance in our treatment decisions.

Second, medicines work. We are not firing blanks. Effective medication is not unique to child psychiatry. However, effecting change, sometimes when we are only vaguely certain of precisely what we are changing, is unique. Some medicines reliably change particular brain functions. And some do not. The effect of stimulant medicines on attention span is fairly reliable and becoming better understood. The panoply of medicines we prescribe to treat angry outbursts are less reliably effective and not as well understood, but sometimes they help. Our interventions have an impact, even if not exactly predictable.

Sometimes we control psychological processes without being certain of whether or not they represent illness. Just as height is increased by growth hormone, attention span is improved by using stimulants. But are we changing pathological inattention or improving the attention of the child who is only relatively unfocused? Is medicine quelling pathological anger or modifying the child who is simply irritable? On the frontier of child psychiatry it is easy to slip unwittingly into using the power of medicine to change what is normal.

Finally, at stake are our most valuable, yet most vulnerable, of resources: our children. Occasionally, the very lives of our children are at stake. But the quality of our children's lives is always hanging in the balance. Will they be happy or sad? Will they have friends or will they be alone? Will they grab the future with confidence or will life be a constant struggle? Will they reach their potential or will they fall short?

This is a book about every parent's desire to control the psychological ills that could befall their child and every parent's wish that his or her child develop without the intrusion of medicine. It is a book that asks provocative questions to guide parents in a search for certainty in a world without definitive answers. It is a book that will help parents decide whether their child should take a psychiatric medicine, but not before it challenges them to consider the role of medicine in their life.

To understand whether psychiatric medicines are overprescribed and to ultimately arrive at a way to decide to medicate a child, we start with the broadest question: By what criteria do we decide to alter our bodies? Do we follow specific criteria, or do we change our bodies until we feel that it's just too far? As we'll see, this is a murky issue. Next, does the brain merit different criteria from the rest of the body? And then, does a child's brain merit still different criteria?

Without firm answers to these questions, parents must rely on their working relationship with their physician, who leans on the age-old maxim of weighing potential benefits against risks. So we next address whether there are benefits to psychiatric medicines and, if so, how to measure them. Then, what of the risks? Are they as simple as a list of physical side effects, or are there subtle risks, such as a child missing the opportunity for personal growth because medicine has solved the problem? Last, how do the benefits and risks of medicine stack up against those of other treatments or against no treatment at all?

Along the way, we'll briefly examine the history of psychiatric diagnosis and the interaction between diagnosis and the use of medicine. Prior to about 1980, diagnosis was minimized, and understanding the child's psychology was emphasized. Joey's mother was often seen as the root of all his difficulties. The past

30 years has been the era of diagnosing disorders. Joey is now diagnosed with you-fill-in-the-blank disorder. A diagnosis always assures the patient that the medicine is truly necessary. But the primacy of diagnosis also has its skeptics. Doesn't it seem like everybody has a disorder these days? Or, at least, a little bit of a disorder? Diagnosing disorders in child psychiatry provides a particular challenge. Can a child's difficulties be reduced to a label? The relationship between diagnosis and treatment is also problematic. Does diagnosis drive treatment, or has available treatment begun to drive diagnosis?

Next, we'll join Mr. and Mrs. Parker as they go through the process of deciding whether to give their daughter, Rosie, a psychiatric medicine. This extended vignette provides a real-life illustration of two parents struggling with the decision to medicate.

Finally, we'll review practical guidelines to help parents weigh the risks and benefits of giving medicine to their child. We'll review the pitfalls parents should avoid and the "Ten Commandments" of medicine, such as always starting with a proper evaluation.

The so-called overprescription of psychiatric medicines grabs the headlines and challenges us to examine the principles by which we change our bodies. As mentioned, child psychiatry provides a particularly provocative arena in which to face that challenge. Ultimately every parent's most pressing need is an answer to the following question: Is my child receiving psychiatric medicine after a careful evaluation and after my physician and I have carefully reviewed all risks and benefits of medicine and compared them with the risks and benefits of alternative treatments, including no treatment at all? Try to fit that on the cover of your favorite weekly news magazine! That question, however, should guide parents as they enter the modern world of child psychiatry.

CHAPTER 1

The Challenge of Change

||||||||||||||||||||||||||||||||||||||||||||||||||||||||||||||||

Daunting Development

Your perfect new baby. Cherub-faced. Napping on your shoulder.
Breathing softly and steadily. All fingers and toes accounted for. You
wouldn't change a hair.

Two months later: You complain to the pediatrician that your baby
is inconsolable at night. He cries and cries. Your pediatrician calls
it colic and reassures you that babies change as they mature. He'll
outgrow it within a few months. *A few months*?! You're already sleep
deprived, running on empty. You can't wait a few months. You're not
asking the pediatrician to change the kid, just calm him down, get him
to sleep. Isn't there something to give him?

Twelve years later: You ordered a cherub-faced, soft-skinned little
butterball, and now your son—with size-12 feet and size-2 head, who
smells like the New York Giants locker room and sports a pimple on
his nose—trips over his lacrosse stick as he runs up the stairs because
once more he forgot to put his math homework in his backpack and
once more he's late, and the bus is coming down the street even as
you're screaming at him to move his butt because you refuse to drive
him to school yet again. You know this is a tough age, but is this a
stage, or does he have some kind of disorder? You wouldn't change a

hair *on* his head, but maybe some Ritalin would help *in* his head? And how about some deodorant?

Five years later: A massive mountain of muscle steps out of the car. He denies using steroids, but he won't swear he hasn't taken an over-the-counter supplement to help him bulk up for football. He says he's had a great weekend with his friends down at the shore. You breathe a sigh of relief to see him in one piece, though you're certain his liver will probably never be the same. You give him a big hug and notice the little lightning bolt tattooed on his neck. And didn't he leave for the shore with his mom's chestnut brown hair? He assures you that platinum looks better with his steel-blue car. Change the hair on his head? Ha!

Initiating Change

Change is the nature of life, the continuous and inevitable certainty of being alive. Our bodies are in constant flux. Our hormones ebb and flow through the day, through the month, and over the years. With age, our bones get longer, our muscles bulkier. We grow hair where previously we had none and lose hair from places we had plenty. Our eyes get weak, and our skin wrinkles. Our bodies change, and we are never consulted.

Here is our dilemma. Are we to accept change passively? Are we to accept whatever life deals? Or are we to initiate change? Are we to learn the mechanics of life in order to master it?

We strive to be initiators, masters of our destiny. With greater understanding, we can replace hormones and lengthen bones. We can enlarge our muscles and replace our hair. We can strengthen our vision and even tighten our skin. Although sometimes wary about where our efforts will lead, we search for the knowledge that will allow us to initiate change or stop it.

We strive to unlock the profound secrets to longevity and health, but sometimes we simply seek to change the mundane. The most basic and noticeable of our intentional bodily changes are rooted in personal hygiene. Every morning I brush my teeth, changing the chemistry in my mouth. I don't necessarily under-stand the chemical changes caused by brushing my teeth, but it is, without fail, an empirically successful experiment, and my wife appreciates the change when she kisses me good-bye.

We initiate changes in our skin chemistry at tanning salons and the beach. I remember Sunday afternoon barbeques at my aunt's house, my older teenage cousins lying on lounge chairs in the backyard, tilting sun reflectors to change the color of their faces. I remember one of them asking her younger brother to straighten her hair by ironing it with my aunt's iron.

Eating is probably the most frequent means by which we ini-tiate change. Like breathing, eating is pretty automatic. We are compelled to eat. We feel the discomfort of hunger pangs. We are taught to set aside specified times at which to eat. We know we'll die if we don't eat.

But more than breathing, we use eating to deliberately change our bodies. An adolescent restricts carbohydrates to look svelte in a new bathing suit for the summer. An athlete adds protein to build muscle. An actor purposely gains weight to better portray a par-ticular character. We've all cut back on cholesterol and saturated fats in an attempt to prolong our lives.

We use eating to change our own body chemistry and that of our child. We apply our knowledge, or our alleged knowledge, to effect change and thereby control outcome. We give our children milk to help their bones grow and carrots to help their eyes see. Sometimes parents try to reach right into the brain, controlling diet in an attempt to control brain chemistry.

Mikey is 5 years old and has been on the move since before he was born. He never stops. Like a heat-seeking missile constantly searching for action, he pulls the dog's ears, takes his little sister's favorite "blankie." It doesn't matter to Mikey. He just always needs something to do. Every night, Mikey falls asleep at 11:30, and, every morning, he bounces out of bed at 6.

Mikey's mom is 35 years old and exhausted. She cannot keep up with Mikey. She searches for a way to intervene. Her friend swears that sugar makes kids hyper. Mikey's mom decides to change Mikey's diet to try to slow him down.

Medicine the Menace?

We do all sorts of things to initiate change or maintain the status quo. We tattoo. We pierce. We eat. We diet. We run. We lift. We cut. We meditate.

Using a medicine to exert our influence can be unnerving to parents. Topical medicines are acceptable, but swallowing pills? Not so fast. Concern starts with the medicine's potential side effects, but then goes beyond, leaving us troubled at a deeper level that can be hard to articulate. Involving medicine makes many of us uncomfortable.

What is it about medicine that makes us simultaneously desirous of its effects yet wary of its power? When does a molecule become a medicine? If a child has difficulty falling asleep, the pediatrician suggests drinking some warm milk at bedtime. He says that something in milk helps some people sleep. Most parents are happy to give it a try. But if some enterprising scientist isolates the molecule in milk that induces sleep and markets it in the form of a pill for children who cannot tolerate milk, we are wary.

The pill opens Pandora's box. We fear using it to control an endless list of bodily functions or to embellish an endless list of traits. All we do is choose the right medicine. It is easy. It is effortless. It is suspect.

In the brave new world, effort is an anachronism. The puritanical maxim "no pain, no gain" becomes the painless but suspicious aphorism "a pill, not will." Using medicine satisfies our need to use science to be what we want to be, to control our own destiny. But we pay with more than a little guilt and fear. We feel dishonest about effecting change the easy way. Medicine lulls us into feeling anything is within our control, a power we do not always want. We want to control disease but would like to leave other characteristics to chance.

Today most medicines treat diseases or symptoms. However, in time, we will have access to medicines that enhance our traits, whether building muscle mass or improving memory.

A few years ago, a team of researchers at Emory University did a small but provocative study with patients who had a fear of heights (Ressler et al., 2004). They treated all patients by exposing them to the sensation of height by using a virtual-reality mask. This is a standard behavioral treatment. However, some patients underwent the procedure having just taken the medicine cycloserine, and other patients having just received placebo. Three months later, the group who had taken cycloserine were less fearful of heights than the group who had taken placebo.

Cycloserine is not thought to treat fear of heights. The researchers hypothesized that it does enhance people's ability to learn—in this case, learning to associate high places with calm instead of excessive anxiety. The authors of the study suggested that this medicine enhanced associative learning. If they are correct, could we use this medicine to teach dyslexic children not to clutch when their teacher takes out a book? As we learn how to affect different aspects of learning, there will be countless possible interventions.

Perhaps we will have access to medicines that improve our coordination or enhance our singing. Over time, these medicines will have fewer side effects. Adapting our value system to incorporate these medicines will become a necessity.

As technology advances, we accommodate our values. When answering machines were first in use, I was reluctant to leave a message. It seemed rude not to talk with the person I was calling. Years later, that view seems silly, and I regularly hope the machine answers so I can leave my message and move on. The invention of the wheel and then the wagon probably brought similar moral consternation, the purists screaming that people who do not have to lug their belongings around would all get fat and lazy.

Similarly, as our understanding of biology leaps forward, our value system will need to accommodate. We are on the cusp of understanding the details of a variety of brain functions. Not far beyond understanding comes control of these functions, but we are without firm guidelines in deciding when to use medicine to change our bodies.

Shelley is 16 years old, and, though she is a bit of a space cadet, she does not have attention-deficit hyperactivity disorder (ADHD). Her little brother, Larry, does have ADHD and takes Ritalin twice daily. Shelley's parents are aware that Ritalin helps minimize Larry's symptoms of ADHD. They are also well aware that Ritalin will help anyone focus, even if that person does not have ADHD.

Dr. Jenkins, Larry's psychiatrist, gets a call from Shelley's mother one Friday afternoon in October. "Dr. Jenkins, I'm calling about Larry's older sister, Shelley. I know you told me that she does not have ADHD. But you know she tends to be a bit spacey. Well, she has the PSATs tomorrow, and I was wondering, do you think it would be okay to give her one of Larry's Ritalins? I probably shouldn't tell you this, but I did give her one last week, and she did her homework so much more easily."

Shelley's mother is not afraid to use medicine to improve her daughter's attention span. But how does she decide? What are her guidelines? Would we object if she had purchased the medicine over the counter?

Molecular Makeover

One way of minimizing the importance of medicine is by focusing on how we obtain it. Over-the-counter medicine gives us less concern. Ibuprofen to stop menstrual cramps? No problem. But if the medicine must be obtained from a doctor, the undertaking is more serious.

Sometimes needing a doctor's prescription reflects the danger of the medicine. Taking a concoction of prescribed chemotherapy medicines is a more serious undertaking than taking your daily over-the-counter multivitamin with extra zinc. Other times, this is an artificial distinction. Medicines that once required a doctor's prescription can now be bought over the counter. When sold over the counter, the medicine is seen in a different light.

But over-the-counter medicines are not innocuous. One can suffer a host of difficulties from taking aspirin and antihistamines and decongestants and every other medicine in the aisles of your local pharmacy. A drug's being sold over the counter is no guarantee of its safety.

Over-the-counter supplements are no different. Although the word "supplement" makes them seem more like food than medicine and keeps their manufacturers from being required to do the rigorous testing demanded of medicine manufacturers, these pills also have risks, if less well documented.

When professional athletes report taking over-the-counter supplements to bulk up their muscle mass, people consider it part of their occupation. The implication is that they are simply enhancing their power through a mundane intervention, without exposing themselves to excessive side effects. Because the intervention is with an over-the-counter supplement, this bodily change is not one that requires consultation with a physician. Confronting criteria for changing body chemistry seems less mandatory.

Similarly, some teenagers regularly use over-the-counter supplements to build muscle mass. Although they often see steroids as potentially dangerous, they rationalize that over-the-counter substances must be safe. In one study of students from a New York suburb, 44% of 12th-grade athletes reported using creatine, a nutritional supplement, usually to enhance their athletic performance or improve their appearance (Metzl, Small, Levine, &

Gershel, 2001). Most of them would probably distinguish between medicines that require a prescription and substances they can pluck from the shelves of their local pharmacy. However, as the authors of the study noted, the safety of creatine is not established in adolescents. Categorizing medicines by whether or not they require a prescription is a useful but artificial distinction.

Are All Changes Equal?

Like virtually all other medicines, psychiatric medicines cause change at the molecular level. Like many other medicines, they involve a physician. Like a few other medicines, they cause a change within the brain. And, like virtually no other medicines, they cause a purposeful change in behavior, mood, or cognition. Ultimately, however, prescribing a psychiatric medicine to a child is simply another example of changing one's body to influence function. As our ability to change this particular organ advances, our values will need to accommodate the increase in our control over the body.

If taking a psychiatric medicine does not seem like such a simple decision, one reason is that our values are not clearly reflected in specific criteria for changing the body. Deciding upon some criteria for changing the body, in particular a child's brain, would help clarify our values and thereby offer guidelines for when to give a child a psychiatric medicine.

CHAPTER 2

The Elusive Criteria for Changing Your Body

||||||||||||||||||||||||||||||||||||||||||||||||||||||||||||||||||||||||

When Is It Okay to Change Your Body?

By what criteria do we determine that a bodily change, by pill or medical procedure, is justified? Let's start with the obvious.

Life-threatening symptoms mandate change, especially if they're immediately threatening. When your child is bleeding, you intervene in any way possible to stop the bleeding. Suturing a bloody gash is a bodily change with which few would argue. Similarly, when you have a history of heart disease and you feel crushing chest pain, you quickly pop a nitroglycerin pill under your tongue. You're saving your life in a very immediate way.

The prevention of disease (a group of symptoms with an identifiable cause and course) mandates change. We vaccinate our children with measles vaccine to prompt the development of antibodies that will prevent a potentially serious infectious disease.

Stopping the progression of disease mandates change. Chemotherapy is our attempt to stop the advance of cancer. Diuretics decrease blood pressure and the negative effects that accompany hypertension.

Physical pain begs for change. "I have a terrible headache. I'd like a painkiller to alter my brain chemistry. Do you have any Tylenol around?"

Physical pain as a criterion for change is not quantifiable, therefore demonstrating the murkiness of standardized criteria. We all have different thresholds of pain; the severity is a function of whose it is. My headache is usually severe. Yours is usually milder. I might change my neurochemistry with Tylenol at the first twinge of pain. To convince me to prescribe a painkiller to change your neurochemistry, you'd better be screaming.

Another difficulty in using pain as a criterion for change lies in legitimizing the cause of the physical pain, which can be tangible or intangible. Is the pain of the tangible tack stuck in the bottom of my foot more legitimate than the 6-year-old's stomachache caused by the intangible anxiety of missing his mother? Do tangible causes of pain justify bodily change more than intangible causes?

The nature of the pain also legitimizes its experience. The pain caused by stepping on a tack is considered legitimate pain. The pin-prick sends a message via specific neurons to the brain, where we experience pain. The anxiety felt by a 6-year-old desperately missing his mom is different and easier for others to minimize. It does not travel by pain neurons. How it works is not exactly clear, but it results in molecular changes in his brain that leave him in deep "emotional" pain. I would hesitate to say that one pain is worse than the other. One who hastens to say that the pain in the foot is worse should speak to someone with debilitating anxiety. Does one pain mandate intervention more than the other?

The Slippery Slope of Psychological Pain and Dysfunction

If physical pain is difficult to assess, psychological pain is even more difficult. Having no measuring stick for pain allows us to become moralistic about whether others should change their bodies.

Joanne is 17. She has a huge, pointy nose. She has a few friends, but because of her nose she is self-conscious about meeting new people. Although she does not suffer from depression, she is chronically demoralized. Her symptoms are not life-threatening and cause her no physical pain. But Joanne hurts, and she feels socially dysfunctional.

Is change justified? Whether Joanne went to a plastic surgeon or used the new medicine Reductonose, if she thought that the change would make her much less self-conscious, is she justified in changing her nose? If she thought it would enable her to be involved with others, should Joanne change her body to relieve herself of psychological pain? Perhaps, if she sticks with her pointy nose, she will learn to overcome adversity and understand people at a deeper level. Or perhaps she'll simply suffer and never learn to adapt.

We have all read about the child who is known to have "overcome his asthma" to become an Olympic swimmer. Asthma, and his battle against it, became a key part of his identity, teaching him valuable lessons about overcoming life's obstacles. The potential gain of developing character by living with the adversity of asthma, however, is quickly outweighed by its life-threatening nature. The danger compels us to use medicine to change his lungs whether or not the change affects the development of his personality.

The psychological pain caused by a pointy nose is more difficult to assess than the pulmonary dysfunction of asthma, and the potential gains of changing one's nose are more difficult to predict. Therefore we have a harder time deciding whether bodily change in this case is justified.

What's in a Name?

Symptoms, by definition, have a subjective quality. They are complaints made by the patient, and, as such, they imply a desire for change. However, when doctors label a group of symptoms as a disorder, they have supplied a justification, perhaps even a mandate, for change.

If 7-year-old Johnny wets his bed every night, his parents might simply see him as a late learner. But if the doctor labels it as enuresis, an elimination disorder, Johnny's parents might feel more justified in using medicine to stop it.

It is a common misconception that the psychiatric establishment easily labels a group of symptoms as a disorder. In fact, it takes years of debate in which psychiatrists question whether a group of symptoms occur together more than would be expected by chance, whether they can be reliably diagnosed, whether they cause significant dysfunction, and the like.

Sometimes the debate is heated, and, although the establishment takes a position, not everyone agrees. This has implications for whether change is justified. Years ago, homosexuality was seen as a disorder, and therefore change through treatment was justified. Then the psychiatric establishment decided, after much debate, that it was not a disorder, so the need to change became less compelling.

Give Me a Life with Quality

Symptoms that lead to loss of function mandate change. Our bodies are intended to function. If they don't, we must find a remedy. Juvenile rheumatoid arthritis is a disease process that includes joint stiffness and predicts difficult movement. We intervene. A cataract impairs the eye's ability to see. We intervene.

Quality-of-life dysfunction can be thornier and more difficult to define, however. It is subjective and dependent on the particular person's needs and wants. If I'm a psychiatrist who doesn't do a lot of physical labor and abhors physical exercise, a bit of shoulder stiffness is not so dysfunctional. As long as I don't have to reach the top shelf for my Corn Flakes, I'm not in much pain, and I'm actually reasonably functional. My orthopedist's recommendation to change my body through anti-inflammatory medicine, much less arthroscopic surgery, is not so compelling. But, if I'm a house painter, my shoulder stiffness is suddenly a major dysfunction.

On the other hand, if the painter becomes hard of hearing, he can still do his job. As a psychiatrist, difficulty hearing causes significant dysfunction and makes my ear doctor's recommendations more compelling.

Is our need to earn a living sufficient reason to change our bodies? If I, as a psychiatrist losing his hearing, began taking Earocine, the latest hearing-improvement medicine, most would probably see it as justified. If Big Joe O'Leary, a football lineman with a chronically sore knee that even rest would not help, took painkillers in order to do his job on Sunday, many would see it as justified.

But what if Big Joe took a medicine to prolong his career? Now we're interfering with the way life should proceed. Should people's careers have a natural life span, with which we don't interfere? At the age of 42, maybe Big Joe should lay off the pills and hang up the cleats.

And what about taking medicines to secure a future career? What about Sidney Stickowicz?

Sixteen-year-old Sidney is 6'8"—skinny, not too bright, but a highly talented high-school basketball player who lives in poverty and expects to go nowhere with his life, except perhaps to prison. Sidney could get a college basketball scholarship if he were a little bulkier. He's tried changing his body by eating the right foods and by taking nutritional supplements, but to no avail. A college player who's taken Sidney under his wing tells him to get the over-the-counter medicine Bulky Man.

Playing ball in college is the only way Sidney will get out of the old neighborhood with its drug runners and violence. It's the only way he'll have a chance at an education and a better life. If he does well in college ball, he is probably good enough to play professionally and earn a very good living. This would assure his children good healthcare, a college education, and a way to stay as far away from the old neighborhood as possible. But he needs to be bigger.

Should Sidney invest in Bulky Man? If it doesn't work, is a supervised trial of steroids justified? Is enhancing a physical attribute, like size, the same as enhancing a mental attribute, like attention? If Sidney's sister, Cindy, is smart enough to win an academic scholarship but having difficulty focusing now that she's in college, should she take a stimulant to improve her focus?

My Fun Is My Life

Quality-of-life dysfunction is not absolute but rather reflects a person's demands on his or her body. Our work puts demands on our body, but so do our other needs. We live in an age in which athletes are gods and advertisers urge us to push our bodies until we sweat purple. We demand our bodies to stand up to the pressures of our recreation.

If the pain in his knees prevents 51-year-old Bill from mountain biking over rocks and tree stumps and skiing on the most difficult slopes in Colorado and playing three sets of tennis against his club's pro, he considers himself dysfunctional. "If I can't participate in my favorite sports, what's the quality of my life?" Bill asks. Rather than adapt his recreation to his aging body, Bill changes his body with a pain reliever prior to engaging in each of these physically challenging endeavors. Now he's functional.

Who determines quality of life? Usually, it's the individual. Changing one's body by taking over-the-counter medicine is a personal decision in which nobody else has a say. If you want a prescription medicine to uphold what you consider to be your quality of life, you have to have your physician's approval. If you want expensive surgery to uphold your quality of life, your insurance company will also have a say.

Good for Me, Good for You

More than physical dysfunctions, psychiatric dysfunction reflects and affects the surrounding people. Bill's decision to ski may disturb his wife, but hopefully their marriage can take the pressure. And Bill's decision to ski or not to ski will have little effect on the mountain.

A family member with a psychiatric disorder, however, will have an impact on everyone in the house. Changing one's body, therefore, influences one's self and the environment. When the environment is composed of people, especially other children, the impact can be significant, if difficult to measure. Does the impact of dysfunction on others fulfill a criterion to change one's body?

Cory is 8 years old and chronically irritable. He is always yelling at his brothers, who resent having to walk on eggshells to help keep Cory quiet. His older brother hates having his friends visit his house, and he looks forward to sleeping elsewhere to get a respite from his brother. Cory's younger brother, though not irritable by nature, is beginning to copy some of Cory's cursing tantrums.

Cory is always battling with his well-meaning but stubborn father, and Cory's mother is forever screaming at her husband about the way he handles Cory. Although their marriage is not perfect, it handles most of the usual stresses. But Cory's behavior has put them both under constant strain, and their marriage is falling apart. Cory is becoming a demanding, self-centered, and irritating presence who is at the center of a family that is slowly disintegrating.

Because of his mood, Cory is dysfunctional. But, as a child living within a family, Cory's dysfunction has served as the most significant in a chain of dominoes, including the effect he has had on the childhoods of his two siblings. Perhaps they will ultimately benefit in some ways by having had a sibling with a disability. Many do. Or perhaps they will grow up angry and resentful and flee their hometown for a more serene place, far away from their brother. Do Cory's parents have an obligation to change Cory's brain to help Cory, his brothers, and their marriage?

Treading Lightly on the Brain

Arriving at a list of firm criteria to guide us in changing our bodies is no simple task. As we consider the brain, we tread even more carefully. What makes the brain so special and the task of defining criteria to change it so much more difficult? Does it merit its own criteria?

Let's bring on the celebrated, if elusive, main character of this book. Let's bring on the brain.

CHAPTER 3

Bring on the Brain

||||||||||||||||||||||||||||||||||||||||||||||||||||||||||||||||||

From the Deep-Down Depths
of the Average Guy's Brain

"Bring on the brain? Whoa! Now we're talking really serious stuff. The lungs are serious. Can't catch a breath without them. The bowels are serious. Not working? Major frustration. The liver? Not quite sure what that big lug does, but too much wine kills it. Can't be good. The heart? Without my ticker, my life is over. I die. Never see my kids again. Gotta keep exercising.

"But my brain? My brain is the reason I need my lungs to breathe and my heart to keep ticking and my bowels to feel relief and my liver to . . . well, whatever. My brain is me! My brain holds my aggravation, my imagination, my consternation, my determination. My brain is the lockbox of my personality. My brain tells me everything I love about my wife, and it reminds me why I can't stand her Uncle Stanley. My brain makes me laugh at *Seinfeld* and cry at the end of *It's a Wonderful Life*.

"Give me a baboon's heart. Give me my brother's kidney. But if you gave me Joe's brain, I'd be Joe. Like a bad movie. No, don't mess with my brain."

Changing Our Bodies, Changing Our Brains

All other organs serve the brain. As the organ that experiences life, the brain gives reason for our bodies. Without the brain's ability to experience, our lives would be no more interesting than that of an amoeba. Without the brain's central role in defining who we are, our differences would be confined to our heights and weights and the sizes of our noses.

So we proceed with caution in deciding when to change the brain. Perhaps we'll improve its individual functions—its ability to remember or focus or relax. But we don't want to lose its primary function; we don't want to lose our identity.

Our struggle over psychiatric medicines and children is therefore unique. We are diving right into the brains of our children, wanting desperately to fix what is broken without changing who they are or who they will become.

To resolve this struggle, we need criteria to define brain malfunction. It is clear that the brain is malfunctioning when a stroke victim cannot lift his left arm. However, it is less clear when a complex function, such as experiencing mood, is malfunctioning. Disabling depression is reasonably straightforward, but irritability can be seen as part of one's personality, and its interference with functioning is subjective. Deciding what constitutes brain malfunction leaves much room for debate.

As we've seen, other organs do not present this problem. We don't think twice about changing the chemistry of our asthmatic child's lungs so that his bronchi dilate and he can breathe more easily. How effectively a child breathes is usually not an inherent part of his identity, and if it is, we don't want it to be. Breathing should be automatic and its effects unnoticed. If the pediatrician tells us to give the medicine twice daily, we do it without much question.

We don't think twice about changing our diabetic child's insulin level to better control her blood sugar. Blood-sugar level is not an integral part of personality. If the pediatrician recommends insulin, we agree to its use with concern, but without the fear of changing the child's self. Changing the brain, on the other hand, leaves us with a queasy sense that our child will awaken the next morning and be a different person.

A Primer on the Brain

Let's briefly review the brain's physical makeup and then try to understand why it is seen as different from the other organs.

The brain sits like a heap of Jello locked inside the skull. It is divided into different lobes. For example, the front of the brain is known as the frontal lobes and the rear as the occipital lobes. Within the center of the brain are a number of smaller, specialized areas, such as the hippocampus and the basal ganglia.

The brain is composed of billions and billions of nerve cells, which are called neurons. To picture a neuron, imagine a child's stick figure without the arms and with thousands of legs. Some of these legs are shorter, and some are longer. All of them connect to the "head" of another stick figure. These trillions of connections make for a highly complex web of neurons composed of a multitude of different tracks. Electrical impulses traverse this web, flowing down one neuron and on to the next. The living brain pulses with electricity flowing in many directions every moment.

The connections between neurons, however, are not actual connections. The "foot" of one neuron does not touch the "head" of the next neuron. Between them is a space called a synapse. The first neuron sends its message across the synapse by sending out chemicals called neurotransmitters. Neurotransmitters, the most well known of which are serotonin, dopamine, and norepinephrine, cross the synapse and plug into receptor sites on the "head" of the second neuron. When they have completed their task, these neurotransmitters are broken down by enzymes in the synapse and sucked back up into the first neuron to be used again. This is called the reuptake of the neurotransmitter.

There are more neurotransmitters than these most famous three, and more are being discovered. And there are a multitude of receptor sites, each designed for a certain neurotransmitter. In addition, even the sites designed for a particular neurotransmitter have unique aspects that make some of them different from the others.

The various neurotransmitters and receptor sites are found in varying concentrations in the different parts of the brain. Some tracks of neurons might have more dopamine receptors, and other tracks might have more serotonin receptors. For now, suffice it to say that most psychiatric medicines change the concentration of different neurotransmitters in the synapse or alter some aspect of the receptor site.

A Different Kind of Organ

That is the brain in a nutshell. What makes the brain different from the other organs? What gives it a special aura unknown to even the most life-sustaining of organs, such as the heart or lungs?

At its simplest, the brain performs defined tasks. It perceives pain. It initiates movement. It remembers. These seem like straightforward functions, akin to those of the other organs. The heart pumps blood. The lungs inhale air. The liver breaks down toxins.

The brain, however, is also the organ through which we experience life. The brain feels a caress and interprets it as coming from a caring parent or romantic lover. It sees a scowl and reads it as one of honest anger or playful tease.

The brain is the seat of our emotions. It feels the excitement of first love and the rage of being violated. It feels the frustration of failure and the joy of success. It feels the comfort of safety and the apprehension of the unknown.

The brain gives us self-awareness. "I guess I am loud and opinionated. I understand why they don't want me on the committee."

The brain connects us to other people. "Honey, remember

strolling along the beach on the night we first met? That beautiful sunset?" The child's brain reaches out to her parent. "Mommy, can't you lie here so we can talk before I go to sleep? Just a few minutes, I promise."

The brain generates theories about the world around us. "My Spanish teacher, Señora Ramirez, always calls on me when I don't know the answer. She must not like me."

The brain makes decisions. "I know it'll be tough, but I've decided to quit my job and study for law school." The brain is the source of our motivation and our diligence. "If I study hard this semester, I think I can earn a place in the Honor Society."

The brain is the source of our spontaneity. "Wasn't little Mitchell adorable when he suddenly bowed at the end of his piano recital? I could just eat that kid up."

No, the brain is not only the body's neurological command center. It houses the mind, the intangible composite of all these functions and the source of our identity.

We are, of course, also known by our bodies. If we just saw Sidney, our 6'8" friend, and he was now 4'7", we would be taken aback. Something very important about Sidney would have changed, but it would still be Sidney. People's bodies change all the time. We count on consistency, but we allow for understandable change. Wrinkles and baldness and gaining a few pounds are usually gradual changes. Amputations and scars, facelifts and nose jobs are more abrupt changes in the way we are known physically. They are not, however, at the core of our identity, whereas the composite of the brain's multiple functions is. Sidney's body plays an integral role in defining his identity, but even if he suddenly had an entirely new body, he would still be Sidney if what he said and did was the same, if his memories and feelings were unaltered, and if he related the way we know him to relate.

If we isolate and change only one of the brain's functions, we lessen the threat of changing our identity. And if we can identify that function as truly disordered, as malfunctioning, we feel more comfortable that we are changing things to how they ought to be, not away from how they ought to be.

Teasing Apart Brain Function and Dysfunction

Memory is a brain function, albeit a complex one. Many types of recall compose what we call memory. Remembering events of 10 minutes ago is a different function from remembering childhood events of years ago. Memories of visual events differ from memories of linguistic events. Some of our memories, like the phone number you just called, are erased from our brains immediately after they've served their purpose. Other memories we hold forever and associate with powerful emotions.

Remembering is a brain function the way metabolizing toxins is a liver function. We can test some functions of Jesse's memory by giving her a battery of tests. But memories are also personal, literally a part of us, and we have difficulty measuring the feelings associated with our memories or the way our memories influence our behavior and mood.

If we can isolate a disordered brain function and tease it apart from our identity, we have less difficulty changing the brain to fix it. Let's use medicine, some real and some fantasized, to hypothetically change an isolated function of an adult's brain. This will seem less threatening than changing the brain of a developing child.

At the age of 55, you begin to have difficulty remembering, and the doctor says you are in the early stages of Alzheimer's. Although your family is upset that you have difficulty remembering new information, they are relieved that you can recall what happened to Grandma in 1958. For now, you have an isolated problem of recent memory, but you are still you. Your doctor recommends Aricept, a medicine that will slow the predicted demise in your ability to remember. You grab the medicine to preserve the brain's function. Your loss of function reflects a brain disease. Taking medicine to fix an isolated problem does not change your identity; it preserves it.

If there is no sign of dysfunction, we have more difficulty. At the age of 55, without any sign of Alzheimer's, you decide to enhance your bridge game. Just before you play, you take Memorocine, a new medicine that will help you better remember the cards. Your wife complains, "What do you need medicine for? Just be the same lousy bridge player you've always been. That's how I know you, and that's how I love you." Suddenly, your loyal spouse feels you're no longer quite you. "The way you've always been" is your identity, and your wife wants it preserved.

As we get closer to the brain functions that are at the core of our personality, we are more reluctant to change the brain. The following year, although you aren't experiencing any difficulties, you decide to take medicine that will change your brain's style of decision-making. After all these years, you suddenly want to become more impulsive, a risk taker. You trade in the four-wheel-drive, steel-girded, seven-airbag Volvo, which you bought after you spent 3 months researching safety data, for the little red Lamborghini that you can afford but have always thought was too flashy, too fast, too risky. Your wife is really beginning to worry. "This isn't the same man I married 23 years ago. I want the old one back." Or maybe she's thrilled. In either case, however, an important part of who she thinks you are has changed.

The patient with Alzheimer's can justify changing himself because he's treating a brain disease that impairs his functioning, but a safety-conscious middle-aged man who wants to be more impulsive does not have a disorder. He is changing who he is, his non-disordered personality, by changing his brain. If the brain is the seat of identity, we need to understand how modern psychiatry defines its disorders. We can then better distinguish between treating a disorder and changing normal functioning.

CHAPTER 4

Psychiatry
Welcomes the Brain

||||||||||||||||||||||||||||||||||||||||||||||||||||||||||||

A Few Definitions

Psychiatrists live in the huge but poorly lit universe of human experience. It is an enormous universe that encompasses everything from people's most observable behaviors to their most intimate thoughts and feelings. Psychiatrists see patients troubled by feelings of anger, anxiety, sadness, and euphoria, bothered by behaviors of punching, stealing, washing, and counting, upset by thoughts that race and thoughts that ricochet. Psychiatrists see patients who are full of grandiosity and patients who feel worthless. They see patients who hallucinate and patients who confabulate, patients who are excessively driven and patients who are thoroughly unmotivated, patients who worry about their choice of sexual mate and patients who worry about their choice of soul mate, patients who are unsure of who you are and who they themselves are. All this and much more.

In this vast expanse of human experience, how do psychiatrists decide what is normal and what is abnormal? And how are the abnormal experiences organized?

Let's start with how any doctor knows if something is wrong. Generally, either the patient comes to a doctor with a complaint, a symptom, or the doctor decides that the patient has an abnormality, a sign. When you go to your ophthalmologist because you're losing your vision, that's a symptom. When your ophthalmologist finds abnormally high pressure within your eyeball, he or she tells you it's a sign of glaucoma.

By definition, a symptom is subjective. It reflects the patient's experience and is rooted in the patient's sense that his or her body is not functioning as desired. The patient sets the standard. Although this emphasis on subjectivity might seem irrelevant in evaluating a patient with glaucoma complaining of a loss of vision, it becomes more relevant in evaluating a symptom such as a child's distractibility, which reflects the parent's expectation, realistic or not, of the child's performance. If a parent complains that his or her 3rd-grader zones out whenever the parent presents the principles of quantum physics, the symptom becomes less compelling to the doctor, though the parent might still be distressed. Because symptoms are subjective, signs that are more clearly objective become crucial.

When you present to your doctor with symptoms, you consider yourself ill, and your doctor searches for these critical signs. If your doctor discovers a combination of signs and symptoms with a known cause that doctors have seen in other patients, then you have a disease. If your doctor discovers a combination of signs and symptoms that doctors have seen before but have only theories about the cause, then you have a disorder. In either case you're ill. But a disorder is not as well understood as a disease.

In medical terminology, the word for cause is "etiology." This word will play an important role in understanding how psychiatrists have categorized the abnormal, so it needs to be understood. The etiology of his pneumonia was a viral infection. The etiology of her hyperactivity was eating lead-based paint that was peeling off the walls. "Etiology" is a crucial word because it can easily be mistaken for disorder. In other words, the cause of the problem can be mistaken for the problem.

If Pattie develops skin cancer after spending years in the sun without wearing sunscreen or a hat, her dermatologist might believe that excessive exposure to the sun was part of the etiology of her cancer, but she would not say that sun exposure was a disorder. On the other hand, Pattie's psychiatrist might think that Pattie's need to be tan is a sign of a psychiatric disorder. He might see Pattie's preoccupation with her appearance as a sign of narcissistic personality disorder. He could only theorize about the etiology of Pattie's personality disorder, but he and other psychiatrists have seen Pattie's signs and symptoms in many other patients.

A Little History

With those definitions as background, let's briefly review the history of how psychiatry has decided what is normal and what is not. Since ancient times, doctors have recognized that people sometimes have maladies of mood and behavior. The Greeks, for example, described types of "madness" and understood these states as being due to the four bodily humors.

Over the succeeding centuries, any interest in mental illness was largely confined to those who were very obviously disturbed. The etiology of these disorders was identified according to the dominant ideas of the age. During the 17th century, for example, mental illness was believed to have a religious cause. People who acted abnormally were seen as having been affected by the Devil. For many years, not much progress was made in describing and differentiating the wide variety of abnormal human mental conditions. During the 19th century, some headway was made, but psychiatry was not yet a well-defined field. Rather, it was an offshoot of neurology.

Enter Sigmund Freud at about the turn of the 20th century. Freud helped the field of medicine appreciate that physical symptoms had psychological causes. He demonstrated that understanding the psychology of children is crucial to understanding the psychology of adults. Freud's writing on the etiology of psychiatric disorders has had an enormous influence on the way we view the entire human experience.

In 1856, the year Freud was born in Austria, Emil Kraeplin was born in Germany. Kraeplin became a psychiatrist and pioneered the use of a classification system for psychiatric disorders. He focused on the signs and symptoms of patients' illnesses, and he described and named what became known as schizophrenia and bipolar disorder. Kraeplin became the father of descriptive psychiatry. He was not interested in etiology as much as in defining illnesses. Although Kraeplin's descriptions became an important foundation for psychiatry's classification of diseases, his descriptive psychiatry was overshadowed by Freud's theories of human psychology that explained how disorders developed.

To the psychiatrists who practiced during and after World War II, theories of how a patient became disordered were more important than whether the patient suffered from a well-described disorder. With a powerful enough theory of etiology, any behavior could be explained, and, if the theory so deemed, any behavior could be seen as disordered. Freud's psychoanalytic theory dominated throughout the 1940s, 1950s, and 1960s. Aberrant behavior was seen as the result of unresolved psychological conflict usually revolving around one's parents, especially one's mother.

Freud's zealous followers sometimes overextended the tentacles of his theory into their understanding of medical illnesses and psychiatric disorders. When autism was first described in the 1940s, psychoanalytic theorists explained the disorder as being due to the mother's lack of warmth. This theory about the etiology of autism became more important than describing the signs and symptoms of the disorder.

Psychoanalytic theory always found some unresolved conflict as the cause of one's behavior, whether one was a patient or not.

People were seen on a spectrum of dysfunction. Virtually all people had milder difficulties, labeled "neurotic," which were the result of unresolved conflict. Some had more serious difficulties, labeled "psychotic," also explained by unresolved conflict. The psychoanalyst asked the question "Are you neurotic or psychotic?" All behavior could be explained by this dominant theory, and so all behavior was subject to being placed on this "diagnostic" spectrum.

As the 20th century wore on, more theories, many of them offshoots of psychoanalysis, developed to explain abnormal behavior. These included social theories about people's behavior in groups, family theories about the influence of family structure on behavior, and behavioral theories about the reinforcers that increased the rate of maladaptive behaviors. The quantity of writing about how patients developed psychological illness far outweighed the writing establishing that certain behavior represented a disorder that could be distinguished from normal.

Although they could be seen as displacing descriptive psychiatry, most of these psychological theories, often spawned by Freud, greatly advanced our understanding of human behavior. One could examine a patient and have lots to say about his psychology or her relationships with others, but one would have little to say about whether the patient's signs and symptoms fit a pattern of signs and symptoms seen in other patients.

A Psychiatric Fable

Once upon a time, as far back as, let's say, 1970, deep in the fabled woods, lived three wise ones. Parents would come from far and wide to allow each wise one to ask them questions. Through these piercing questions, the wise ones would come to know the family and discover what was ailing the parents' child.

Oliver was a rambunctious, impulsive 9-year-old who had been sent to the principal too many times for cursing at the teacher. In class, Oliver was constantly out of his seat, taunting his frustrated teacher, who would regularly argue with the sharp-tongued Oliver in front of the class. At home, Oliver would sometimes hit his mother and pull the cat's tail. Mrs. Oglethorpe had heard of the wise ones at a PTA meeting, and, desperate to understand her child, she begged her husband to accompany her and seek their help. Mr. Oglethorpe was angry about having to miss 2 days of work, but he reluctantly consented. The next day Mr. and Mrs. Oglethorpe sat before the wise ones.

The first wise one asked for lots of personal information. "Tell me, vas Oliver breast-fed? Ah, for 18 months, you say. And he showered vith Mr. Oglethorpe until he vas 6. Hmm. And you say you leave the door of your room open at night . . . even ven you are having relations. This is all very interesting." Mr. Oglethorpe demanded to know what the wise one thought. There was an edge to Mr. Oglethorpe's voice, and the first wise one noted that the edge made him uncomfortable, as if he were being attacked.

Then the second wise one began. She carefully noted that Mrs. Oglethorpe's chair was slightly behind Mr. Oglethorpe's chair. When the wise one asked for information, Mr. Oglethorpe took charge with a forceful tone and described how he and Mrs. Oglethorpe were very cooperative in their parenting. This was difficult for the wise one to imagine, as Mrs. Oglethorpe remained quiet throughout the session.

Last, the third wise one asked his questions. "Mrs. Oglethorpe, tell me exactly what happens after Oliver hits you. Yes, I understand that you send him to his room. But what happens immediately after he hits you—the next moment? Oh, you tell him to stop. I see. And then he says, 'Make me!' And then for approximately 3 minutes you argue with him about going to his room? And then, when you realize you can't get him to his room, you try to calm him down by taking him to Howard Johnson's for ice cream? This is all very interesting."

Mr. Oglethorpe was now ready to burst. "I took off 2 days from work for this. Will you please tell me what the problem is?"

The first wise one began. "It is very clear that Oliver vas allowed to nurse at his mother's breast for too long. He has never learned to be his own person and is angry that his needs are never satiated. Yet he feels powerless and impotent that he cannot protect his mother from the aggression he imagines his powerful father is inflicting upon her during the night. He hits his mother because he, in fact, loves her, and he identifies with his intimidating, aggressive father, vich is vhy he hits the other children in class. He does not allow himself to realize these feelings but instead acts them out. I believe I can help him understand these feelings, if I see him four times each veek over the next 2 to 3 years."

Next, the wise one with long frizzy hair and wearing sandals and a colorful print peasant shirt spoke. "This is a family that is ill configured. Instead of both parents feeling like equals, we have a hierarchy in which all the power resides in Mr. Oglethorpe. Mrs. Oglethorpe feels like one of the children, and therefore she is not respected by Oliver. We need to reconfigure this family in weekly family therapy, so that Mr. and Mrs. Oglethorpe are at the top of the hierarchy as equals, and so that Mr. Oglethorpe is comfortable playing with Oliver without worrying that he is relinquishing control by doing so."

Last, the third wise one took out his clipboard. "I've done some calculations. It seems that every time Oliver hits you, Mrs. Oglethorpe, over the next 3 minutes you reinforce him with your attention approximately every 4 seconds. This comes to approximately 50 reinforcers. I know you don't realize you're doing this, but every time you respond, whether by yelling or arguing or taking him for ice cream, you are increasing the probability that he will hit you again. We need to graph how many times this happens each day and then give you—and the teacher, by the way—an alternative approach."

Mr. and Mrs. Oglethorpe were confused. Each wise one sounded convincing to them, but no wise one seemed to give the others any credence. They all sounded right. They were about to wander back into the forest, more confused than when they arrived, when Mrs. Oglethorpe asked, "What about a diagnosis? None of you told us Oliver's disorder." The three wise ones glanced at each other in dismay and dismissed Mrs. Oglethorpe's question. The second wise one spoke. "There is a movement afoot to label rambunctious children like Oliver as having a hyperkinetic reaction, but that is a meaningless diagnosis. We all agree it explains nothing. It's just a label."

The wise one with the accent spoke with authority, "Ve have to understand vhy the boy acts this vay. Vut is going on in his head?"

Mrs. Oglethorpe was stunned. "You mean he has a problem with his brain?"

"Ve said nothing about the brain. Ve are talking about his head, his mind. This is what ve must understand to decide on his treatment."

In the 1960s and 1970s, the tradition of Kraeplin was down, but it was not out. Like a spore that withstands the harshness of a cold winter, the legacy of Kraeplin was surviving in places like Washington University in St. Louis. There, descriptive psychiatry was beginning its comeback, as psychiatrists focused on describing signs, symptoms, and the courses of psychiatric disorders rather than theories of etiology.

Begin the Revolution

Enter the *Diagnostic and Statistical Manual of Mental Disorders*, third edition (*DSM-III*), in 1980. The American Psychiatric Association (APA) had published the second edition (*DSM-II*) in 1968. It listed all the diagnoses in psychiatry and gave a brief description of each. It was a short book, and, though doctors used the names of the disorders listed in *DSM-II*, the descriptions of the disorders were sparse. Psychiatrists and the public were still far more interested in the etiology of the patient's problems. What unresolved intrapsychic conflicts of early life led to the disorder?

DSM-III established the revolution. The APA tried to wipe the slate clean of theories of etiology. It published a compendium of all the disorders in psychiatry, each with a list of observable signs and symptoms that would serve as criteria for the diagnosis. That way, using the criteria, doctors of different schools of thought would arrive at the same diagnosis for a given patient. They might disagree about his psychological conflicts, but at least they'd agree on diagnosis. In short, the APA tried to define psychiatric disorders by observable signs and symptoms and establish their primacy over theories of etiology.

For example, *DSM-II* defined "hyperkinetic reaction of childhood (or adolescence)" in one sentence as a disorder "characterized by overactivity, restlessness, distractibility, and short attention span, especially in young children." *DSM-III* changed the name to attention-deficit disorder with hyperactivity and defined it as follows:

The child displays, for his or her mental and chronological age, signs of developmentally inappropriate inattention, impulsivity, and hyperactivity. The signs must be reported by adults in the child's environment, such as parents and teachers. Because the symptoms are typically variable, they may not be observed directly by the clinician. When the reports of teachers and parents conflict, primary consideration should be given to the teacher reports because of greater familiarity with age-appropriate norms. Symptoms typically worsen in situations that require self-application, as in the classroom. Signs of the disorder may be absent when the child is in a new or a one-to-one situation.

The number of symptoms specified is for children between the ages of eight and ten, the peak age range for referral. In younger children, more severe forms of the symptoms and a greater number of symptoms are usually present. The opposite is true of older children.

A. Inattention. At least three of the following:
   1. often fails to finish things he or she starts
   2. often doesn't seem to listen
   3. easily distracted
   4. has difficulty concentrating on schoolwork or other tasks requiring sustained attention

    5. has difficulty sticking to a play activity

B. Impulsivity. At least three of the following:
1. often acts before thinking
2. shifts excessively from one activity to another
3. has difficulty organizing work (this not being due to cognitive impairment)
4. needs a lot of supervision
5. frequently calls out in class
6. has difficulty awaiting turn in games or group situations

C. Hyperactivity. At least two of the following:
1. runs about or climbs on things excessively
2. has difficulty sitting still or fidgets excessively
3. has difficulty staying seated
4. moves about excessively during sleep
5. is always "on the go" or acts as if "driven by a motor"

D. Onset before the age of seven.

E. Duration of at least six months.

F. Not due to Schizophrenia, Affective Disorder, or Severe or Profound Mental Retardation.

In addition, *DSM-III* set criteria for the diagnoses of attention-deficit disorder without hyperactivity and attention-deficit disorder, residual type.

One can see the profound change in diagnostic criteria. *DSM-III* demanded that explicit signs be observed. It also offered different subtypes of attention-deficit disorder. Using this new, descriptive model, *DSM-III* also set out criteria for types of depression, anxiety disorders, impulse disorders, sexual disorders, schizophrenia, and so on. Over the subsequent two decades, the criteria of *DSM-III* were modified, and they will certainly be modified again and again. Nevertheless, psychiatry had entered the world of observable and measurable signs. Etiology was almost never part of the diagnostic criteria.

Psychiatry was looking to model other specialties in medicine that could measure dysfunction. If cardiologists could agree upon criteria for a dysfunctional heart, what prevented psychiatrists from establishing criteria for a dysfunctional brain? Plenty.

We would never want to insult it, but the heart is a relatively simple organ. It is a pump. You can measure how much it pumps and how efficiently it pumps. When it pumps inadequately, the person becomes dizzy or faint. The brain is far more than a pump. What is it? How does one measure the dysfunction of behavior or feelings? How does one recognize, much less agree upon, the pathology of the human experience?

Defining the structural pathology of the brain—that is, the structural abnormality that causes a malady—is a relatively straightforward task. Even before CAT scans and MRIs, doctors could perform an autopsy and find the brain tumor that killed the patient. This didn't help that patient, but doctors could discover and classify different structural maladies of the brain. Defining the functional pathology of the brain is a more philosophically difficult, time-consuming, and, needless to say, highly contentious task. It is also still a work in progress.

Even the seemingly observable signs are easily debated. For example, "difficulty staying seated" is still a subjective call. *DSM-III* tried to build safeguards into the system, such as relying on the teacher's viewpoint, as teachers generally have experience with a broader range of children than parents have. To be sure, it is an evolving, imperfect system based on subjective judgment, not yet on objective lab tests.

At the start of the 21st century, researchers are beginning to make objective measurements of the brain to see if patients with the same disorder have the same brain dysfunction. Such research often includes measuring the concentration of different neurotransmitters, enzymes, and receptor sites; using an MRI to visualize and measure the different lobes and spaces within the brain; or employing a PET scan to measure the amount of glucose used in different parts of the brain during specific tasks.

Understanding Behavior Yesterday, Understanding the Brain Today

The psychological theories of the mid-20th century were plagued by a gaping hole. They focused on behavior and the psychological antecedents of emotional states, but they rarely acknowledged the organ in which all this was happening. It was as if the brain was in charge of moving our limbs and controlling our intellectual functioning, but all the psychology floated apart from the body, like an invisible helium balloon tethered to one's belt. It was as if theorists had been trying to describe a rash without mentioning skin.

To be sure, these earlier theorists were aware that they were describing theories of brain function, and they could not benefit from technology that was not yet available. Still, there was no connection between theories of mind and function of the brain.

If blood flow is insufficient, we intuitively trace it back to an inefficiently pumping heart. But we don't immediately connect our moods, our thoughts, or even our actions to our brain function. Rather, we blame our parents, or we rail about personal responsibility—important etiological factors, to be sure, but an incomplete understanding of human behavior.

Today's researchers are beginning to connect brain and behavior. Scientists can compare the brain chemicals of people with and without certain disorders, and they can measure the changes in brain chemistry before and after medicine is taken. Today's view of the brain, the world's most complicated contraption, is still rudimentary but far superior to any previous understanding. Researchers now have a foothold. Disorders of behavior are now known to be disorders of the brain. With this in mind, psychiatric medicine begins to make sense. Medicines are an efficient way to change the brain.

Now, we will explore a surprising twist.

Nature and Nurture: Not So Different After All

A look inside the brain shows us how its functioning is affected by environmental factors. One fascinating study by Lewis Baxter and Jeffrey Schwartz and their team at the University of California, Los Angeles, used PET scans to examine the brain functioning of patients with obsessive-compulsive disorder (OCD) before and after treatment with medicine and before and after treatment with a nonpharmacological behavioral treatment (Baxter, 1992). The PET scans of patients who responded to either medication or behavioral treatment showed a change: a decrease in glucose utilization in a part of the brain known as the caudate nucleus. Patients who did not respond to these treatments, as well as those treated with placebo, did not show this change.

This study demonstrates that although medicine can change the brain, so does successful learning through a talking/doing therapy. A type of psychotherapy, without the concomitant use of medicine, changed the patient's brain functioning and helped diminish the patient's symptoms. What happens in the environment has an observable effect on the brain.

Let's extend the principle one startling step. If learning through an interaction with another person changes the brain, then the brain is probably being changed whenever one interacts with others in a way that leaves a lasting impression. When you teach your child to ride a bike, you are changing his brain. When you teach your child not to steal, you are changing her brain. When you model politeness to your child, you are changing his brain. And when you scream at your child that she is a fool, you are changing her brain.

Every time a child learns, tracks of neurons are being modified with a resulting effect on the child's brain. These changes are highly complex and still undefined, but the principle that experiences have an effect on the brain is beginning to be scientifically validated.

That is not to say that all human behavior is the result of learning. The brain also comes prewired. Children are born with different traits that reflect their inborn wiring. That wiring is also barely understood. But that's life in a young science. We have only taken the first steps toward a biological understanding of this most complex condition called human psychology.

Fluidity between nature and nurture must be acknowledged. Life experiences are encoded on the brain. Medicine is not the only way of influencing the child's brain, but it is the most easily measured and best-understood method. The behaviors of those around the child also influence the child's brain, and parents in particular exercise this influence all the time in thousands of ways. The evidence of this is seen in a child's learned behaviors.

A Twist of Irony

The brain simultaneously is affected by and affects the world around it. An infant's brain experiences irritability, causing the baby to cry. The sound of the baby crying, in turn, affects the brain of the vigilant parent, who feels the need to nurture and therefore picks up the baby. This, in turn, soothes the now comfortable baby, whose brain is encoded with a memory of this sequence of events.

If a child's brain experiences a chronically irritable mood, this, in turn, affects the brain of the mother, who might be chronically irritable herself. The mother becomes frustrated and screams. The child feels angry and hurt and calls his mother a fat jerk. An increasingly frustrated mother slaps her child. An increasingly resentful child kicks his mother. The brain of the child initiates behavior. The environment (in this case, the mother) responds to the child's behavior, thereby affecting the child's brain, which responds to his mother's behavior. Round and round and round we go. All this is set into the child's developing brain. Run this sequence hundreds and hundreds of times. Make it more complex, adding in the little sister taunting her brother and the father demanding that his wife simmer down. All these mold the child's brain and determine who the child becomes. Yes, parents, too, affect their child's brain.

Where in this story is the boundary between nature and nurture? When is the screaming mother no longer an environmental factor but a biological cause of neurological change in her child's brain? When is the child's decision to kick no longer a brain function but an environmental factor, as it infuriates his mother, who screams longer and louder?

What a twist of irony if the parent who would not permit her child to take psychiatric medicine for fear of changing his brain was the parent who was changing his brain through her constant screaming.

The brain changes the world around it. The brain is changed by the world around it. This is the dynamic process that makes us who we are.

A More Complicated World

The dimly lit world of human behavior in which psychiatrists live is slowly becoming illuminated. The modern classification of disorders offers an imperfect but slowly improving diagnostic structure by which to categorize mental maladies. Medical technology offers a look inside the human brain in an attempt to discover the biological correlates of the newly described disorders. The theories and observations of Freud and his successors, although no longer dominant, still bring a deeper understanding to human psychology and will be tested scientifically.

Psychiatric disorders are being defined, but the boundaries between these disorders and normalcy are sometimes poorly delineated. Although the symptoms of psychiatric disorders are troubling, the signs are sometimes less than perfectly objective. Psychological symptoms, without a clear disorder, present a dilemma. Patients want their pain resolved, but they are concerned that changing the brain is not quite like changing the kidneys or lungs.

So What's a Parent to Do?

Discussing the criteria for changing one's body, the nuances of symptoms and disorders, and the netherworld between mind and body could keep philosophers busy for years on end.

In real life, decisions must be made and made now, before a child becomes an adult. Parents have one trip through with each child and must decide whether to intervene or to defer.

Rob is 7 years old. He lives in a small, cramped apartment in the city with his overworked, chronically tense parents. His teacher is a strict control freak. Rob's parents and school can no longer tolerate Rob's high energy level. A child psychiatrist concludes that Rob has mild ADHD. He informs Rob's parents that in another environment Rob might do a little better, maybe would even fall just short of the criteria for ADHD. Yes, Rob is inherently active, but living in a cramped apartment with two highly stressed parents makes Rob's activity level seem more problematic. The teacher's style is not helping matters, and neither is being in a class of 32 children.

The child psychiatrist says Rob does not have a life-threatening illness. He is not in severe pain, and his mild dysfunction is, in part, a function of his environment. If his parents agree, Rob could be treated with Ritalin. Rob's parents initially decline.

They struggle with their decision. Should they move out of the city? They could move to two acres in suburbia, where Rob would be free to spend the afternoons running around the property. In the suburbs, Rob would have fewer children in his class, and his teacher would be better able to keep Rob busy and reward him for completing his work. Rob would still be more active than his peers, but he would be more tolerable and less dysfunctional. Maybe getting out of the city would lighten his parents' moods as well. Then they'd be able to cut Rob a little slack.

Rob's parents don't want to move to the suburbs. Moving out of the city would mean a longer commute and less time with Rob. And there's no guarantee that Rob would get a well-trained, easygoing teacher in the 'burbs. They can't afford a private school within the city. Can they change who they are? Should they be on medicine? No, they conclude, we're stressed but not dysfunctional. We don't need medicine. In short, controlling the environment might be helpful, but there's no certainty, and it isn't going to happen.

Rob's parents inform the doctor that they're not moving to a new home and they're not changing schools. They have a problem, and they have it here and now. They see Rob as dysfunctional, and they want to consider medicating him. "Doctor, how should we decide?"

CHAPTER 5

A Duty to Treat

|||||||||||||||||||||||||||||||||||||||||||||||||||||||||||||||||||||||||

A Doctor's Duty

Different forces drive the decision to treat. Symptoms bring the patient to the doctor. Doctors are guided by the patient's signs of illness. In the sometimes blurry world of signs and symptoms, what duty drives the physician?

Hippocrates, in his famous oath, promised to act "for the benefit of my patients." That's about it. That's about as specific as the great physician of ancient Greece ever got. Sure, he promised to pass his knowledge on to the next generation. He promised to keep confidences and not to be mischievous or corrupt. He promised to "abstain from . . . [treatment that] is deleterious" (*Guthrie, 1990)* In terms of what he would actually do for his patients, however, he only promised to do what benefits them. In a nutshell, Hippocrates promised to do what is beneficial and not what is deleterious.

He certainly left lots of room for judgment. Not a word about liposuction. Not a word about steroids. Not a word about Ritalin. No mention of pain or dysfunction or quality of life. He left us to fill in the blanks. He didn't worry about overprescribed or underprescribed. Nevertheless, in essence, he gave us the principle that guides physicians in their decisions to prescribe medicine for their patients. Weigh the potential benefits against the risks. It's that simple.

Raj is a 19-year-old college freshman. He has been severely depressed for the past 3 years. He has made two suicide attempts, each resulting in a psychiatric hospitalization. He has been on four different antidepressants, but none of them has helped. His parents and his psychiatrist are very worried about him but don't know what to do next.

Raj's psychiatrist would like to consider one of the effective, but more infrequently used, tricyclic antidepressants, which have fallen out of favor since the advent of the SSRIs due to their higher likelihood of side effects. The possible side effects of tricyclics include dry mouth, constipation, dizziness, blurry vision, and even heart-rhythm changes. The psychiatrist discusses the possibility of side effects versus the possibility of benefit from the medicine with Raj and his parents. They decide to proceed with a trial of medicine.

Putting Pen to Pad

Writing a prescription looks easy—just scribble illegible markings on the almighty prescription pad and hand it to the patient. But much lies below the surface. The prescription is the culmination of a series of steps, each of them crucial yet often assumed or ignored. The process includes establishing a trusting relationship with the patient, evaluating the patient's complaints, discussing possible treatments with the patient, and then helping the patient decide what to do.

In years past, the doctor, in his paternalistic wisdom, decided on the patient's care. He (most doctors were men) was the holder of wisdom and good judgment. He spoke with (sometimes not so) tender authority to unknowledgeable patients who were expected to follow his directions without question. This provided the patient with a sense of security, a sense that the doctor was in control of an anxiety-provoking situation.

Today, the patient is more knowledgeable and takes more responsibility for some of the difficult decisions. Doctors are forced to acknowledge that their wisdom is finite, that every treatment has at least a little of the unknown. Patients participate in deciding whether to proceed. The doctor is one source of information, though perhaps not the ultimate source.

Some patients feel empowered by this opportunity, and others are overwhelmed. Some patients hit the Internet running, researching their disorder and its treatment, familiarizing themselves with the travails of every person from London to Los Angeles who has shared common symptoms.

Other patients look longingly for the fatherly physician of old who would simply tell them what to do. They miss the feeling of security they got from following their doctor's advice. The more their physician tries to drag them into the 21st century by making them a part of the decision-making process, the more they long to rely on their doctor's experience and judgment.

Most physicians attempt to accommodate a patient's style and needs. Some are more accommodating than others. What all physicians share is a duty to do, as Hippocrates said, what the physician believes will benefit the patient. And yes, there is a lot of wiggle room for discussion about what is painful and what is dysfunctional. Whether our relationship with our physician is longstanding or fleeting, whether we look for the physician to decide or whether we demand a say in our own care, ultimately the physician has a duty to do what benefits the patient. The physician has a duty to weigh potential benefits against risks.

Risk versus Benefit: And the Winner Is . . . ?

Every prescription does not require a 3-hour deliberation regarding the risk-benefit ratio. That would bring a halt to the delivery of medical services. Usually we rely on our doctors to quickly assess risks and benefits and make a decision. When we consider certain medicines, however—for example, those that we expect to take for longer than a few days and affect our brain chemistry—we often want a more careful analysis.

Some benefits and risks are more difficult to assess.

Daryl is 12. His parents are considering the use of Adderall. Dr. Ortega has said the medicine will probably help Daryl quell his impulsivity. She has reviewed the likelihood of diminished appetite and the medicine's possible effect on Daryl's weight.

Daryl's parents now have a more difficult disagreement to resolve. Will medicine prevent Daryl from learning to compensate for his inborn characteristics? Daryl's father reports that he was just like Daryl: impulsive, often in trouble, always clowning to fit in with his peers. Although he does not want his son to experience the same growing pains, he feels that he learned from his struggles. He understands himself better and believes his experience made him a stronger person. Daryl's mother contends that her son's current self-esteem is in jeopardy. If he's constantly in trouble, he'll continue to feel bad about himself. He'll be more likely to hang out with other kids with self-esteem problems and maybe end up abusing drugs and alcohol.

Dr. Ortega appreciates each parent's viewpoint. Both parents question the subtle effects of medicine and suggest a potential course of events. The mother's viewpoint is palpably relevant, given Daryl's current problems at school, at soccer, and on the bus. The father's viewpoint is intriguing, if difficult to test. In 30 years, will Daryl have learned to turn his impulsivity, a current liability, into an asset? Will medication prevent him from learning to do so? And will this long-term benefit be worth the predictable pain of Daryl's childhood and the risk that he will never learn to do so? Dr. Ortega doesn't really know.

Weighing risks and benefits is an imperfect solution when risks and benefits are not fully understood, but it is our only solution. Doctors are obligated to do what benefits their patients. If that includes the use of medicine, a doctor's duty is to answer the patient's questions with his or her best understanding. That is all he or she can do.

"So, Here's What I Need, Doc!"

Many patients now independently pursue and evaluate medical procedures, especially those of an elective nature. In fact, when the decisions are less medically crucial, some patients bypass the doctor-patient relationship and arrive at their own conclusions. When doctors are overly compliant with this approach and abdicate their judgment, medical care is jeopardized. The writing of the prescription is done not with due care but rather with due expediency, a simple rubber-stamping by the physician. Although this probably happens infrequently, it is a dramatic representation that flames the fears of overprescribing. The decision to prescribe is best made within the context of a trusting doctor-patient relationship.

I'm sitting in my office on a Tuesday afternoon. A mother I've never met calls requesting an immediate appointment for her 16-year-old son so that I can prescribe Ritalin. This does not sound like a psychiatric emergency, so I ask her why the appointment has to be immediate. The SATs are this Saturday, the mother responds with a hint of indignation.

Stories such as this are infrequent, but they represent instances in which parents see the physician as the gatekeeper to the treatment they have already decided their child needs. There is no doctor-patient relationship.

This patient resists benefiting from the physician's experience or listens with a biased ear, minimizing the physician's opinion. These patients often end up avoiding appointments, seeing them as superfluous and preferring to run their own treatment. Because modern psychiatric medicines can be easy to use and because the target symptom is often very subjective, some patients begin to play with the dose themselves.

As elective medical procedures become more available, patients often feel empowered to act on their own research and to seek medicine. Paradoxically, the doctor-patient relationship is more threatened. The patient feels comfortable defining the problem and initiating an elective treatment without the guidance of the physician. The patient's happiness is the immediate goal of treatment. More traditional medical criteria such as severe pain or significant dysfunction are bypassed.

The decisions here are grayer—less certain and more subject to debate—and this can appear to characterize child psychiatry in particular. The public sees many psychiatric medicines as elective, necessary only in that they help an overwrought parent or teacher. Even when problems are severe, even when there is significant dysfunction, many are quick to stand in judgment and quick to assume medicines are unnecessary and overprescribed.

Difficult Decisions

Sometimes the calls are tough, but ultimately decisions must be made.

Susan is 14 years old. She is an attractive young woman, but something seems wrong. She has no eyebrows and no eyelashes. She has pulled them out. Beneath Susan's bandanna are large bald patches where she has pulled out her hair. Although she is fully pubescent, Susan has no remaining pubic hair.

Susan has trichotillomania, a vexing disorder to treat. She feels compelled to pull out hair. In addition, she has some mild symptoms of obsessive-compulsive disorder. Psychotherapy has not helped. Behavior therapy has helped minimally. The scientific evidence that medicine might help trichotillomania is equivocal at best. My first thought is to do nothing. That is always a possibility, though sometimes not a comfortable one. Instead, after consulting with Susan and her parents, and taking her symptoms of obsessive-compulsive disorder into account, I decide that the possible benefits of medicine outweigh the risks.

Medicine is started. Susan has a mild side effect of tiredness. We decide to continue the medicine. After 3 months at a reasonable dose, Susan has not changed. We decide to discontinue medicine and resume our attempts at behavior therapy. If Susan does not improve, we might consider a trial of a different medicine. For now, Susan and her parents decide to defer that possibility.

CHAPTER 6

The Challenge of Children

‖‖

"Dr. Kalikow, I've felt terrible for the past 4 months or so. I'm moody and irritable. I've been feeling down in the dumps. Sometimes I even wonder if life is worth living. I awake in the middle of the night and can't get back to sleep. Nothing is fun anymore. I don't feel like playing tennis, and, even though I love my wife, I've got to be honest with you, when we're in bed, I'm just, you know, going through the motions. I just don't know why I'm feeling this way. Work is stressful, but that's always been true. Can you help?"

This is not the voice of a child or an adolescent. This is a married adult. He paints a textbook picture of depression. Clear and precise. He's able to compare how he felt last week and how he feels now. He comes voluntarily, of his own accord, looking for help.

Most children do not present their symptoms so obviously. They are usually less insightful and less articulate than adults. In addition, because they are dependent, children present at the behest of others. Although they are not necessarily unwilling, usually their parents, not the children themselves, have decided there is a problem. Children are also in a state of constant change and reflect the behavior of those around them.

Our understanding of the psychiatric disorders of children and adolescents is a work in progress and therefore presents another difficulty in evaluating children. Diagnostic criteria have changed drastically over recent decades and continue to change. Many children present with a textbook picture of a particular disorder, and the decision to medicate is clear. But many children do not. In our struggle to understand a complex array of factors affecting the child's psychological status, we may find certainty where it does not exist. In doing so, we run the risk of prescribing medicine for what begins as a diagnostic dilemma and concludes as a diagnostic delusion.

In short, children are subject to a host of confounding influences. These make the psychiatric evaluation and therefore the decision to medicate a trying task.

Whose Symptom Is It Anyway?

Most children and teenagers do not initiate a visit to the local child psychiatrist. Their parents do. Most children come willingly. Some come reluctantly. A few come very grudgingly. Though the parent might think there is a problem, the child does not necessarily agree. Although most children abide their parents' wishes and are cooperative, adolescents, in particular, often have their own ideas about what is or is not a problem.

Yoni is 17 years old and a senior in high school. His liberal-minded parents are worried that he has been smoking too much marijuana. They suggest to Yoni that maybe he should "see someone." Yoni responds, "You mean a shrink? I don't think so."

After much cajoling and arm-twisting, Yoni comes to see me. Yoni is polite but far less than enthusiastic. He is willing to talk about his plans for college, but he cannot countenance the possibility that his marijuana smoking is causing him trouble. After the second visit, he digs in his heels. "Forget it, Mom. I'm not going. You're just throwing away your money. Kalikow's a nice guy, but I don't have a problem. If you think there's a problem, see him yourself. Later."

57

Whose problem is it anyway? Sometimes teenagers do not see the problem and assert that this is really their parent's problem. I'm perfectly fine, thank you. Their frustrated parents, looking desperately for something that will help their child, want to exert their control in their child's best interest.

Devin is 16 years old. When he was 14, his mother, Mrs. Phillipo, brought him to the doctor for an evaluation. The doctor concluded that Devin might have ADHD and might benefit from Adderall, which Devin took reluctantly for 2 years. Now Mrs. Phillipo complains that Devin is refusing to take the medicine.

Sitting in the doctor's office, Devin shoots back, "Mom, I'm 16 years old. It's my life, and I don't need medicine to help me in school. There's nothing wrong with B's and C's for a musician like me, who's not going to college. I'd rather get C's on my own than A's by taking some artificial chemical cooked up in a lab. And that stuff stifles my creativity. I can't write my music. I lose my imagination. I'm no longer inspired, and I'm not going to take it!"

Who's the patient? Symptoms are by definition the patient's subjective sense of a problem. Devin would argue that he has no subjective sense of any problem. His mother would argue that Devin is not in a position to judge. He's being defensive because, after all these years of hearing that he is not living up to his potential, he doesn't want to see himself as damaged goods. Maybe he's even depressed. Devin would respond that his mother is being offensive because she's so hung up on grades and that although he has ADHD, they say that Einstein did too. To what extent is a parent's complaint considered the child's symptom?

Throughout childhood there is a tension between diminishing dependence and increasing independence. The wise parent tries to maintain control and simultaneously allow for growth. Medical decisions, however, push the limits of this process.

Marco is 17. He has always been a bright but unmotivated student, happier watching *Star Trek* reruns than doing homework. This has never sat very well with his highly educated parents, who expect Marco to live up to his potential. Marco's mother is supportive but very anxious about her son and constantly asks Marco if his schoolwork is done. Of course, it never is.

Over the course of his high school years, Marco becomes increasingly depressed. He is not suicidal, but he is more argumentative with his parents, is falling further behind in his schoolwork, and has not worked an iota on his college applications. This is making his mother nuts. Marco has had two trials of antidepressants, both discontinued because of side effects.

Though Marco's parents continue to hound him about his college applications, in fact, they are more worried about his depression. His mother imagines life a year from now. Marco's friends will be away at college, while Marco will sit at home watching TV, unable to muster the energy to get a job. She wants Marco to try another antidepressant. Marco acknowledges his depression but adamantly refuses to try another antidepressant.

Parents differ about what constitutes a compelling need to medicate. If a teenager is depressed and suicidal, most parents feel a compelling need to treat. If a high-school student is a bit unfocused and not achieving to his potential, only some parents feel a compelling need to treat. As such, the decision to medicate an adolescent reflects both the adolescent's struggle for independence and the values of the parents. This challenge is unique to working with children and adolescents.

Listening with a Grain of Salt

Oh, the challenge of listening to a child! Sometimes brutally honest, other times using smoke and mirrors, a child seeks to protect himself or herself from a painful reality. Talking to a child can be like talking to a convincing con man or a lousy liar. The child can be very believable or painfully transparent. You wonder, "Did that actually happen or is this wishful thinking?" Sometimes the superficial smile belies the child's hurt, which the child is loath to share with a doctor he or she does not know and whose services he or she did not request. The smile becomes the mask of equanimity, the child's attempt to convince you, and often himself or herself, that all is well.

A child might feel embarrassed about sharing problems with the doctor. Maybe he or she is not even aware of the difficulties. Ask the child who will not fall asleep without a parent lying next to him about bedtime, and you might hear a simple, "I fall asleep okay." Ask the child who has no friends what she does at recess, and you might hear a confident, "I play with my friends." Ask the teenager who can't remember where he put his homework about his organizational skills, and you might hear the assurance that everything is under control.

Children do not have the same facility with language as adults. They do not have the same level of insight, the same skills of self-observation, or the same perspective on time as adults. Children are more prone to say what they wish to be true and then believe it is so.

Mr. and Mrs. Sorrel report that Timmy is spending more time by himself. He doesn't want to see friends, doesn't enjoy his toys, seems sad most of the time, and talks about dying. When I see a reluctant Timmy in my office, he seems quiet and demoralized but denies ever feeling sad or angry or guilty or hopeless. Timmy does not come right out and say, "I sure feel hopeless, Dr. Kalikow. I need some help."

The desperation of the child's cover-up can reflect an obvious defense against the pain of taking responsibility.

Jenny is sitting between her parents. Her father, Mr. Smith, reports that 8-year-old Jenny has fits of rage. He says that earlier that morning, she punched her sister and scratched her mother. Mrs. Smith sits, holding back her tears, scratch marks apparent on her left forearm. Jenny immediately snaps back at her father, "Mandy punched me first. And I never scratched Mommy. She poked herself with a fork."

This indirect and less than accurate manner of communicating does not mix well with the pace of modern medical care. Understanding a child takes time and patience, both lacking in the 15 minutes some allot for talking with the child. Additional information must also be obtained from parents. In not allowing the time to understand the child's symptoms more accurately, we run the risk of reducing our evaluation of the child to our first impression and preventing our understanding from growing over time.

Fourteen-year-old Eli is a raging bull. His parents consult Dr. Westervelt about the possibility of using medicine to treat Eli's anger. During the evaluation, Eli is belligerent and obnoxious and flings the toy basketball against the wall of the doctor's office. Whenever Dr. Westervelt suggests a reason for Eli's anger, Eli responds by throwing the ball harder against the wall, closer and closer to the doctor's framed diplomas.

Dr. Westervelt, already graying and losing his hair, feels like telling Eli's parents that Eli would be better served by another child psychiatrist. He recognizes his own frustration, however, and decides to stay the course. Over the upcoming months, Eli eventually calms to a dull roar. Dr. Westervelt learns about Eli's anxiety about his health and his angry confusion about whether his parents are progressing with their stalled divorce proceedings. The use of medicine is deferred.

Responsible adults usually supply accurate, even insightful information about the child, but sometimes parents have their own agenda and can unwittingly give biased information.

Mrs. Solaro has a long history of anxiety. Although Lexapro has changed her life, nobody would accuse her of being laid back or mellow. She is dramatic, effusive, ever talkative, and oblivious to the invisible boundaries that separate people.

Sandra is Mrs. Solaro's 8-year-old daughter. Sandra is a demanding and defiant little girl who is prone to intense rages. In describing Sandra to Dr. Nathanson, Mrs. Solaro continually refers to Sandra's anxiety, almost unaware of Dr. Nathanson's specific questions. Sandra has had some symptoms of anxiety, but Dr. Nathanson realizes that she is far more complex. Nevertheless, her mother plugs away at the possibility of an anxiety disorder like a lobbyist pushing for a pet project. She insists that she herself has been transformed by Lexapro, and she's sure her daughter will be too.

In short, children are a challenge to evaluate. The evaluation can sometimes be frustrating but should always be multifaceted, involving talking to the child, taking a detailed history from the parents, and obtaining some information from, or at least about, the school. If time is not taken to do a proper evaluation, including understanding the dynamics of the child's family, the use of medicine can be hurried.

If Only You Were a Better Parent

Over recent years, the nature-nurture debate has swung toward the importance of nature, but the influence of nurture looms large. Parents still too often feel a level of responsibility beyond what is reasonable. Blaming the child's parents is a national pastime, the subject of countless movies and books, a cultural truism from the 20th century. For decades, parents have been seen as the cause of the child's problems. Understanding the role of the environment is crucial. If the environment is overly represented, however, biological influences, for which medicine might be an appropriate treatment, will be overlooked.

Harvey is 11, and, like his mother, a bundle of nerves. He worries about anything and everything. He gets sweaty palms and palpitations. Harvey's father blames his wife for having taught their son how to worry. He therefore will not consider using medicine to diminish Harvey's anxieties.

After further discussion, Harvey's father begins to appreciate that, although Harvey has been influenced by his mother's anxiety, he was also born with a biological predisposition toward anxiety, a propensity he demonstrated even as a toddler. He acknowledges that Harvey's 13-year-old sister spends lots of time with her mother yet is as cool as a cucumber.

Parents influence their children in powerful ways, but they do not write on blank slates. Each child arrives biologically wired for certain traits and sometimes with a predisposition for a psychiatric disorder. Understanding this wiring is the frontier of child psychiatry but should only be the starting point of understanding a child.

Tina is 6 and has been hard to console since birth. She is the "difficult" child. Tina's parents are rigid and demeaning. When Tina screams, her mother ignores all her psychologist's advice and screams back.

Tina and her mother have to leave the house in 15 minutes. Tina's mother tells Tina to put on her sneakers. Tina refuses. Tina's mother demands that Tina put on her sneakers this minute. Tina refuses. Now Tina's mother screams, "Why are you so difficult?! I can't take it! Why can't you be more like your brother, Alex?"

Tina's father comes running down the stairs in his wife's defense. He tells Tina, "Stop being such a baby, and just do what you were told, damn it. If you're going to act like a baby, we'll put you back in your crib. Is that what you want? Huh?"

When Tina's grandparents are over at the house on Sunday and ask what the psychologist has been saying, Tina's mother reduces the psychologist's explanation of Tina to the highly oversimplified statements: "She has a difficult temperament. She was born that way. We might have to start her on medicine."

Tina's parents find it easier to see Tina as having a biological problem than to acknowledge the negative influence of their insensitive parenting. If she does not improve, they will too quickly consider medicine, instead of taking a hard look at their own behavior. If the 20th century left parents feeling overly responsible for each of their child's foibles, the 21st century runs the risk of convincing parents that their children come completely prewired and that their own impact is minimal.

Reflecting the World around Them

Children are influenced by their upbringing and their biology. They also reflect what is happening in their immediate world, making diagnosis difficult.

Patty Brown is 9 years old. She is brought to see me by her mother, who is in the midst of a brutal divorce with her husband, who refuses to participate in Patty's evaluation. Mrs. Brown reports that Patty has been crying more over the past 2 months. She doesn't want to see her friends and is clingy at bedtime. Despite the obvious recent family upheaval that is overwhelming Patty, Mrs. Brown thinks Patty has depression and wants her started on an antidepressant.

Despite her forceful initial presentation, Mrs. Brown ultimately confides that she herself has been feeling hopeless, betrayed, and angry. She hasn't been sleeping and spends hours crying when Patty is in school.

Is Patty depressed, is she responding to the devastation of a divorce, or is she simply reflecting her mother's depression? Is Mrs. Brown's report about Patty more a projection of her own difficulties? Who is really the patient here? Who, if anyone, should be started on medicine? Evaluating a child sometimes challenges the doctor to differentiate the child's problem from that of the parent.

The Right to Choose Your Work

Adults can choose where they want to work. A multitude of factors determine what we each do, but rarely are we legally bound to a specific job. Not so for children. Children are legally mandated to attend school. As adults, we can pursue a job that plays to our strengths. Good with numbers? Go into accounting. Friendly and outgoing? Consider sales. Are you a very slow reader? Think twice before you apply to law school. If you decide on law school, it will be your choice.

Children do not have a choice. The law demands, and our culture expects, that children will attend school. Furthermore, the school environment places a premium on certain types of learning but not others. Reading is emphasized more than constructing, and writing valued more than designing.

Children present a challenge because they are being evaluated within a context to which they are legally mandated. Functioning reflects an interaction between our biology and the demands of our environment. The school environment plays a powerful role in determining whether a child is dysfunctional.

Sal is 13 years old and in seventh grade. He is a quiet but curious boy who loves to take things apart to see how they work. Sometimes he can even put them back together. Sal can sit for hours investigating the wiring of a radio or fax machine or anything else his mother designates as permanently broken. Despite being irritated by the mess in the basement, Sal's mother admits that Sal is becoming quite adept at understanding and fixing things.

Unfortunately, Sal's school does not offer a hands-on course on dismantling appliances. Instead, Sal is expected to master language-based tasks, such as reading his social studies book and writing a composition with an introduction, supporting paragraphs, and a conclusion. Sal has a hard time staying focused on these activities. They all play to his weaknesses in language. Sal is fairly focused if he's interested, but without that motivation Sal tends to drift off into oblivion. He dreams about the day when he'll be able to own a repair shop and spend his time tinkering with and fixing appliances.

Sal's mother understands her son. He is just like his grandfather, who owned a successful TV repair shop. She tries to buoy Sal's flagging self-esteem. She wants him to do well in school, but in the back of her mind she plans on getting Sal into a vocational school when he's eligible in the 11th grade. Until then, Sal will continue slugging it out with his pencils and books and save the tinkering for weekends.

Mandatory education is not the villain, but we must acknowledge that our system of education places a premium on certain language-based skills, such as listening to lectures, reading texts, and writing essays. These demands highlight the cognitive weaknesses of some children and often fail to reveal and reinforce their unique strengths.

The Evolving Child

Children are, by their very nature, constantly changing. As they change, so do their responsibilities. Children who do not seem symptomatic at one stage might during the next. Differentiating symptoms from normal development can be a challenge.

At 7 years old Ben was a reasonably attentive child. He listened to his teacher's lessons about addition and subtraction and was as organized as a second grader needed to be. Four years later, Ben's parents complain that he could lose his shadow on a sunny day. They say he is always leaving his baseball glove at the field and never knows where to find his windbreaker. He always seems to be leaving his homework sheets in his locker and doodles with his pencil when he should be focusing on his homework. Ben's father has a novel idea for Ben's next birthday party. He's going to send all Ben's friends into the community on a scavenger hunt. Whoever returns to the house with the largest number of Ben's belongings wins the prize. Ben's parents ask themselves if Ben has ADHD or if he is just a normal 11-year-old boy.

As children grow, so do our expectations of them. We expect them to be organized and responsible students. We expect them to be level-headed and in control of their moods. But sometimes our expectations are beyond the child's capabilities. If a child isn't able to perform a task, we don't know whether the child might outgrow the problem or adapt on his or her own. We can only wait and see.

CHAPTER 7

The Evolving Diagnoses of Children

||||||||||||||||||||||||||||||||||||||||||||||||||||||||||||||||

Driven by anticipation, I head into the bar. The guys of my old neighborhood are reuniting 20 years after our high-school graduation. I glance around and recognize no one. We must have the room in the back. Sitting at the bar are a bunch of middle-aged men, some bald, some with heavy jowls, others with bellies hanging over their belts. I don't remember going to school with kids who looked like that.

"Kevin!" One of the bald guys is suddenly embracing me. Who is this guy, and how do I get him off? He doesn't look like anyone I've ever known. I take a step back. This guy has a moustache and is balding and kind of gangly. He doesn't fit anyone in my memory bank. Hold it just a second. His eyes, nose, and mouth look familiar. Oh, my . . . I can't believe. . . . It's Sam.

I look at the attractive blonde next to Sam. She looks kind of familiar, but I'm less certain. She looks a bit like Erin, Sam's old girlfriend and the girl in the class most responsible for sending guys walking into closed doors. I'm about to give Erin the big hug I always dreamed of giving her during high school when Sam says, "Kevin, I'd like you to meet my wife, Claudia." Oops! I immediately change my plans and make a new mental file for Claudia. Mistaking Claudia for Sam's old flame, Erin, is a mistake I'm going to be sure to avoid.

Examining patients and identifying their disorders is a bit like meeting old friends. Some patients have disorders with all the expected features, recognizable right off the bat. Others present with some unexpected characteristics, and you look carefully for the telltale signs that help you draw the correct conclusion. Still others you're not sure about at all. You try to fit them into some known category. Sometimes you're right, and sometimes you're not. There are always consequences, however, so you try not to make any serious errors.

Of the many challenges in evaluating the child, among the most difficult is that many children do not fit neatly into the evolving diagnostic system, which is largely borrowed from adult psychiatry and adapted for use with children. Textbook cases of obsessive-compulsive disorder and attention-deficit hyperactivity disorder are easily recognized. Unfortunately, however, many children have not read the textbook and present with a combination of symptoms that are difficult to pigeonhole. They look a little like this or a little like that, but "to tell you the truth, Mrs. Bernstein, I'm just not sure."

With confusion and uncertainty comes vulnerability. Both parents and doctors want to organize the cacophony of symptoms under a recognized diagnostic label that carries the power of knowledge. Although receiving a diagnosis is painful, it brings the hope of relief and a potential understanding of cause, prognosis, and treatment plan.

However, in the world of child psychiatry, a world of complex patients and evolving diagnostic criteria, the hidden enemy is premature diagnosis and incorrect treatment plan. Given the confusing presentation of some children and the difficulty of applying adult diagnostic criteria to children, diving in too soon is easy to do.

Deepening Our Understanding
of Childhood Disorders

Since the publication of *DSM-III* in 1980, child psychiatrists have been increasingly trained to look for disorders, even if their etiology is not fully understood. Particularly if your patient wants to submit your bill to the insurance company, you had better find a disorder for the appropriate box on the claim form. These disorders serve as a kind of collective memory bank for psychiatrists. Yes, we have seen that constellation of symptoms before. It's called such-and-such disorder.

After 1980, psychiatrists relied on *DSM-III* and, since 1994, *DSM-IV*. As one can see from the titles of these books, however, the *DSM*s are works in progress, influenced by the most recent research. *DSM-II* preceded *DSM-III*. And, in 2013, *DSM-V* will follow *DSM-IV*. The current *DSM* system tries to include different aspects of a person's life in its diagnoses, but *DSM-IV* is not the final word. It is an evolving construct and subject to revision.

Child psychiatry tries to make sense of the complaints of parents and their children. *DSM-IV* is our collective memory bank for when we run into those complaints again. Putting a picture of Claudia in my memory bank was simple. Putting the criteria for some psychiatric disorders in our collective memory bank is more difficult because they have yet to be firmly established in children. And if you say, "What the hey! Let's have criteria that are broad and general and so what if I label some people with a disorder they don't really have?" then you might also end up treating with medicine that the patient doesn't really need.

Let's take a look at attention-deficit hyperactivity disorder and then bipolar disorder to see how this problem plays out in the real world.

The Better Defined, the More You Find

ADHD presents an enlightening demonstration of the evolution of a diagnosis. It is an atypical diagnosis of child psychiatry in that it was not extrapolated from adult psychiatry but rather developed as a disorder of children. Only in recent years has it been extended for use in adults. ADHD provides a good example of how symptoms are first identified and criteria are slowly developed to help organize those symptoms into a recognized disorder. The development of the diagnosis of ADHD demonstrates how one can catch a lot of fish and then go to work at sorting them out afterward. As we better define disorders by noting the obvious, we improve our ability to look critically at the subtle.

The thread of what we now call ADHD formally began in the early years of the 20th century. In 1902, Dr. George Still, an English pediatrician, described children with impulsivity and defiance. After the worldwide flu epidemic of 1918, symptoms such as hyperactivity were noted in children who had a known history of neurological illness—in particular, flu-associated encephalitis. In the decades that followed, these same symptoms of hyperactivity and impulsivity were noted in children who were never known to have had a neurological disorder. Because they did not have a history of an obvious neurological illness, these children were labeled with the fairly meaningless label of "minimal brain dysfunction" (MBD).

Eventually, with the publication of *DSM-II* in 1968, the label of MBD was discarded in favor of a descriptive word that said nothing of the unknown etiology or source of the problem. These children were diagnosed as "hyperkinetic reaction of childhood (or adolescence)" and became known as "hyperactive" children. Although the name allows teenagers to have this disorder, the text of *DSM-II* stated that "the behavior usually diminishes in adolescence." The text also noted that in addition to overactivity and restlessness, distractibility and short attention span are characteristic.

By 1980, with the publication of *DSM-III*, inattention was

viewed as the "prominent" symptom. Excess motor activity was seen as more often present in younger children and frequently diminishing in adolescence. Because attention span was now identified as the cardinal feature, the conglomerate of symptoms became known as attention-deficit disorder (ADD). Three subtypes were noted: ADD with hyperactivity, ADD without hyperactivity, and ADD, residual type.

Since the early 1980s, children with these symptoms have been studied more closely, and additional features have been noted. For example, many of these children are disorganized, procrastinate excessively, and have difficulties with planning. Some lose control of their anger too easily. In addition, it has been noted that the attention spans of these children fluctuate and are very dependent on the level of stimulation of their task. More recently, studies indicate that these children exhibit differences on various brain scans and blood tests.

We are witnessing the slow evolution of the criteria of a disorder. As more children are diagnosed, doctors better appreciate the subtleties previously missed and the ways in which children with ADHD are similar to and different from one another. As these similarities and differences are clarified, so too is the disorder.

By 1994, with the publication of *DSM-IV*, the mounting information led to yet another, if subtle, name change. The disorder became known as attention deficit hyperactivity disorder (ADHD) with three subtypes: ADHD, predominantly impulsive/hyperactive type; ADHD, predominantly inattentive type; and ADHD, combined type (that is, both impulsive/hyperactive and inattentive). Research over the upcoming decades will probably lead to even greater understanding and with it still more name changes, and the ADHD label may be divided into different diagnoses.

With better-delineated criteria, the disorder is being observed in people not originally suspected of having it. Previously, ADHD was rarely recognized in girls, as they are typically less active than their male counterparts. Today, with an improved understanding of inattention and impulsivity, the disorder is more often diagnosed in girls. Similarly, the disorder was previously thought to have run its course by early adolescence. Because our understanding of how these symptoms progress into adolescence and adulthood has improved, ADHD is now more frequently found in these age groups. Differentiating ADHD in preschoolers is also beginning to be explored significantly. When does the normal hyperactivity of a 3-year-old become the early signs of ADHD? This presents another frontier for fine-tuning the subtle nuances of this disorder.

During this stage of defining the disorder, as more people read about ADHD, they perk up and consider whether they might suffer with it. Many consult their physicians about this possibility. With an expanding supply of complaints from patients, doctors develop a more sophisticated understanding of who fits the criteria.

At the same time, however, doctors are wary about labeling anyone who does not quite fit the criteria. If criteria are interpreted too liberally, some people might be labeled with a disorder they don't have. *DSM-IV* seeks to minimize this risk by stipulating that the symptoms must cause impairment in two or more settings, rather than just one. Yet, driven by patients looking for answers and trying to organize a messy world of symptoms into a unifying diagnosis, doctors are vulnerable to stretching the criteria, to making a diagnosis even though the criteria are not quite met.

During the evolution of a psychiatric diagnosis, researchers face the question of whether a diagnosis is on a spectrum or stands as a distinct category. Whether ADHD is a spectrum diagnosis—some people being very inattentive but not quite meriting the diagnosis—or a categorical diagnosis—you either have it or you don't—is unclear at this time. An intriguing study by Shaw and colleagues (2011) found that those with ADHD, those without ADHD but with a moderate number of ADHD symptoms, those without ADHD but with only a mild number of ADHD symptoms and those without any symptoms of ADHD are on a biological spectrum. Children's brains are known to normally "thin" or "prune" the neurons of their cerebral cortex. In this study, the rate of this thinning was inversely proportional to the child's number of ADHD symptoms. That is, those with ADHD have the slowest rate of thinning the neurons of their cerebral cortex. Those with a moderate number of symptoms of ADHD were slightly faster. Those with only a mild number of symptoms were faster. And those without any symptoms of ADHD pruned at the fastest rate. This study points to ADHD being on a biological spectrum.

Research aside, however, the spectrum model is quite seductive. One can diagnose patients as borderline ADHD, namely as having "a bit of ADHD" or as being "kind of ADHDish." A diagnosis of ADHD justifies treatment with medicine. It's easy to use the spectrum model and diagnose patients as borderline ADHD. Whether you have "a little" ADHD or "a lot" of ADHD, the medicine will still work, at least to some extent. Because stimulant medicine improves the attention span of those with and without the disorder, the patient benefits anyway (Rapoport, Buchsbaum, Weingartner, Zahn, Ludlow, & Mikkelsen, 1980).

ADHD provides a good example of an evolving diagnosis with characteristics that are slowly becoming apparent and will gradually be incorporated into the criteria for the disorder. Now let's take a look at bipolar disorder, a disorder whose criteria in children are at a different stage of evolution.

The Example of Mood

Disordered mood has been recognized for millennia in adults. Children, however, were never seen as worthy of study. Even throughout most of the 20th century, while theories developed about adult mood disorders, children were seen as incapable of depression. Although psychiatry now recognizes that children can experience depression, it is still attempting to accurately describe different types of depression. As in all of science, debate drives progress. Bipolar disorder in children finds itself the focus of contentious debate.

When I worked on an in-patient psychiatric hospital unit during my psychiatric residency training, the concept of bipolar disorder, previously called manic depression, seemed relatively straightforward. These patients had prolonged periods of depression, during which they were burdened with unbearable sadness, lethargy, and a total lack of motivation, except for possibly the contemplation of suicide. These periods of depression alternated with prolonged bouts of mania, during which patients were full of energy, apparent mirth, or extreme irritability. They spoke faster than they could think, instigated laughter in those around them, had wild sexual encounters and drinking sprees, required almost no sleep, and lived life on the edge. These periods of depression or mania could last months at a time.

For years, these images of patients with bipolar disorder guided my evaluation of new patients. I looked for the textbook characteristics I had come to know. I found classic cases of bipolar disorder in teenagers infrequently and in children rarely. Bipolar disorder was said to be unusual in childhood, and I concluded that this must be true.

Artie is 17 years old. He tells me that throughout 10th grade he felt morose and sullen and frequently contemplated suicide. Constantly lethargic, he often couldn't make it to school. This is hard to imagine about the fast-talking young man currently sitting in my office. He is now brimming with energy. He seems pressured, and, although I am fascinated by his story, I'm not really relating to him. I am unable to take notes fast enough to keep pace with all the colorful details of what he's telling me. He seems bright and articulate. But every few minutes I remind myself of the question I originally asked, because Artie seems to have gone off onto yet another tangent. He seems full of confidence and talks about his plans to save America's homeless. He has me convinced, until I recall that he can't organize his math homework, much less a national campaign. He reports feeling just so happy and "oh so great." Yet, when I confront him, my radar detects irritability. Fearing an explosive outburst, I stop my line of questioning. He tells me he's been getting by on about 4 hours of sleep each night. What is he doing instead, I ask. He reports that he sneaks out of the house and meets some girl he's just gotten to know for drinking and wild sex. I think to myself, *Some disorder!*

Even with the wild escapades that might evoke envy in others, bipolar disorder is malignant, dangerous, and disabling. Concluding that Artie suffers from it is not a stretch. However, over recent years researchers began conjecturing about a different presentation of bipolar disorder in children.

All child psychiatrists are confronted with parents who bring in their extremely irritable children. This is perhaps an understatement. These are children who are slaves to their irritability. They often have prolonged and intense meltdowns and can be unfocused and impulsive, reminiscent of children with ADHD. Child psychiatrists struggle with how to diagnose these children.

Recently, some have conjectured that these children have bipolar disorder, as they fit many of the criteria, including restlessness, excessive talking, distractibility, decreased need for sleep, and, most important, irritable mood. These psychiatrists are trying to prove that, although these patients have symptoms that overlap with those of ADHD, they can be distinguished from those children. They further assert that, though not proven at the highest scientific standard, the medicines that are effective in adult patients with bipolar disorder are also often effective in children diagnosed with this disorder.

Others argue that because these children do not fit the important timing requirements of bipolar disorder, namely the alternating episodes of depression and mania, these children do not have this disorder. These doctors contend that the lack of discrete episodes of mood change contradicts a core element of bipolar disorder and that eliminating this timing requirement lowers the diagnostic threshold and has led to the overdiagnosis of the disorder. They feel that the frequent, intense emotional outbursts that have come to characterize bipolar disorder in children is a nonspecific problem, characteristic of many difficult children, and that many children diagnosed with bipolar disorder do not fit many criteria beyond extreme irritability.

Do these children have bipolar disorder? Perhaps, but the current thinking leans away from this possibility. Over recent years, research has shown distinctions between children with more strictly defined bipolar disorder (namely those with episodes of mania that include extreme elation, silliness, or grandiosity) and those with nonepisodic severe irritability, intense meltdowns, inattention, and anxiety. This latter group is currently being described as having severe mood dysregulation disorder or temper dysregulation disorder with dysphoria, a diagnosis that is being considered for inclusion in *DSM-V*. Researchers (Brotman et al., 2007) have shown that the parents of children with severe mood dysregulation disorder do not have a higher rate of bipolar disorder than those of a control group, whereas parents of children with more strictly defined bipolar disorder do have a higher rate of bipolar disorder. Other research (Althoff, Verhulst, Rettew, Hudziak, & van der Ende, 2010) has shown that, unlike those with strictly defined bipolar disorder, those with severe mood dysregulation disorder, although likely to have psychiatric difficulties as they get older, are no more prone to develop bipolar disorder than a control group.

Researchers have also shown that, unlike those with severe mood dysregulation whose symptoms are fairly consistent, children with bipolar disorder are symptomatic episodically. Unlike the episodes of adults with bipolar disorder, however, the episodes of children can be very brief, so that they cycle through mania in less than a day. Given the ongoing symptoms that provide a perpetual backdrop, distinguishing these very brief episodes can be extremely challenging and leaves enough diagnostic wiggle room that parents looking for answers can find them by using the popularized diagnosis of bipolar disorder.

Molly is nine. She is an unfocused, immature, anxious, self-centered child. When she can't deal with what life throws at her, which is daily, Molly gets fussy and pouty and stomps away. This is very difficult for her parents, whose younger son is a likable, bright, highly empathic little boy. Molly has few friends, and those relationships are always tenuous because of Molly's behavior. Molly's mother, a child psychologist, is overwrought and, after many evaluations, flustered about what to do next.

At her annual checkup with the pediatrician, Molly is fidgety and silly. The pediatrician is having a hard time performing the physical exam and is struck by Molly's hyper, giddy state. She knows Molly's mother is troubled by Molly's difficulties. Maybe Molly has bipolar disorder, she suggests.

Full of dubious hope, Molly's mother goes home and immediately calls me with the question of whether Molly could "be bipolar." I tell Molly's mother that Molly is certainly not typical of patients with bipolar disorder. I believe that Molly has elements of both ADHD and an anxiety disorder. She was probably silly because she was nervous. But I ask myself, *Amid all the family turbulence Molly causes, am I missing the micro episodes of childhood bipolar disorder? Maybe I'm being too conservative. Maybe the pediatrician is right, and I should be treating Molly with Depakote for bipolar disorder.* Now I'm starting to feel insecure. I can't let my patients and their pediatricians see me as less than cutting edge in my knowledge of psychiatric disorders, but the cutting edge is not necessarily correct. I don't want to needlessly expose a child to medicine.

Because children diagnosed with bipolar disorder are irritable, a bit hyper, and somewhat grandiose, it is easy to imagine the symptoms of childhood bipolar disorder being used broadly enough to include a great many difficult children. Bolstered by popular books and magazine articles, the parents of these children first question, then sometimes become convinced that their children suffer with this disorder. If they do, should medicines, some with significant side effects and others with minimal research proving their usefulness in children with bipolar disorder, be prescribed?

As with ADHD, the diagnosis of bipolar disorder in children is evolving. Although there are degrees of bipolar disorder and doctors refer among themselves to a bipolar spectrum, bipolar disorder appears for now to be a categorical, not spectrum, diagnosis in youth. However, some of the medicines used to treat bipolar disorder are less liberal than those used to treat ADHD—that is, these medicines are not known to be effective whether one has the diagnosis or not, and they are more dangerous. Other medicines are possibly more liberal, but also carry more significant risk.

In years to come our current understanding will seem unsophisticated. But we must make decisions based on what is known now. While research plods slowly forward, parents seldom want to be left in the waiting room of academia while their children suffer. If medicine might help, they want to know the risks and benefits. The responsible use of medicines to treat children's symptoms when the exact diagnosis is murky is not ideal but can still be a valid choice.

CHAPTER 8

The Burden of Proof

||||||||||||||||||||||||||||||||||||||||||||||||||||||||||||||||||

Are There Benefits?

To decide whether to prescribe medicine, doctors must first be convinced that medicine could benefit the patient. Do children benefit from taking psychiatric medicine? How are we to know?

In 1978, Dr. Clark is treating Tim, a 16-year-old boy who has been having a hard time for the past 3 months. Tim's girlfriend broke up with him 4 months ago, and Tim's grades have been falling during the entire school year. At home Tim has been sullen and morose. These concerns led Tim's parents to Dr. Clark.

Dr. Clark diagnoses Tim as having depression. He tells Tim's parents that, although he's not sure, he strongly believes that Improvil, the antidepressant he has been using to treat adults, will help Tim. All agree that Tim should give it a try. About 2 weeks later, Tim is feeling much better. His parents agree that their old Tim has returned.

Dr. Clark has never read anything about the use of Improvil in adolescents, and so he writes a case report detailing what happened for the medical journal he reads every month. Other doctors read Dr. Clark's report. Some find it intriguing. They, too, have been wondering if antidepressants like Improvil would help adolescents with depression, and, now, because of Dr. Clark's report, they begin to use this antidepressant in adolescent patients.

However, Dr. Kaplan, from Missouri, is dubious of Dr. Clark's results. Dr. Kaplan is not sure that he agrees with the diagnosis of depression. He knows lots of jilted, morose teenage boys. He knows lots of adolescents whose grades have fallen. Maybe Tim's curriculum is more challenging this year. Maybe Tim has been a bit sullen, but maybe his parents are overly sensitive, worried parents, and Tim has only been a little bit more morose than the usual teen.

Dr. Kaplan is also unsure that Improvil helped. Maybe Dr. Clark was so enthusiastic that the medicine would work that he convinced himself that it did. Maybe his enthusiasm infected Tim's parents, and they're seeing improvement that does not exist. Maybe Tim was so convinced of the power of the big blue capsule that he feels it must be helping, and the more he feels it must be helping, the better he feels. In short, Dr. Kaplan is not about to start any of his depressed adolescents on this antidepressant. He writes a skeptical letter to the editor about Dr. Clark's results.

Undaunted by Dr. Kaplan, Dr. Clark continues to treat depressed adolescents with Improvil. By 1983, he has treated 15 teenage patients with it. All meet criteria for depression as listed in the relatively new *DSM-III*. Dr. Clark writes of his series of successfully treated patients for the psychiatric journal.

The ever-skeptical Dr. Kaplan reads the report. He acknowledges that 15 successfully treated patients are a whole lot more convincing than one. He is impressed that Dr. Clark has used *DSM-III* and is more assured that all these teenagers are depressed, but he still has plenty of questions.

Do these patients also have other diagnoses? Maybe they are all suffering with anxiety disorders, and the medicine is actually treating the anxiety disorder. And maybe Dr. Clark's unabashed enthusiasm is becoming an epidemic, infecting 15 more families who desperately want help and are convinced that their children improved because of the antidepressant Dr. Clark prescribed. He expresses his thoughts in another letter to the editor.

Dr. Clark is frustrated and furious when he reads Dr. Kaplan's letter. What ever will it take to convince the skeptic from Missouri? Dr. Clark decides that this means war and that he will prove to Dr. Kaplan that Improvil helps depressed teens.

The following year, the industrious Dr. Clark convinces a national foundation to fund a research project investigating the use of Improvil in depressed teenagers. Dr. Clark employs a team of doctors and psychiatric nurses. He convinces the local mental-health clinic to send him their next 200 depressed adolescents. Every adolescent is seen by one of the child psychiatrists on Dr. Clark's team who decides whether the patient meets *DSM-III* criteria for depression. They also must determine that the patient does not meet criteria for other diagnoses, such as psychosis, drug and alcohol abuse, and mental retardation. Because so many of the teenagers with depression also have an anxiety disorder, Dr. Clark and his team decide that adolescents with depression and an anxiety disorder will be included. After the first psychiatrist establishes the diagnosis, a second child psychiatrist then confirms the diagnosis. As it turns out, only a hundred of the 200 teens fit these strict criteria and are allowed into the study.

Dr. Clark discusses his project with each of the 100 adolescents and their parents. Using his superlative persuasive skills, he convinces all 100 families to participate. He divides the teenagers into two groups. One group is treated with Improvil, and the other group is given placebo, a pill identical in appearance to Improvil but filled with an inert substance. No teenager, no family member, and no treating physician knows who is receiving Improvil and who is receiving placebo. A team psychiatrist monitors the progress of each patient weekly.

After 10 weeks of treatment, Dr. Clark and his team break the code. They reveal to themselves and their patients who is taking medicine and who is taking placebo. Dr. Clark discovers that 60% of the patients taking medicine improved and that 25% of those taking placebo improved. His statistician confirms that this is a significant difference and that therefore the medicine was more effective than placebo in treating adolescents with depression.

Dr. Clark secretly breathes a sigh of relief and once again writes his results for the medical journal. Dr. Kaplan reads the report. Although not convinced, he is now very intrigued. He is still not sure if Improvil treats depression or anxiety, but he thinks the medicine must be helping some patients with some of their symptoms. He wants to know if any other team has been able to replicate this study's powerful findings. He wants to know what would have happened if the teenagers had received higher doses of medicine or if they had received medicine for a longer time. He wants to know how many people improved a little and how many improved a lot.

Dr. Kaplan is beginning to consider that Improvil might be effective for adolescents with depression. He will consider prescribing it to his next depressed teenage patient.

And so the wheels of medical progress grind slowly forward.

Over the past 50 years, the previously nonexistent field of psychiatric pharmacology has developed into a bona fide science. The number of available medicines increased from the 1950s into the 1960s, then jumped again during the 1990s. Clinicians have had more medicines to treat patients with more widely recognized disorders, as well as patients with troublesome symptoms that might not fit neatly into our current characterization of disorders. But are these medicines effective in children and adolescents? How does a clinician know if a particular medicine will be effective for a given individual?

In order to be approved for use by the Food and Drug Administration (FDA), a drug company must prove that the medicine has been adequately studied and that it effectively and safely treats a given population with a given disorder. Although some psychiatric medicines are FDA-approved for certain disorders in children over a certain age, most are not. Most have only been sufficiently tested in adults, but these medicines can still be used in children. Using a medicine for an age group for which it is not approved or for a disorder for which it is not approved is called the off-label use of the medicine. This is legal and ethical and is done commonly by physicians in all fields of medicine.

Before prescribing a medicine for an off-label indication or to an off-label group, a physician asks, "What evidence do I have that this medicine will benefit this patient?" This seemingly straight-forward question masks what can be a highly personal decision-making process. Different doctors, in no small part dependent on their personality, have different standards of proof that they feel must be met before they are willing to prescribe a given medicine. This is especially true in child psychiatry because many of the medicines we prescribe are not FDA-approved for use in children and safety data in children are not always available.

Some physicians will prescribe a given medicine as long as the FDA has approved the medicine for anybody of any age for any disorder. Others will prescribe the medicine if they have read of other doctors' successful case reports using the medicine for a specific disorder. Some are satisfied if they have seen a report of a group of patients who have been prescribed the medicine without significant side effects, even though the trial was not of the highest scientific caliber. Still others want to have read the results of one or more well-constructed, double-blind, placebo-controlled stud-ies proving the medicine's efficacy and safety in the age group and for the disorder for which he or she plans to prescribe it. Some-times, although double-blind, placebo-controlled studies prove a medicine's efficacy, the medicine is still not FDA-approved for that disorder. This might simply reflect the drug company's decision not to pursue the expensive endeavor of seeking FDA approval. This does not diminish the strength of the proof by double-blind, placebo-controlled research.

The double-blind, placebo-controlled study is the gold stan-dard of most drug studies. In a placebo-controlled study one group of patients receives active medicine, and a matched group of patients receives placebo, an identical pill without medicine in it. A double-blind study is one in which neither doctor nor patient knows which patients are taking active medicine and which are taking placebo. Everyone is "blind" to the medication status of a given patient. If significantly more people respond to the pill with medicine, we presume they have responded to the medicine and not simply to having taken a pill.

Although this research sounds simple enough, doing it is plagued with a number of difficulties. A researcher must find parents and children who are willing to participate in research. The researcher must find enough children who fit the criteria for the disorder being studied and, ideally, who do not have other diagnoses that might cloud the issue. Because many children with one psychiatric disorder also have another diagnosis or diagnoses, this presents significant difficulty. Parents must also be comfortable with the idea that their child might be "treated" with placebo—namely an inactive pill.

The researcher must decide how long the trial of medicine should be. If medicine usually begins to work after 4 weeks, then doing a 2-week trial is pointless. If medicine begins to work after 4 weeks but picks up momentum after 8 or 12 weeks, one would ideally follow these patients the entire time. This takes a lot of time, money, and manpower, as well as the patience of parents and children. If the children are not improved in the process, the parents will itch to flee from the study and try another treatment approach. Researchers must also decide on an adequate dose of medicine. Although no researcher wants to give subjects too high a dose, neither do they want to underdose, thus dooming the trial to failure.

This research is hampered by other problems as well. For example, how do you measure a patient's improvement? Measuring a decrease in hyperactivity is relatively easy because this is an observable symptom. Measuring an improvement in a child's mood is more difficult. Does one rely on the child's reports about his or her mood? Children can be unreliable reporters of mood. Does one rely on a parent's report? Parents can misinterpret a child's behavior, and they are particularly inaccurate in picking up the depressed moods of their teenagers. When a parent reports improved focus, does one confirm that observation with the child's teacher? Parents and teachers often disagree. Researchers frequently use rating scales to measure improvement. Often they use more than one rating scale. Sometimes improvement is indicated on one rating scale but not another. In which rating scale do we put the most stock?

In deciding whether psychiatric medicines are overprescribed or underprescribed for children and adolescents, we must know whether these medicines are effective, and we must ask how doctors know. We must appreciate that the research that establishes a medicine's efficacy is often difficult and expensive. Further, there are a multitude of medicines for a multitude of problems, and the efficacy of each is not proven with the same level of precision.

CHAPTER 9

The Benefits of Medicine

|||||||||||||||||||||||||||||||||||||||||||||||||||||||||||||||||||

The Name Game

Before looking at the benefits that psychiatric medicines offer, let's clarify the wide array of medicines being discussed. This is not a comprehensive review of all the medicines used by child psychiatrists. Rather, it's a brief guide to the different families of medicines.

Psychiatric medicines are usually categorized by the type of symptom or disorder they most commonly address. For example, there are antidepressant medicines, antianxiety medicines, and antipsychotic medicines, which treat depression, anxiety, and psychosis, respectively. Some medicines are categorized under names that seem less specific, such as mood stabilizers, which treat bipolar disorder, and some medicines use names based on their specific cellular action, such as the beta (receptor) blockers and alpha (receptor) agonists. Other families, such as the stimulants, are named for the medicine's original therapeutic effects—in the case of stimulants, namely stimulating the bronchi to allow greater airflow or stimulating those who have narcolepsy. And still other families use names that only make sense in relation to the names of medicines that preceded them. For example, the atypical antipsychotics are atypical relative to the antipsychotic medicines that had been used in the 30 years that preceded them.

The point is to be careful of the name game. The names of medicine families have a variety of origins and do not necessarily describe all the medicine's uses. Antidepressants are sometimes also antianxiety agents, and stimulants, despite their name, effectively treat hyperactive children. Some mood stabilizers are also antiepileptics and don't stabilize everyone's mood, and anti-hypertensives (for high blood pressure) are sometimes used as sleeping pills.

Why the confusion? Medication names often originated decades ago, when less was known about the many effects of the particular medicine. As years went by and the use of the medicine was better defined or even expanded, the old name stuck even though it didn't necessarily convey the medicine's modern use. A medicine is marketed to solve a specific type of problem and therefore is categorized in that family of medicines. As new uses are developed, the medicine could be placed in other categories but typically isn't.

The confusion is increased when a drug company markets the same medicine under different names for different purposes. For example, bupropion is marketed as Wellbutrin for depression and as Zyban as a medicine to help people stop smoking cigarettes.

With that warning in mind, let's review the families of medicines that are generally used by child psychiatrists.

The most commonly prescribed family in child psychiatry is the stimulants, which include medicines such as Ritalin, Concerta, and Adderall and are used most often to treat attention-deficit hyperactivity disorder. Although they do stimulate people when taken in higher doses, at therapeutic doses they lengthen attention span and decrease hyperactivity.

Strattera, a norepinephrine reuptake inhibitor, was the first nonstimulant medicine approved for the treatment of ADHD. And, recently, two alpha agonist antihypertensives, Intuniv and Kapvay, were approved to treat this disorder. The short-acting forms of the alpha agonists, Tenex and Catapres, had been used for many years to treat mild tic disorders and childhood insomnia, albeit off-label.

The next group of medicines is the antidepressants. There are a few families of medicines under this heading. The most commonly used today are the selective serotonin reuptake inhibitors, or SSRIs. These include medicines such as Prozac, Zoloft, Paxil, and Lexapro. They are labeled as SSRIs because they inhibit the reuptake (that is, reabsorption) of serotonin in the synapse between neurons.

There are other antidepressants, such as Wellbutrin, that primarily affect the norepinephrine and dopamine, rather than serotonin, in the synapse, and still others, like Effexor, that affect norepinephrine and serotonin. There are also older families of antidepressants dating back to the late 1950s and early 1960s. These include the tricyclic antidepressants, such as Tofranil and Norpramin, named for their chemical structure, and the mono-amine oxidase inhibitors (MAOIs), such as Parnate, named for the synaptic enzyme they inhibit.

Next are the atypical (or second-generation) antipsychotic medicines, such as Risperdal, Zyprexa, and Seroquel. They are atypical because they differ from the "typical" (or first-generation) antipsychotic medicines that had been in use in preceding decades. Interestingly, some of these medicines have been more commonly used to treat bipolar disorder, tic disorders such as Tourette's disorder, and severe agitation.

The mood stabilizers are used to treat bipolar disorder. Lithium is the oldest of these, but Depakote is also used. Because Depakote was initially used as an antiepileptic medicine, other antiepileptics, such as Tegretol, Topomax, Trileptal, and Lamictal, have also been tried in the treatment of bipolar disorder, albeit with differing levels of success.

The antianxiety medicines, or anxiolytics, include medicines such as Xanax, Klonopin, and Valium. Note that the antianxiety medicines are not antidepressants, but many of the antidepressants, including the SSRIs, the tricyclics, and the MAOIs, are also antianxiety medicines. To confuse you further, there are many types of anxiety, and none of these medicines treat all types. Finally, over the years, the tricyclic antidepressants, which are used for some types of anxiety, have also been used as effective medicines for bedwetting.

The important point here is that given the enormous complexity of the brain and our incomplete understanding of the way these various medicines affect its functioning, parents need their physician's help in determining which, if any, is best suited to treat their child.

The Benefits of Medicine

Now that we've reviewed the names of the different categories of medicine, let's return to the more important question of benefit. Do these medicines benefit children? If so, at what level of proof? And what are the criteria for using these medicines? Let's start with some of the psychiatric medicines that are FDA-approved for use in children. Although there aren't many, the past few years have seen an increase. This chapter will review them group by group.

The stimulants are FDA-approved for use in treating attention-deficit hyperactivity disorder, although the minimal age criteria differ from one stimulant to another. Several of the SSRIs are FDA-approved for use in children with obsessive-compulsive disorder, and two, Prozac and Lexapro, are approved for use in youth with depression, again with differing age criteria. One of the tricyclics, Anafranil, is also approved to treat OCD. Lithium is FDA-approved for the treatment of mania in adolescents. Two first-generation antipsychotics, Haldol and Orap, are approved for the treatment of Tourette's. And, over the past few years, a few of the second-generation antipsychotics were approved for the treatment of schizophrenia and mania in adolescence or extreme agitation in children with autism. (For a more complete discussion of the FDA-approved versus off-label uses of these medicines, see my book *Kids on Meds*.)

Remember that although a particular medicine might be approved for the treatment of a specific disorder, the use of that medicine can be considered off-label if the patient's diagnosis is unclear.

Putting the Brakes on ADHD

The stimulants have been the mainstay of treatment for attention-deficit hyperactivity disorder for decades, Strattera being introduced in early 2003 and Intuniv and Kapvay around the end of that decade. Many controlled studies have proven the short-term efficacy of stimulants in ADHD. Approximately 70% of children with ADHD respond to the first stimulant they are prescribed (Elia, Ambrosini, & Rapoport, 1999; Spencer, Biederman, Wilens, Harding, O'Donnell, & Griffin, 1996), and a large proportion of the balance respond to a second trial with another stimulant. Only about 25% or less of these children respond to placebo (Wilens & Biederman, 1992).

Other medicines, such as Wellbutrin and the tricyclic antidepressants, are FDA-approved for disorders other than ADHD in different age groups. They are sometimes prescribed for children with ADHD, based on the clinical experience of many practitioners and a small amount of double-blind, placebo-controlled research (Conners et al., 1996; Connor, Fletcher, & Swanson, 1999; Spencer et al., 1996). The tricyclic antidepressants, however, are more often avoided because of their side effects.

Paul is 5 years old and in an extra year of preschool. His mother complains that he's always on the go. He's constantly pulling books off the shelf or toys out of the cabinet. He uses each one for about

30 seconds and then moves on. When he's outside, his mother is in constant fear that he'll dart into the road and get hit by a car. This already happened when Paul was 4 years old. He ended up with a broken arm and a concussion. That was only a few weeks after Paul let himself out of his seat belt and thought it would be fun to grab the wheel while his mother was driving.

In school, Paul is a lovable terror. His teacher says he cannot sit for circle time. He's constantly touching the other children, testing Melanie's response when he pulls one of her pigtails, hugging his friends vigorously when they least expect it. When the teacher is reading a story, Paul is up off the carpet trying to push the buttons on the computer or running over to gleefully knock down the replica of the Empire State Building that his good friend, Keith, just completed before story time. The other kids are forever yelling, "*Paaaaul!* Stop it!" and the teacher has used up all her tricks for controlling Paul and managing a class of 15 other children simultaneously.

Paul's pediatrician has noted Paul's frequently risky behavior and has considered starting Paul on Ritalin for the past 2 years, but she is uncomfortable prescribing a stimulant to such a young child. She refers Paul for a psychiatric consultation. Though his parents are initially reluctant, Paul is started on Ritalin. Paul's parents are shocked at the change. Their son's activity level diminishes substantially, and he is able to inhibit much of his impulsive behavior. He is able to sit for circle time, though he does do better when he is sitting near the teacher. All the adults in Paul's life are still constantly on their toes, but Paul can function in an age-appropriate setting.

Paul has ADHD, combined type—that is, he is both hyperactive/impulsive and inattentive. This is causing him significant dysfunction and is completely altering the classroom experiences of all his peers. Paul cannot attend to the teacher's lessons. He cannot form age-appropriate social relationships. He is frequently being yelled at and is in need of constant supervision.

ADHD is not thought to be a life-threatening illness, but we see that it can be. Children with ADHD are at greater risk for more severe injuries and for emergency room visits (DiScala, Lescohier, Barthel, & Li, 1998; Leibson, Katusic, Barbaresi, Ransom, & O'Brien, 2001; Rowe, Maughan, & Goodman, 2004). Paul is not in physical pain from his ADHD, but indirectly it has caused the physical pain of a broken arm and countless bumps and bruises.

It has also caused him the indirect psychological pain of hearing his name screamed in a disappointed, "What am I going to do with you?" tone of voice. This does not happen a few times each day. It happens a few times each minute, every minute, every day. Paul is beginning to see himself as someone who always frustrates others and never lives up to his potential. Paul's symptoms have a very negative impact on his entire family. His parents are learning not to scream, but Paul has caused significant stress in a previously happy marriage. His sister complains that Paul does not get punished when he does something wrong, and she is embarrassed about having friends visit her house.

Paul's behavior has improved by taking medicine. He is at less risk for accidents, and he can participate in the classroom without a one-to-one aide. He gets along better with his peers, and both his teacher and his parents find him more manageable.

Medicine has made a significant difference in the lives of Paul and his family. This change is supported by countless studies, many of them double-blind and placebo-controlled, which document the improvement in the symptoms of ADHD while taking a stimulant. Most of these studies have been done in elementary school–age children. Some have been done in preschoolers and adolescents.

These studies demonstrate that stimulants diminish the symptoms of ADHD immediately and for up to 1 to 2 years when taken continuously. Clinical experience is that stimulants most often continue to be effective for much longer than 2 years. Therefore, for most people, as long as they are taking a stimulant, the medicine will control their symptoms of ADHD.

Does this improvement assure a good long-term prognosis? Unfortunately, no. Long-term follow-up studies of people with ADHD who were treated with stimulants for a few years as children have shown a wide range of possible outcomes for those with this disorder (Hechtman, 2004). Although approximately a third or more of people with ADHD will go on to have significant problems as adults, the effect of stimulants on changing this outcome is still unclear. Stimulants seem to improve social skills and lower the risk for dangerous events, such as car accidents; however, the extent of their influence on more global success has not been proven. Possibly stimulants need to be taken on an ongoing basis in order for patients to accrue long-term benefit.

Some children with less severe ADHD or sufficient compensatory strengths—or perhaps simply some good luck—eventually turn their symptoms into beneficial personality characteristics.

Thaddeus was always in trouble. Never afraid to take a chance, he would risk failure, punishment, or a trip to the principal's office on a moment's notice. Thaddeus would accept the consequences, which always seemed modified because of his affable, "aw shucks" manner. Thaddeus was never very interested in schoolwork and rarely did it, but he had the intellect to get by with reasonably good grades. Still, he never achieved the academic success of which he was intellectually capable. In high school Thaddeus had a few brushes with the local police department but always narrowly escaped punishment. A psychiatric evaluation concluded that Thaddeus had many symptoms of ADHD, but he was never treated.

Thaddeus made it through college in much the same way. After college, he took a job as a real-estate agent. He loved being out and about, never confined to a desk. When the opportunity arose, he jumped into a deal to buy himself a piece of property. He had a good feel for calculating the numbers involved in real estate and loved interacting with the workers who helped in the upkeep of his properties.

Although he rushed into some deals that ultimately failed, over the years he did quite well, scoring far more successes than failures.

Medicine might have helped Thaddeus in school, and we'll never know if that would have changed the course of his life. But Thaddeus never did take medicine. He drove his parents absolutely crazy and cost them some money in legal fees. He somehow averted disaster after disaster and ultimately, on the strength of his assets, earned a good living and raised a family.

Attending to Attention

The concept of ADHD is a work in progress. For now, however, children in the hyperactivity/impulsivity spectrum are distinguished from children who primarily exhibit inattention. With the current emphasis on academic performance, the public is becoming more aware of the negative impact of ADHD, predominantly inattentive type. Research is also proving the detrimental effect it has on social relationships and the risk of psychiatric disorders.

Eddie is a 13-year-old space cadet. He is very bright but very disorganized, always losing his books and his sneakers. In early elementary school, Eddie easily mastered the three R's. When he entered middle school, with the demand for organization, independence, and self-motivation, Eddie began to struggle. He stares out the window during class, and when the teacher calls for homework to be handed in, Eddie has forgotten that his half-completed homework is crumpled at the bottom of his book bag, under last Monday's tuna sandwich. Eddie's report card is a row of C's and D's with comments such as "not working to potential" and "missing assignments."

Eddie's mother used to teach children with learning disabilities, and over the years she has worked with Eddie to improve his organizational skills and stay focused. Now, during middle school, she sits with Eddie every night to help him attend to his homework. Although Eddie is a good sport, he is also a young adolescent who is not happy about his mother's interference in his life. He asks his mother to cut him some slack. Eddie's mother, ever frustrated, responds that if he could do his homework in the hour it should take, she wouldn't sit with him. Even with her help, homework takes 3 or 4 hours each night, and who knows how long it would take without her involvement.

Eddie's teachers see Eddie as the classic underachiever. They realize he is bright but consider him lazy. They have had conferences with Eddie and his parents, sat Eddie in the front row in the classroom, reminded him to write down assignments, and given him extra credit to do basic work. All to no avail.

Eddie's parents take him to a psychologist who diagnoses attention-deficit hyperactivity disorder, predominantly inattentive type, and recommends that Eddie be seen by a child psychiatrist for medication. Eddie's mother knew this recommendation was coming. She had resisted the idea of medicine but finally agrees to start Eddie on a stimulant.

On medicine, Eddie is focused and attentive. He no longer loses his belongings and is able to listen and respond when spoken to. He is less argumentative with his parents, and when it is time for homework, he approaches it with motivation and insight. His mother reports that on the plane to New Mexico, Eddie read a hundred pages of his English book. At his job at the Y, where he helps to take care of younger children, his supervisor sees him as more deliberate in his behavior with the children and "less likely to act without thinking." His parents feel like this is too good to be true, and even Eddie refers to the medicine as his "magic pill."

Before Eddie took medicine, his parents sometimes feared he'd cross the street without looking for cars, but they did not consider ADHD, predominantly inattentive type, to be a life-threatening illness. Eddie was not in physical pain, and, although he was becoming demoralized about his schoolwork, he was not in deep psychological pain.

Although Eddie was able to get through elementary school on native intellect, at 13, he was experiencing dysfunction. His organizational skills were being challenged. He had to be more responsible for the tools of his trade, and he had to be more organized in his academic work. Although Eddie could zero right in on a book about fantasy action heroes, he had difficulty staying focused when reading about the Civil War or the parts of an atom.

Medicine has helped Eddie focus. It has also improved his motivation. On Sunday morning, Eddie takes his medicine and within a half hour marches off to do his homework with drive and enthusiasm.

I was once asked the following question by a teenager: "Dr. Kalikow, how does the Ritalin know that I should focus on the teacher and not the cute girl sitting in the next row?" I explained that there is no magic pill and that he would have to supply the direction of his focus. But the truth is that for some children, the pill does seem like magic. Some children do seem more motivated and energetic about their schoolwork.

Deciding who should benefit from this sometimes magical pill is often difficult. An often-heard fallacy is that only those with ADHD respond to stimulants like Ritalin. This is untrue. A study by Dr. Judith Rapoport and her team at the National Institute of Mental Health demonstrated that children and adults without ADHD are also more attentive when taking stimulants (Rapoport et al., 1980). So, if one falls short of meeting the criteria for ADHD but still has dysfunction, one might benefit from using a stimulant.

Ramon attends a prestigious university. He was very unfocused as a child, and the pediatrician recommended a trial of Ritalin. His parents decided against this. In high school, Ramon continued to be inattentive, but he overcame this difficulty through hours and hours of very hard work and graduated near the top of his class. His freshman year of college went poorly. Ramon did not fail out of school, but despite his best efforts, his grades were mediocre. Ramon and his mother come in for a consultation.

Ramon complains that although he loves college, has friends, and finds the schoolwork fairly interesting, he cannot concentrate well enough on the amount and type of work college presents. After much deliberation, Ramon, his mother, and I decide on a trial of Ritalin.

Ramon is able to focus better on his reading, but he does not like the idea of taking medicine. When he is home from college, he comes in and presents me with his solution. Although studying for exams is difficult, he has decided he can always work harder and longer, something to which he is accustomed. Exams, however, are time-limited, and, despite knowing the material, he does poorly on tests because he can never finish in the allotted time. He is always the last person sitting in the room, having spent the previous 2 hours battling his tendency to glance around the room while carrying on an internal monologue to stay focused on the questions.

So Ramon declines special testing accommodations and decides to use the Ritalin for exams only. This, in fact, works for about a year, before Ramon decides to forgo the use of medicine altogether, change his major to one requiring less sustained focus, and simply battle with inattention.

What were the criteria Ramon used to decide to take a medicine that was clearly effective? His life was not in jeopardy. He was not in physical pain. He was not depressed. He was demoralized about the possibility of leaving his university and upset that he might not be able to complete his planned major in biochemistry.

Was Ramon treating a disorder? That's difficult to say. Certainly, years ago his pediatrician thought Ramon had ADHD, but 10 years later, it is difficult to determine exactly how he made that diagnosis.

Did Ramon meet criteria for the diagnosis of ADHD as a college student? His style was certainly marked by inattention. And he did fit a few of the descriptive characteristics of people with ADHD, predominantly inattentive type. This inattention clearly affected his ability to function in school, but it did not significantly affect other spheres of his life.

Was there "clear evidence of clinically significant impairment," one of the *DSM-IV* criteria to diagnose ADHD? With his high degree of persistence and his ability to marshal great effort to keep up academically, Ramon was functioning reasonably well relative to most people his age. He was getting mostly C's in a tough program in a highly competitive university—not great, by his own standard, but not "impaired."

However, is "clinically significant impairment" an objective measurement or a subjective judgment? The writers of *DSM-IV* placed this requirement in the criteria for most disorders to help distinguish pathological conditions from milder presentations of symptoms. They did so admitting that this "is an inherently difficult clinical judgment" (*DSM*-IV, p. 7) but wanting to maintain a reasonably high threshold for labeling someone with a psychiatric disorder. In a book sometimes colored by controversy, a book with accessible criteria that we all enjoy applying to our friends and family, this criterion of "clinically significant impairment" is often overlooked and sometimes difficult to apply. It is also necessary in the task of establishing what constitutes a psychiatric disorder.

So maybe Ramon has ADHD, and maybe he's just a very inattentive young man enrolled in a program whose intensity exacerbates his inattention.

Does one need a diagnosed disorder to use medicine? A disorder is certainly one of the reasons to take a medicine. However, people take medicine for symptomatic relief all the time. If I take medicine for a headache, it isn't to treat a disorder. It is to stop my symptom of pain. Whether or not it is a sign of an underlying disorder, Ramon's symptom of inattention improved while taking medicine.

As Dr. Rapoport discovered, stimulant medicines improve attention span whether one has a diagnosis of ADHD or not, although the attention span of a person with ADHD will improve to a greater degree than the attention span of a person without ADHD.

One might argue that Ramon's symptom is environmentally induced, that it is a function of studying a difficult curriculum in a competitive university. Ramon has a long-standing difficulty with inattention, however, and in a less competitive program in a less competitive university, he would still have been inattentive. The change Ramon ultimately makes by switching programs diminishes the effect, but he is still inattentive. Symptoms are frequently the result of an interaction between our biology and the environment we choose to live in or our style of living within that environment.

Symptoms that are partly a function of the demands of the environment are more difficult to assess. Attention span is not a static quality that one either has or doesn't have. If I'm 67 inches tall, I am 67 inches tall any place on earth under virtually any circumstances. If I'm inattentive, however, I might be more inattentive in noisy places, and less in quiet places. I might be more inattentive when reading about molecules, less when reading a Stephen King novel, and still less when working in my woodshop.

Neuropsychologists attempt to define and measure the characteristic of attention. Although it is a complex trait that is dependent on the task at hand, some of us are more globally inattentive. Because of its complexity and because those with inattention suffer silently, often slipping through the cracks, the potential benefit of medicating this impairment might be among the most slippery slopes in psychiatric pharmacology.

Ratcheting Down Rituals

Terry is 9 years old. He is very ritualistic. Before going to bed each night, Terry's mother must say "goodnight" to Terry using the exact same words in the exact same order. His mother must then check that each dresser drawer is closed in a standard way. Every night, Terry doubts his mother did the process correctly, and every night, the whole procedure must be done again. This can take up to 2 hours. When he walks, Terry counts his steps in groups of six. Over and over he counts. In class, Terry counts the number of times the teacher says the word "read." This makes it impossible to catch the meaning of the teacher's instructions.

Terry has obsessive-compulsive disorder. Although many people with OCD respond to cognitive-behavioral therapy, a type of talking/doing therapy, Terry did not. Terry is started on Zoloft. Within a few weeks, the anxiety that fuels his rituals has diminished, and he is better able to resist them. Instead of saying to himself, "If I don't count six steps, my mother will be hit by a car," he now says, "If I don't count six steps . . . well, whatever."

Obsessive-compulsive disorder is a debilitating, though not life-threatening, disorder. To say it causes dysfunction is an understatement. To say it causes mental pain is obvious. Terry, therefore, fits at least some criteria for using psychiatric medicine to change his brain chemistry, and he has improved by using it.

Obsessive-compulsive disorder manifests in many ways. Some people, like Terry, have checking and counting rituals. Some become extremely fearful of germs and develop hand-washing rituals. They wash their hands over and over, always doubting that they washed adequately. Some are obsessed by the fear of being gay, and others are obsessed by the possibility of a loved one dying. Some are obsessed by the worry that they acted in a less than scrupulous manner, and others are obsessed by an unreasonable fear of AIDS.

Many but not all of these people develop rituals to attempt to prevent the feared consequence. For example: "If I say my mother's name before my left foot gets under the bed covers, she will return home safely," or "If I tap my pencil three times with the correct cadence, I will answer the next math problem correctly."

These patients know that these conclusions are unreasonable, but they feel compelled to perform the ritual anyway and are plagued by the fear that they might not have done it correctly. They therefore repeat it over and over, always trying to get it exactly right.

Performing a ritual is not abnormal. Some religious rituals have been performed by millions of people over thousands of years. Many children also engage in rituals, such as not stepping on cracks or bouncing the basketball three times to assure your foul shot will go in. These people do not have OCD. They are happy to perform their ritual and see its performance as serving a useful purpose, or they know it's silly but do it a few times and forget it.

Individuals with OCD, however, are plagued by anxiety if they do not perform their ritual. Each time they do perform the ritual, their anxiety plummets, and they enjoy relief—for a moment. Then the doubt creeps in, and they feel compelled to do the ritual again. Or they have a thought they cannot shake. It's as if their brain is covered in flypaper. I often tell children with these obsessions that they have "sticky thinking," that their thoughts get stuck on their brain. If we talk about medicine, I often compare it to spraying cooking oil on a frying pan before you fry eggs. It helps the eggs slide off the pan, the way unwanted thoughts should slide off their brain.

Does medicine help people with OCD? Yes. There are a growing number of double-blind, placebo-controlled studies indicating that medicine, in particular the SSRIs, is significantly better than placebo in lowering the symptoms of OCD (Geller et al., 2001; March et al., 1998; Riddle, 2001). Although all the SSRIs might be equally helpful, only some SSRIs are FDA-approved for the treatment of OCD in children.

Not all OCD is absolutely debilitating. As with most disorders, doctors often gauge the degree of illness by labeling it as mild, moderate, or severe. So where do we draw the line? Whom do we treat? Who will benefit from medicine?

Meryl is 13 years old and the second of four children in a warm, tightly knit family. Her parents originally consulted me when Meryl was 8 and extremely fearful that some vague ill would befall her mother, who had to travel frequently for business. I saw Meryl for a few visits to discuss her fears and the ways she could manage them. She improved.

About 2 years later, Meryl returned with more worries, this time about her younger brother's safety on a summer trip. Again, Meryl and I spoke. Meryl felt better and decided not to return. Although Meryl had an obsessive quality to her thinking style, I did not diagnose OCD but rather saw her as demonstrating a more generalized type of anxiety.

Now Meryl returns again. She is obsessed with stabbing her best friend. She has no plan to do this and realizes that this would be a terrible thing to do, but when she is not otherwise occupied, she can't stop thinking about it. She's fine while she's playing volleyball and pretty much okay when she's engaged in class, but when given the opportunity to wander, her mind returns to this terrible obsession. Meryl reports this happens continually through the day. Despite these persistent thoughts, Meryl achieves A's and B's in school and has plenty of friends. Normally a happy, if anxious, young woman, Meryl is beginning to become demoralized and fears spiraling into a depression because she can't shake these thoughts. Her parents and I discuss whether to prescribe medicine or to give Meryl some cognitive tools to try to deal with her anxiety and hope that it blows over.

Meryl has mild OCD. Never let the word "mild" fool you. Meryl still has a disorder, and she is still in pain. In discussing whether to use medicine, Meryl's father wants to know what will happen if we do not. That seems like a good criterion for deciding whether to use medicine. If the symptoms will improve without medicine, let's hold off.

Unfortunately, as you might expect, there's no clear answer to that question. For some people, OCD becomes an ongoing, life-long disorder. For others, it is an intermittent disorder that lasts for years. For still others, the symptoms lessen, and they learn to manage the obsessions or compulsions by one of a number of techniques. They fall into the category of "subclinical"—that is, less than mild in the range of severity. Which will Meryl be? I don't know.

Whereas Meryl has mild OCD, others are called obsessive by their friends and family but do not have OCD. They are not plagued by obsessions. Rather, they have obsessive personality traits. For example, they like order and neatness. They like to be organized and punctual. When this style characterizes an adult's entire personality and interferes in his or her functioning, we might diagnose obsessive-compulsive personality disorder.

A child's personality is still forming, however, and we usually don't diagnose personality disorders. However, children do have their own personality styles. Sometimes these styles are rooted in their temperaments. How temperament affects personality style or one's predisposition to developing a disorder is only beginning to be studied.

Chet is 10 years old and has always been fussy. He needs everything to be "just so." When he was younger, Chet needed his socks to feel exactly right, and he would slowly and deliberately adjust them until he was satisfied. Now, when he puts his coat on, Chet has to adjust his sweatshirt sleeves to feel "just so," and when he combs his hair before school each morning, he takes 5 or 10 minutes to gel his hair and put every hair in place.

Chet is hardworking and a perfectionist about his homework. He takes painstaking effort to make it look just right. Because Chet likes everything just so, he is considered the rigid member of the family. Chet prefers routine, familiarity, and predictability. He is often seen as controlling of others, but his family understands that this is Chet's way of assuring that he will not be faced with a change that would make him anxious.

Chet's obsessive style is explained to his parents. They learn how to deal with Chet's traits. No medicine is used.

A few years later, Chet is seen again. He is still obsessive, but now he is taking longer to do the homework of middle school. He stays up at night, deleting and deleting until he thinks his homework assignment is just so. His mother is trying to get Chet to be a little less diligent, and the evening sometimes ends in a battle between Chet and his mother, leaving Chet crying that he can't stand handing in homework that is less than perfect.

We can debate whether Chet has OCD, or whether he's going to eventually receive a diagnosis of obsessive-compulsive personality disorder, or whether he'll outgrow this and be your typical highly successful, diligent, orderly accountant. Though he falls short of dysfunction, Chet and his parents are battling. Chet's parents want to know if medicine could make life easier for Chet and themselves. Maybe it would, but I'm torn between wanting to assuage the family's pain and wanting Chet to learn how to successfully manage his personality characteristics, which I think he probably can do.

The FDA has approved some of the SSRIs for the treatment of OCD in children and adolescents. Chet might not have OCD, however, and therefore our decision to use one of these medicines to treat him will be based more on clinical experience with other children like Chet than on double-blind, placebo-controlled studies.

Dealing with Depression

Bob is 14 years old. He was previously an easygoing, happy young man who had lots of friends and did well in school. But over the past 6 months, Bob has been despondent for no apparent reason. He cries at the drop of a hat, is irritable over trifles, feels worthless and hopeless, and thinks the world would be better off without him. He has been reading about the lethality of his mother's heart medicine and wonders how long it would take to slowly pilfer enough to kill himself. He feels this way for the better part of each day. He has withdrawn from his friends and stopped doing his schoolwork.

Bob is being seen by a competent psychotherapist on a regular basis. He likes the therapist and is learning about himself, but he is not improving. Bob is started on an antidepressant. After about a month, Bob's mood is improving. He is socializing more. He cares about his schoolwork and is optimistic about his life.

Bob was suffering with major depression, and his case demonstrates but does not prove benefit from the use of psychiatric medication.

Depression is a disorder characterized by a group of symptoms endured for a protracted period of time. It is not "having a bad day." It is not feeling lousy because you were rejected by your prom date or because your parents have threatened to divorce. It is not being demoralized because you failed the math midterm.

We have all felt sad. Sadness is a normal response to loss. If we leave our favorite umbrella on the train, we feel mildly sad over that small loss. If we endure the death of a parent, we feel deeply sad over a far more significant loss. When we are sad, we often cry. We might sleep restlessly for a while, and we might lose interest in food or in enjoying ourselves. Extreme sadness is mourning. Mourning is time-limited and has a clear precipitant.

Often we can find a precipitating loss when we feel sad. Perhaps it is not the loss of an object or person; perhaps it is the loss of an idea or expectation. For example, I might feel sad when I'm expecting to have dinner with my entire family and am disappointed to learn that one of my children has made other plans.

Sometimes we just feel moody. We can't put our finger on what it is, but we're just sad. Maybe we're sensitive and start to cry upon hearing a certain song on the radio. Sometimes we just want to be alone. Other times, we are irritable and snap at whoever crosses our path.

During these times, we often say we're depressed, but we're not. We're sad or demoralized. We're disappointed or dejected.

We're gloomy or just plain bummed. These are all different from depression.

When a psychiatrist diagnoses depression, he or she is diagnosing a disorder, not a normal and transient state of mood. Depression is characterized by a group of signs and symptoms that have been the person's predominant experience over at least the past 2 weeks. People who present to a psychiatrist, however, have usually been suffering with their symptoms for much longer than 2 weeks. The signs and symptoms that characterize depression include a feeling of sadness, disordered sleep and appetite, an inability to experience pleasure, difficulty concentrating, lethargy, a sense of hopelessness or worthlessness, and a lack of motivation. Often, the depressed person feels that her life is not worth living, or he actually acts to end his life.

To merit a diagnosis of depression, one must have a minimal number of symptoms, and the symptoms must interfere in the person's functioning. Clearly, Bob suffered with these symptoms, and functioning was impaired. Clearly his symptoms diminished and his functioning improved after he started the medicine. Most would argue that Bob met criteria to take medicine to alter his brain chemistry. He suffered from a painful, life-threatening disorder.

Did the medicine stop his symptoms, or would a little blue pill filled with sugar have done as well?

Pass the Placebo, Please

As we saw in Chapter 8, single case reports can be simple and dramatic. Is there more scientifically based evidence that antidepressants are effective in children and adolescents? Do we need to examine the response of children apart from the response of adolescents?

One of the vexing issues in answering this question is the placebo response. That is, if a researcher gives antidepressant medicine to one group and placebo to the other group and 60% of the group taking antidepressant improve, but 50% of the group taking placebo also improve, one has a dilemma. Did the medicine help, or was it simply the taking of a pill that helped?

This sounds far-fetched. After all, how could 50% of a group of depressed adolescents improve simply by taking a little pill containing no active medicine? Nevertheless, this does happen.

The most commonly used antidepressants in the United States, prior to the advent of Prozac, were the tricyclic antidepressants. Research had clearly shown that they were superior to placebo in treating depression in adults. However, research in children and adolescents never really showed a difference between the efficacy of placebo and the efficacy of the tricyclic antidepressants. Sometimes the response rate to active medicine was high, but so was the response rate to placebo. Sometimes the response rate to medicine was less impressive and no better than placebo.

Research over the past 10 years has begun to show that children and adolescents with depression respond at a greater rate to some of the SSRIs, like Prozac, than to placebo (March et al., 2004). But here's the rub. Even in these studies, sometimes about 30% or more of children and adolescents respond to placebo. That doesn't mean that medicine doesn't work. It means that lots of people respond to placebo. This is true in studies of many types of medicine, not just psychiatric medicine. People often respond to placebo. Interestingly, people also get side effects to placebo. When researchers study the prevalence of side effects, they always find that varying percentages of the group that takes placebo complain about a variety of side effects, though they have not taken active medicine.

Some have half jokingly suggested that with such a high response rate to placebo, why not prescribe it to depressed adolescents? There are a number of problems with this idea. First, it would be unethical to lie to a patient, to tell him or her that you are prescribing an active medicine when you are not. Second, although a 30% response rate is not bad, clearly 60% or 70% is better. If a study found that 70% of the group responded to medicine and 30% responded to placebo, my guess is that you'd choose to be on active medicine.

Over recent years, studies have begun to demonstrate that some of the SSRIs are effective in treating depression in children and adolescents. For example, the recent Treatment for Adolescents with Depression Study (TADS), studying over 400 teens, demonstrated that Prozac is superior to both placebo and cognitive-behavioral therapy. In 1997, Dr. Graham Emslie and his research group also showed that 56% of children and adolescents taking Prozac, but only 33% of patients taking placebo, were improved or much improved after an 8-week trial (Emslie et al., 1997). Though there is a fairly high response rate to placebo, this is a significant difference.

These are considered encouraging results—enough so that more research studies are under way for these and many of the other newer antidepressants. Unfortunately, some of these studies are finding negative results. For example, although initial research (Keller, 2001) about the use of paroxetine was favorable, later research (Berard, 2006) reported a lack of effect. Overall, however, the data is still forthcoming.

However, there are practical difficulties in studying the response to the SSRI antidepressants. These medicines take a long time to work and often seem to pick up momentum over the course of months, long after the study has ended. This makes estimating the benefit of medicine more challenging. In one uncontrolled study by Paul Ambrosini and colleagues (1999), the response rate to Zoloft 6 weeks into the study was 65%. The response rate at 10 weeks was 84%. Although this study did not have a control group on placebo, and thus is not the gold standard we ultimately want, it does suggest that 10 weeks of medicine is better than 6 weeks. Interestingly, although the TADS also showed an increasing response to Prozac over the subsequent 36 weeks, it showed a similar improvement for those treated only with cognitive-behavioral therapy (March et al., 2007).

Nine months later, Bob is still taking his antidepressant. He continues to do well. He is dealing with the usual trials and tribulations of being 14 and seems happy, enjoys his friends, and is playing on the school baseball team. He complains about schoolwork in a passing manner but is diligent about completing it. He is looking forward to his family's summer trip to Alaska and says of his suicidal ideation, "I was like another person back then." When we begin to discuss tapering the medicine, both Bob and his parents become antsy. His parents still shudder to recall their son's considering how to end his life. Nobody wants to return to life in the dark shadow of depression.

The Pain of Misery

Not all people with depression fit the criteria that Bob fits. Bob's episode of depression was just that, an episode. He seemed to have a fairly clear onset of significant dysfunction preceded by years of good functioning. Other people with depression live in a chronic state of misery and irritability. They are able to function, but they are moody, unhappy, and difficult to live with. Adults who suffer from this form of chronic, low-level depression, sometimes called dysthymic disorder, often look back and say it started when they were kids. When they start medicine as an adult, they make comments like, "I haven't felt this good since I was 12" or "I forgot what it was like to feel normal."

Children often don't have the opportunity to look back at their lives and pinpoint the date of onset of their depression. Some are simply reported to have "always been that way."

Darla is 8 years old. Her parents report that she has always been irritable and pessimistic. Often seen as the black cloud that blocks the family's sunshine, Darla is belligerent and oppositional, so her parents are always careful not to disturb her. She becomes easily frustrated when faced with any unexpected change. She does adequately in school but does not have many friends.

Darla is clearly functioning, but she is not happy. After 4 weeks on Prozac, Darla seems like another person. "She just seems happier, more cheerful, more pleasant," her mother says 3 months later with tears in her eyes. "I've never seen her like this. I enjoy being with her now. I've always loved her—after all, she's my daughter. But I've only started to like her over the past couple of months."

Darla has never been suicidal. Her life has never been in danger, but she is in pain—not the physical pain of a stomachache but the emotional pain of a dysphoric mood. Darla lives a discontented life. She has endured no stress to make her unhappy. She simply is. Her functioning seems reasonable at first glance. She is going to school and has a few friends. At a deeper level, however, Darla's social functioning is impaired by her irritability, and her self-image is affected by her negative view of the world and herself.

Now we again carefully approach the slippery slope of diagnosis in children. One could look at Darla as suffering from a lifelong bout of dysthymic disorder and, by labeling her difficulty as a disorder, justify treatment with medicine.

Or one could diagnose Darla with oppositional defiant disorder (ODD) or severe mood-dysregulation disorder, a feature of each being irritability. There is no medicine for ODD and no proven medicine for severe mood-dysregulation disorder. However, medicine might be used to treat one of the symptoms, in this case Darla's moodiness.

Or one could say, "Darla is just a sourpuss. That's who she is. It's her personality. That's what makes the world go round." Regarding the possibility of treating Darla with medicine, one might say, "Darla's parents don't want to do the tough job of parenting. They just want to make their lives easier."

That may be "who Darla is," but if we leave it at that, we are bypassing the challenge to understand the differences among children and allowing ourselves to beg the question of whether to use medicine. If it's just who she is, we would be using medicine to tinker with her personality. On the other hand, if we accept that Darla's moods are causing emotional pain and may be the sign of disorder, we will attempt to learn more about children and their moods. For the near term, we will still struggle with when to use medicine. However, in the long term, we will develop an understanding of where to better draw the line between what is normal and what is disordered, and this should help guide us in our use of medicine in the future.

The view that simply accepts Darla for who she is callously fails to appreciate the pain that Darla experiences, as well as the pain of Darla's caring and sacrificing parents, who see a possible solution just a prescription away. Even if we do not see Darla as suffering from a disorder, she is still suffering. If medicine diminishes that suffering, Darla's parents will consider using it.

Darla benefits from the use of Prozac. She is in less pain. She is functioning better. So within the realm of the relatively primitive science of medicating children who suffer from lifelong moodiness, our case report indicates that the patient has improved. This is not a placebo-controlled study. Because of our relative lack of sophistication in diagnosing and treating these children, this is the best we can do for now.

In summary, we are slowly developing an understanding of mood disorders in children. We have a small but growing body of studies showing that specific antidepressants are more effective than placebo in treating major depressive disorder in children and adolescents. We have no such studies on the use of medicine to treat debilitating moodiness or irritability, even if diagnosed as dysthymic disorder. Nevertheless, we have case reports and lots of clinical experience to demonstrate that antidepressants can alleviate some symptoms of depression in these children and adolescents.

Beating Bipolar Disorder

Ten-year-old Perri has always been prickly. Over the past year, however, her mood has been morose, punctuated by intense temper outbursts. Perri cries easily and screams at her mother that she'd be better off dead. Although she is predominantly depressed, during the course of the day Perri periodically gets very giddy and silly. Her parents are relieved that the screaming has stopped, but the silliness feels excessive and out of proportion to anything that has recently happened. Couched in her usual ongoing irritability, it's hard to distinguish the silliness from the emotional noise that surrounds it. Usually very self-conscious, Perri periodically seems full of herself. During one such episode, she refuses to write down her homework, threatening her teacher with having her fired.

Perri is taken to a child psychiatrist and diagnosed with bipolar disorder. She is started on Abilify and over the next 2 weeks her irritability and silliness lessen.

As we've discussed, the diagnosis of bipolar disorder in children is reserved for those who have episodes of manic symptoms, including excessive silliness, elation, or grandiosity. Unlike many children with severe irritability, Perri meets those criteria. She is started on an atypical antipsychotic medicine that is FDA-approved for children.

The Autistic Child

Arnold is 12 years old and was diagnosed with autistic disorder, commonly known as autism, at an early age. He is in a class of five children with two teachers in a highly specialized school. Arnold rarely makes eye contact and cannot make conversation. His language skills are like those of a young child, and he reads at a beginner level. Arnold does not stay focused on any task for more than a few moments.

When he enters the office, he does not acknowledge the doctor he has known for 4 years, despite the doctor's attempts at social contact. Rather, he paces quickly and repeatedly back and forth across the room.

Stimulant medicines were prescribed in an attempt to lessen Arnold's hyperactivity, but they only excited him. Now Arnold is beginning to bite his fingers until they bleed, punch himself, and occasionally strike out at others in his class.

Arnold is started on Risperdal. He becomes less agitated and less aggressive. His self-injurious behavior diminishes. He is still uncommunicative, inattentive, and highly dysfunctional, but he and those around him are safer.

Arnold was in physical pain and a danger to himself and others. He and those around him benefit from his use of medicine. The scientific basis for the use of medicines like Risperdal in children with autism rests on well-executed studies demonstrating a benefit that clearly exceeds that of placebo. For example, in one study, 69% of those treated with risperidone (the generic of Risperdal) improved, whereas only 12% of those treated with placebo improved (McCracken et al., 2002). Even the nonstatisticians among us can appreciate that powerful difference. Risperdal and Abilify, both atypical antipsychotics, are FDA-approved for the treatment of this extreme irritability in children with autism.

No medicine cures autism. For many years, haloperidol (the generic name for Haldol) was the only medicine to have passed the threshold of a double-blind, placebo-controlled study. But, as we've seen, recent research has shown that atypical antipsychotic medicines, like risperidone, are also helpful (McCracken et al., 2002; McDougle et al., 2005). In these studies, medicine has been shown to decrease some of the characteristic behaviors of autism, such as severe tantrums, self-injury, and repetitive behaviors, but did not improve the social relatedness that is a core element of the disorder. Other medicines are prescribed to children with autism in an attempt to alleviate a particular symptom, such as stimulants to lessen hyperactivity, albeit with less dramatic improvement.

In its most textbook form, autism is fairly easy to diagnose. Dustin Hoffman's character in the movie *Rain Man* is the classic presentation. However, over recent years, clinicians have begun identifying more children with subtle signs of autism. Some of these children have groups of symptoms that are now discussed as being on the autistic spectrum. Clinicians regularly use this label among themselves. Although this is not a diagnosis, this label helps the clinician organize his or her thoughts about the patient and therefore makes it easier to medicate the child's symptoms, even though the child's difficulties don't quite qualify as a disorder.

CHAPTER 10

Let's Be Practical

||||||||||||||||||||||||||||||||||||||||||||||||||||||||||||||||

Now that we've looked at some of the FDA-approved uses of psychiatric medicine, let's review some of the medicines that are effectively used, albeit without FDA-approval—the so-called off-label use of medicines. Some of these are only beginning to be tested by well-constructed studies proving the medicine's efficacy in children. Again, my goal is not to catalogue all the uses of psychiatric medicines in children but to demonstrate that medicines that have been studied less thoroughly also benefit children.

When a medicine becomes available, it is often prescribed for children for whom other medicines have not been helpful. When this is successful, the physician sometimes writes a case report that stimulates more methodical research on a particular medicine. The vignettes in this chapter describe medicines that, although not as rigorously researched as the medicines in Chapter 9, are used regularly by many clinicians based on their own experience or the accumulated reporting of success by other physicians. The benefits of these medicines have passed the valued, but not always to be trusted, criteria of agreed-upon clinical wisdom.

Prescribing for Panic

Peter is 10. He is with his family at the amusement park, standing in line to get on the Ferris wheel he's been on many times before. Suddenly, he starts getting a queasy feeling. He feels his heart racing. He is short of breath. He feels shaky and sweaty. He is in an unexplainable panic and fears he is going to die. Despite the fact that he and his brother have been waiting in the long line for 15 minutes, he refuses to proceed. After about 30 minutes, the symptoms dissipate, but he refuses to return to the Ferris wheel. He doesn't feel like doing much of anything else at the park that day. He only wants to return home.

Peter begins having these attacks daily. Between attacks, Peter anxiously anticipates the next attack. At home, Peter wants to be near his parents, and, at night, he needs the door open so that he doesn't feel closed in. Peter especially fears being stuck in his classroom, unable to leave. The teacher lets him sit near the door, but Peter's constant need to open the door to step out of the classroom is disrupting the class.

After about 2 weeks, Peter is refusing to go to school for fear of having an attack. His parents try coaxing, threatening, and pleading. Sometimes Peter makes it to school; increasingly he does not.

A visit to the pediatrician does not reveal a physical cause of these episodes. So the pediatrician suggests a consultation with a child psychiatrist.

The psychiatrist says Peter is experiencing panic attacks and, given the frequency and ongoing nature of the attacks, diagnoses Peter as having panic disorder. He prescribes Klonopin, an antianxiety medicine, which Peter is to take each morning and each evening. After Peter starts taking Klonopin, the panic attacks stop. Peter reluctantly, slowly, cautiously returns to school.

After about a month, the psychiatrist recommends stopping the Klonopin. Although a very low risk in children with an anxiety disorder, he is concerned about Klonopin's potential for addiction. Peter and his parents, who were initially reluctant to start the medicine, are now reluctant to stop it. Nevertheless, they do so, and about a week later the panic attacks return. The psychiatrist resumes the Klonopin, which gives Peter immediate relief, and simultaneously starts him on Zoloft. About 2 months later, the Klonopin is again discontinued, even though Peter and his parents are reluctant. This time, however, the panic attacks do not return, and Peter remains on Zoloft.

Though Peter feared dying, his life was never in danger. Though he experienced uncomfortable physical symptoms, he was never in significant physical pain. Peter did experience severe psychological pain, in the form of acute panic anxiety, and anticipatory anxiety as he awaited the next panic attack. This anxiety caused significant dysfunction, as it inhibited Peter's ability to attend school, go to his friends' houses, and feel comfortable in his own home.

Peter was treated with two types of medicine. Klonopin, the first medicine prescribed, is an antianxiety medicine that worked immediately. When it was discontinued and the panic attacks returned, Peter was given Zoloft, an antidepressant that over time prevents panic attacks and only needs to be taken once daily. Neither of these medicines is FDA-approved for the treatment of panic disorder in children, although each is approved for use in children with other disorders.

Has Peter benefited from taking these medicines? It certainly seems so. They stopped the anxiety that was impeding his ability to lead the life of a normal 10-year-old. Peter's parents experienced a common change of heart about medicine. Though they reluctantly permitted the doctor to start medicine, once Peter improved, they were fearful of stopping it. This phenomenon reflects parents' exquisite recall of the pain of watching their child in psychological distress and their relief when the child slowly regains normal functioning. All of this speaks to the benefit of medicine.

Any physician who has treated patients with panic disorder will quickly attest to the dramatic benefit medicines afford. We readily use these medicines even though we do not have large double-blind, placebo-controlled studies to prove their benefit to children.

Salvaging Sociability

Amy is 12 years old. She has always been very timid. As a toddler, she clung to her mother when faced with a stranger. The pediatrician assured Amy's parents that Amy would outgrow her timidity. As a first grader, Amy remained quiet and socially removed in class. Her warm and supportive teacher assured her parents that she had seen many quiet children in her 30 years of teaching and that Amy would outgrow her shyness.

Now Amy is in sixth grade. She is painfully shy and has no friends. She speaks minimally in class. She is afraid to eat in the cafeteria because she fears she will look stupid if tuna fish falls out of her sandwich. She fears the other kids will laugh at her. She sits alone on the school bus each day, imagining the critical stares of her peers.

Her mother encourages her, bribes her, threatens her to be more outgoing, but to no avail. After 6 months of psychotherapy, Amy still sits timidly in her chair answering the therapist's questions with one-word responses. Amy's parents take Amy to a different therapist, who uses a more behavioral approach, reinforcing Amy for the slightest improvement in socializing. She has minimal success.

Amy's behavioral therapist suggests a psychiatric consultation for the possible use of medicine. Amy is started on Paxil. She also continues in therapy. After about a month, her anxiety in front of others begins to lessen. After two or three months, she is speaking in class and has begun to develop a friendship. She is not running for class president, but she is more socially engaged. And she is happier.

After Amy has been taking Paxil for about 18 months, the psychiatrist begins to taper Amy off the medicine. This is fine with Amy, who says she no longer needs the medicine and that she just wants to be normal. Although the medicine has helped Amy, she is now preoccupied, at age 13, with being like all the other kids. The medicine is tapered, then discontinued. Amy continues to see the behavioral therapist, albeit less often, and she continues to do well.

Like Peter, Amy was never in physical danger. Like Peter, she was in significant psychological pain. Although Amy's parents were also in pain and were the driving force behind getting Amy help, Amy's discomfort should not be minimized. She was not content to be alone. On the contrary, she desperately wanted friends. She was simply too petrified to pursue them.

Amy benefited from Paxil, a medicine approved for social anxiety disorder in adults. The medicine lowered her anxiety and allowed Amy to make use of behavioral therapy. Amy remained socially reluctant, but she began to make slow progress. The benefit seemed clear. The double-blind, placebo-controlled research proving the efficacy of Paxil and other SSRIs in treating children with social anxiety disorder and other anxiety disorders (Rynn, Siqueland, & Rickels, 2001; Wagner et al., 2004; Walkup et al., 2001; Walkup et al., 2008) is stronger than the research on the use of SSRIs to treat other childhood disorders, including depression and obsessive-compulsive disorder. Yet these medicines are not FDA-approved for use in these anxiety disorders in children.

You Can't Hear Me with the Water Running

At age 14, Chelsea Burns is spending more time in the bathroom than she should be. The tub water always seems to be running. She insists that she needs to shower after breakfast and again after dinner, though her hair is rarely wet. Mr. Burns says she's just a teenager. Mrs. Burns finds it peculiar, especially when she begins finding cookie crumbs on Chelsea's carpet and empty cookie bags stuffed in a corner of her closet.

Mrs. Burns consults the pediatrician, who finds rubbed areas on the back of Chelsea's knuckles and suspects that Chelsea has bulimia. After a tearful struggle, Chelsea admits to vomiting every time she eats, three or four times daily, and masking the sound with running water. She says this started in an attempt to lose weight and that now she is unable to stop. She gorges on pints of ice cream, boxes of donuts, and bags of cookies, then heads to the bathroom to vomit. She lives in fear of being caught by her parents.

The pediatrician sends Chelsea to a child psychiatrist, who sees Chelsea in therapy and simultaneously starts her on Prozac. After a few months, Chelsea's need to vomit is diminishing. Resisting the urge to vomit is still a battle, but she feels confident that she can do it.

Prozac is FDA-approved for the treatment of adults with bulimia nervosa. It is not approved for use in children and young adolescents with this disorder. Nevertheless, knowing the medical risks of the disorder, including potassium depletion and consequent heart-rhythm disturbances, and the psychological pain Chelsea experiences, her physician feels Prozac is a reasonable intervention. Whether because of the Prozac or not, Chelsea improves.

Mad Max

Max is 12 years old. He lives with his divorced mother and a younger brother. Max's mother works as a teacher's aide so she can be at home after school. She is calm and patient and understands children. Max's father has not been seen in 6 years. His mother has heard that he was in a psychiatric hospital in another state.

Sometimes Max is delightful—articulate, funny, helpful. More often, he is a terror. Max is very easily frustrated. When he does not get what he wants, Max explodes with anger. He rants and raves and storms around the house like a wounded bear. Max's little brother runs for cover. Max's mother used to be able to physically contain him. Now Max weighs 125 pounds.

Max is beginning to stay up later and later at night. Sometimes he is up all night in a chat room, does not awaken the next day until 2 PM, and misses school. If his mother awakens him, he erupts and refuses to go to school.

Max is exploding with increasing frequency. He throws furniture, threatens to kill his mother, and recently picked up a baseball bat and waved it menacingly at his brother. He cries, screams, and feels like others are talking about him, which, because of his behavior, is true. On one occasion, his mother is so scared that she calls the police, who bring Max to the emergency room. After he tears up the ER, Max spends the night in a psychiatric hospital.

The psychiatrist in the hospital diagnoses Max as having bipolar disorder and starts him on Seroquel. Within a few days, Max's behavior becomes more reasonable. He is less explosive and more able to be with others. His thinking is clearer and less pressured, and he has a better understanding of others' intent to help him.

Max is discharged from the hospital after a week. He remains on Seroquel. After about a month, his psychiatrist starts him on Depakote. Over the subsequent few months, Max continues to improve. Although he requires a special school that can deal with his periodic aggression and low frustration tolerance, he slowly becomes one of the more functional students in the school.

Max also has benefited from medicine. Although he was not in danger of hurting himself, he was in danger of hurting someone else. He was not in physical pain, but he was in substantial psychological pain. He was not sleeping, often missing school, not getting along with his peers, and generally dysfunctional.

As we've already seen, the diagnostic criteria of bipolar disorder in childhood remain a debate within child psychiatry. But in the real world of pain, doctors sometimes have to use the available remedies despite having inadequate information. Seroquel is approved to treat adolescents with bipolar disorder, but Depakote is not. We have some data on the use of these medicines in adolescents and adults, and, for now, that will have to suffice.

Max had to be treated, and so he was. He improved while taking medicine, and therefore we unscientifically, but probably accurately, ascribe the benefit to the medicine. The powerful effect of the hospitalization, however, cannot be discounted.

The Schizophrenic Child

Barney, 11 years old, lives in a residential school. Barney's mother has schizophrenia and lives in a halfway house. She has never been able to adequately care for Barney. Barney's father is absent.

Barney has lived with his mother intermittently, depending on her ability to function. When Barney was 8, he made odd noises in class. These were not the explosive noises that a child with a tic disorder tries to suppress. Rather, they were the weird, outer space–like sounds of a child who did not seem to realize that his classmates found him bizarre. Barney had no real friendships. He was usually alone, and sometimes the teacher would find him mumbling to himself, although he would not tell her what he was saying.

Barney begins cutting up his schoolbooks with a scissor. He is evaluated by a child psychiatrist who thinks that Barney is hearing voices telling him to cut up the books. The child psychiatrist diagnoses schizophrenia and hospitalizes Barney. During his hospitalization, Barney is treated with Zyprexa, an antipsychotic medicine approved for use in adults. The hallucinations begin to recede, and Barney is sent back to the residential school.

Barney is not in physical pain. His life is probably not in jeopardy, though because of his mental state, this can be difficult to evaluate. He is arguably in psychological pain and certainly dysfunctional and therefore merits treatment.

Schizophrenia is a rare but debilitating disorder in children. It is typically characterized by the presence of hallucinations, most commonly auditory, or delusions, the false and often bizarre beliefs to which the person clings. Schizophrenia is most often a progressive disease characterized by a slow downward spiral of dysfunction.

There have been a few small studies showing the efficacy of the atypical antipsychotics in treating schizophrenia in children and adolescents (Findling, McNamara, Youngstrom, Branicky, Demeter, & Schulz, 2003; Kumra et al., 1996). These studies have been sufficiently convincing that some of the atypical antipsychotics are FDA-approved to treat schizophrenia in adolescents, although not children. Nevertheless, Barney has been treated with apparent ensuing benefit.

Aggressive ADHD

Lee is 12 years old. He is fidgety and unfocused. Nobody has ever considered that he might have ADHD. Lee is best known in school for being reactively aggressive. If he feels threatened by another child—and it doesn't take much for him to feel threatened—Lee's fists go up, and he's ready to rumble.

Lee is exquisitely sensitive to embarrassment, and when Mrs. Janus, his teacher, unwittingly put Lee on the spot in class about his missing homework, Lee shot back with an angry tirade of four-letter words that left Mrs. Janus speechless. After regaining her composure, she marched Lee down to the principal's office.

A psychiatric evaluation reveals ADHD but also notes Lee's hair-trigger temper and flying fists. Although Lee does not fit all the criteria for conduct disorder, he is certainly aggressive, albeit in a reactive, not predatory, manner. Psychotherapy has been useless in the short run. Lee is bright and in some ways extremely sensitive, but he is also a rigid young man who sees the world in black and white terms. Although he grudgingly admits that the child psychiatrist is not a jerk, he stubbornly refuses to return after a few visits.

Because of his diagnosis of ADHD, Lee is given a trial of Adderall. He is more focused and less fidgety, and, most notably, he is getting into fewer fights. Although he superficially resists the medicine, which represents an affront to his self-image, Lee allows himself to take it from his mother every morning. He reluctantly agrees to occasionally see the child psychiatrist to monitor the medicine.

Stimulant medicines, as we have discussed, are FDA-approved for the treatment of ADHD in children. Although they are not approved for the treatment of aggression, some children experience this benefit from stimulants. We are still learning about the range of symptoms that are ameliorated by these medicines.

Appreciating the Change

We have just reviewed the histories of many children who have benefited from the non-FDA-approved use of medicine. Klonopin is not approved for children with panic disorder. Paxil is not approved for children with anxiety. We could list all the approved and nonapproved indications of each of our many medicines, and our list of benefits would be incomplete. Let's expand our thinking.

Medicine does more than stop a symptom or defeat a disorder. It changes a mindset. When Allegra stops my allergic nose from running like a faucet, it is also changing the way I feel. My nose stops running, and the sun comes out. My entire outlook is changed. This is an indirect but powerful effect of the antihistamine.

Children experience these indirect benefits of psychiatric medicine all the time. The FDA does not approve a medicine because it offers this psychological benefit, but it is perhaps the most meaningful benefit of all.

Seventeen-year-old Ellen is starting her senior year of high school. For years, Ellen had been painfully shy. She was able to talk only to her closest friends whom she had known for years. She was unable to sit in the cafeteria with a larger group of peers.

Ellen has been on Lexapro for the past year and now feels more comfortable with peers. She feels she'd like to discontinue the medicine at this time but acknowledges that, if she had never taken Lexapro, she would still be quiet, withdrawn, and afraid to speak up in public. Ellen appreciates the change.

Sixteen-year-old Jonah has been on Zoloft for about a year. He reports, "I'm not used to happiness. I used to see the world as gray and dreary. I was cynical, gloomy, and pessimistic. I used to be ticked off by this little Miss Mary Sunshine who sits near me on the bus. Now I'm happier. I like being with people better, and they like to be with me."

Sixteen-year-old Jeremy, with depression and obsessive-compulsive disorder, says, "It's hard to admit that the medicine is responsible for my improvement because I don't like to think it has control over me. But I know it helps me. I can move along, and that's good."

Some children can detect the subtle changes in others when they are on medicine, and this is an indirect benefit.

Tyesha has been on Prozac for 9 months. She is less rigid, happier, more willing to try new activities and foods. Tyesha expresses, with poignancy, how her life has improved. "I have a new attitude," she says proudly. "And with my new attitude, my mom likes me better."

This is not a judgment of Tyesha's mother, who surely loves her daughter. Rather, it demonstrates that Tyesha's change has positively affected her mother and allowed for more pleasant interactions between the two of them. Her mother's change has subsequently been positive for Tyesha.

Many children with ADHD also readily give testimony to the efficacy of medicine. Their reports are insufficient for proving the medicine is effective at improving focus or diminishing impulsivity, but they demonstrate the positive effect of the medicine's effectiveness on the child's life. These are benefits of medicine.

"Without the medicine," says 11-year-old Carl with ADHD, "I'd never be able to get my work done."

Eleven-year-old Carrie, with lifelong inattention, reports that "whenever I start to zone out, the medicine helps me focus on the teacher." She loves the idea that she's no longer the class space cadet.

Ten-year-old Brandon echoes Carrie's sentiment about listening to the teacher. "I used to watch the clouds out the window. Now I know I'm in math class."

Fifteen-year-old Reggie has been spacing out in school for years. After 2 months on Concerta, he reports improved grades and more confidence. Reggie states, "When the teacher asked a question, I used to raise my hand just to feel smart. I didn't even know what the question was. Now I raise my hand because I know the answer."

Testimonials are notoriously unreliable for proving a medicine to be effective. However, they do demonstrate the patient's appreciation of the positive change since starting medicine.

Looking Past the Horizon

Although children are not known for worrying about the future, their parents do. When parents consent to give their child medicine, they are not only looking for relief of the current symptom, they are also looking toward the future. Will the medicine harm my child in 20 years? This is a valid question, but parents would do well to also ask how medicine could benefit their child by reducing the malignant long-term effect of the disorder.

Without studies examining patients who have taken medicine over many years, the perception of the likelihood of improved prognosis is based largely on the knowledge that medicine helps in the short run and on the increasing realization that, if left untreated, the psychiatric disorders of many children will become chronic. The assumption, therefore, is that medicine will continue to help these children, thus improving their long-term outcome.

There are indications that different medicines improve prognosis in a variety of ways. For example, it is known that depression is a very recurrent disorder (Birmaher et al., 1996; Fleming, Boyle, & Offord, 1993; Lewinsohn, Clarke, Seeley, & Rohde, 1994) and that children with dysthymic disorder are at an even greater risk than children with major depression for developing a subsequent mood disorder (Kovacs, Akiskal, Gatsonis, & Parrone, 1994). Emslie and colleagues (2004) have shown that depressed children who have improved on antidepressants are more likely to relapse when changed to placebo than when continued on medicine. If medicine taken during childhood or taken in an ongoing manner into adulthood prevented perpetuation of illness, millions would benefit.

In addition, some have argued that in some countries an association existed between a declining adolescent suicide rate and the advent of the SSRI antidepressants (Gibbons, Hur, Bhaumik, & Mann, 2005; Olfson, Shaffer, Marcus, & Greenberg, 2003). Others have shown that adolescents with bipolar disorder committed far fewer offenses when they were taking medication than when they were not (Dailey, Townsend, Dysken, & Kuskowski, 2005). Again, if medicine helps decrease the chances of self-injurious, illegal, or dangerous behavior, many would benefit.

Adults with ADHD are known to be at greater risk for such difficulties as divorce, drug abuse, and problems with the law. An interesting review by Wilens, Faraone, Biederman, and Gunawardene (2003) showed that, contrary to popular belief, children with ADHD who were treated with stimulants had a significant reduction in their risk for drug- and alcohol-use disorders in later adolescence compared to children who were not medicated with stimulants. If the medicine was even partly responsible for this decrease, these patients and all society benefited significantly.

How medicine could improve prognosis is open to speculation. Do medicines change the parts of the brain responsible for the progression of these disorders? Does medicine help the child improve relationships with others, thereby improving self-esteem and lowering the risk of psychiatric illness in adulthood? The answers to these questions are unknown. In their concern for their child's future, parents must consider the possibility that medicine could have a powerful beneficial effect on their child's long-term outcome.

Summarizing the Benefits

Children can be painfully anxious or depressed. They can be disruptively irritable or hyperactive. Although child psychiatry is a young and evolving science, minimizing the importance of children's dysfunction simply because they are not adults is scientifically unsophisticated. Underestimating the pain caused by the psychiatric disorders of children and their families is callous. These people hurt and greatly appreciate the relief medicine affords them. Although we sometimes lack the highest standard of proof, we treat children with medicines based on clinical experience, and many patients are benefiting.

CHAPTER 11

The Risks of Medicine

||||||||||||||||||||||||||||||||||||||||||||||||||||||||||||||||||

There's No Such Thing as a Free Dinner

The side effects of any medicine are a bit like uninvited guests. You ask good friends over for dinner, and without telling you, they bring along their boorish cousin Seymour, who's been staying with them for the past month. You enjoy having your friends over, but you didn't count on listening to Seymour groan on about the details of his nasty divorce and how his ex-wife ran off with the milkman and on and on. So you ask yourself, "Was it worth it? Was dinner with close friends worth putting up with Seymour?"

Similarly, you take a medicine for a particular beneficial effect. You also get effects that you did not want and that might be harmful. These are called side effects, and every medicine causes them in some people. Usually, like Cousin Seymour, they are unwanted and unpleasant. They include rashes and headaches and diarrhea and sedation.

Before considering these negative side effects, let's remember that sometimes side effects are useful. Sometimes, they're like your friends' cousin Leo, who turns out to be a witty, charming dinner guest, possibly more fun than your friends. If you invite your friends for dinner because you know that Leo is in town, whom are you really inviting? Is Cousin Leo a side effect or the main event?

Sometimes doctors prescribe a medicine because the side effect is desired.

Harry is 8. He has insomnia. He doesn't fall asleep until about 1 A.M. He's tired the next day because he has to wake up for school at 7. His parents and doctor don't know why Harry can't fall asleep; he just can't. He's always been this way. He's not depressed or anxious. His pediatrician says there's no medical problem.

The doctor tells his parents about clonidine. She explains that this is a medicine used to treat high blood pressure in adults but also used for children with tic disorders and ADHD. One of the side effects of clonidine is lethargy, so many doctors use it to help their patients with insomnia. For Harry, it works like a charm.

Was the sedating effect of clonidine a side effect? In Harry's case, it was the desired therapeutic effect. In the 1960s, Obetrol, a stimulant medicine, was marketed to help people lose weight. In the 1990s, the same medicine was renamed Adderall and marketed to treat attention-deficit hyperactivity disorder. Weight loss went from being the intended therapeutic effect to a problematic side effect. Whether an effect is therapeutic or a side effect depends on one's perspective.

Usually, however, side effects represent negative events. Given that they are negative, let's consider how they factor into the decision to take medicine.

Gauging Probability

When deciding whether to prescribe a medicine, the physician must gauge the likelihood of different side effects. Is the chance that Billy's hair will turn blue 1 in 1000 or 1 in 3? This makes a big difference. In addition to being a function of the particular medicine prescribed, the probability of side effects can reflect the dose prescribed, the duration for which the medicine is used, or the other medicines the patient is taking concomitantly. It can also depend on the age of the child.

Pedro is 4 years old. He is extremely hyperactive and is started on Ritalin. He becomes irritable on the medicine, however, so his mother discontinues it, and the next day Pedro is back to being his lovable, if hyperactive, self. Two years later, Pedro's physician prescribes Ritalin again. This time Pedro becomes much less active and more focused, without side the effects he experienced earlier.

Pedro's side effects were most likely a function of his age. Not all 4-year-olds react adversely to Ritalin, but some do.

Gary is 13. He is very shy and has an anxiety disorder. He is started on Zoloft. At 125 milligrams daily, he is no longer anxious and timid. In fact, he is uninhibited and confronts the assistant principal, which lands him in detention. His dose is decreased to 100 milligrams daily. Gary is once again his usual sweet self but a bit less shy and a bit more outgoing and socially involved. Thank goodness, he remains reasonably inhibited.

Gary developed the side effect of disinhibition, which was probably the result of too high a dose. At a lower dose, Gary benefited from the medicine without the side effect.

Wai's pediatrician recommends Tylenol and Phenergan for Wai's upper-respiratory symptoms. Knowing Wai had recurrent illness all last winter, her father continues this regimen, without informing the pediatrician, on a two- to three-times-per-day basis for about 9 months per year over about 3 years. Wai starts showing increasing agitation, and her parents are referred to a child psychiatrist. Careful examination reveals that Wai is having visual hallucinations. Both medicines are discontinued. Within a few weeks, the hallucinations stop, and Wai is much improved.

Wai's side effects were probably due to the length of time for which she took the medicine and perhaps the combination of medicines she was taking.

Any medicine can cause side effects. Although medicines with fewer side effects are being developed, no medicine is specific enough to cause only the desired effect in the correct organ. However, just as one can gauge the probability of a chair collapsing before one sits in it, one must gauge the probability of a particular medicine causing a particular side effect. Knowing that a medicine causes pancreatitis in 1 in every 50,000 patients is less alarming than knowing it does so in 1% of patients. A 1% chance of pancreatitis is less alarming than a 25% chance. A list of possible side effects is essentially meaningless without understanding their probability.

For medicine to be seen as causing a side effect, the probability of experiencing that side effect must be greater in patients taking medicine than in those taking placebo. Adverse events, such as heart failure, also occur in the general population who do not take medicine. If medicine is going to be held responsible for causing a side effect, the risk of that adverse event must be higher than in a group of patients who have taken placebo and higher than would be expected in the general population.

Gauging Danger

One must also consider the type of side effects. Just as it's unusual to be lucky enough to catch Cousin Leo in town, it's unusual for side effects to be desirable, though sometimes they are, making the medication a particularly good choice. Dangerous side effects, such as hepatitis or loss of platelets, can be unlikely but scary. Luckily, most side effects are nuisance-level, such as headaches and stomachaches. The physician doesn't want to cause them but knows they'll only be a nuisance; if need be, the medicine can be discontinued, and the side effect will disappear.

Physicians always have the well-known creed "first do no harm" in the back of their minds. That advice is time-honored and valid, but it should caution the doctor to consider carefully the benefits and risks before prescribing a medicine, not handcuff the doctor into doing nothing at all.

My rule is not to have the patient's side effects keep me awake at night. This rule may be a bit self-serving, but I think it also serves the patient well. The three types of side effects that keep me awake at night are life-threatening side effects, irreversible side effects, and very painful side effects. However, if the benefit of the medicine outweighs these risks, I will consider prescribing it. If I can then sleep well, I consider it to have been the correct decision. This doesn't mean the decision is risk-free—it just means that I consider the potential benefits to be worth the risk.

Valerie is 16. She is an intelligent, creative young woman who lives with her divorced mother and three sisters. Valerie has dramatic mood swings that interfere with her life at home and school. When frustrated, after she finishes throwing books and clothes and picture frames around her room, she cries inconsolably. Other times, Valerie is buoyant and engaging. Psychotherapy has not controlled these episodes. Her mother is at her wits' end. Valerie's psychotherapist suggests a consultation for medication.

Dr. Pincus evaluates Valerie. She does not really fit the criteria for bipolar disorder, but her mood swings hint at the swiftly changing mood, or mood lability, seen in patients with bipolar disorder. Dr. Pincus thinks about prescribing Depakote, and she considers the warnings that this medicine can cause pancreatitis and suppress the production of platelets, albeit rarely. She is also aware that Depakote is linked to causing polycystic ovary syndrome, with its risk of obesity, menstrual irregularities, and acne. Dr. Pincus considers the side effects and then decides that, if the medicine works, they are worth the risk. Valerie and her parents agree.

Side effects such as pancreatitis and bone-marrow suppression are potentially life-threatening. The benefit of a medicine that can cause these types of side effects must clearly outweigh the risk. Life-threatening side effects, even if very rare, weigh very heavily.

Potentially irreversible side effects, though not life-threatening, are also concerning.

Hank is started on Haldol for schizophrenia in the mid-1980s. He requires a large dose to function in a highly supervised residential treatment facility. After 3 years on the medicine, Hank develops an involuntary movement of his mouth called tardive dyskinesia. Haldol is discontinued. A year later, Hank continues to demonstrate this involuntary movement. It is unknown whether it will ever disappear.

Most medicines used in child psychiatry do not cause life-threatening or irreversible side effects, but some do. Child psychiatry has had to deal with some pre-Prozac antidepressants causing heart-rhythm disturbances and lately the question of whether some antidepressants cause suicide. Perhaps the most infamous of irreversible side effects has been tardive dyskinesia. Fortunately, the risk of many of these side effects is low, and newer medicines, such as the atypical antipsychotics, have been developed with a much lower risk of side effects like tardive dyskinesia.

Extreme pain is another troubling side effect. Pain thresholds vary, however, and evaluating the level of pain is always a tough call, especially in some children who can be overly dramatic.

Sasha is started on Dexedrine. Her mother calls to report that Sasha is responding to the medicine but that she has had a headache for the past few days. Sasha wails every morning and refuses to leave for school. Her doctor is unsure if Sasha is in terrible pain or being very

135

dramatic about a little pain. He tells Sasha's mother that headaches generally pass after a few days. A week later, Sasha's mother calls back. The headaches are continuing, unresponsive to pain medicine. Together, she and the physician decide to discontinue the medicine.

Some side effects are dramatic but reversible. These, if carefully monitored, need not be alarming.

Sandy is started on Adderall for ADHD. After 3 months, she has lost 15 pounds off her starting weight of 90. This is a significant weight loss. Adderall is discontinued, and Sandy regains and maintains her weight.

Henry is 14. His diagnosis is uncertain, but his inability to control himself is not. He is explosive and constantly fighting. He is started on Risperdal. The medicine is helpful, but Henry starts gaining weight. At first, his parents are thrilled with the new, better-behaved Henry. Because "he was always so skinny," they're not even bothered that he's gained a few pounds. Then Henry's face starts getting round, and his body starts looking chunky. Henry is embarrassed and his parents are worried. Risperdal is discontinued, and Henry's weight slowly returns to normal.

Weight change is a significant, potentially dangerous, but ultimately reversible side effect. Weight gain is sometimes associated with elevated cholesterol, triglyceride, and sugar levels. These metabolic changes are generally thought to be reversible, but this may not be true. This does serve as a reminder that these medicines can cause a range of effects, and we are currently aware of only some of them. It also reminds us that children taking these medicines need to be monitored.

Given that what we know is incomplete and always growing, one must consider the depth of our knowledge about a medicine. Is it based on our experience of seeing 100 children take the medicine over the past 6 months? Or is it based on seeing thousands of children who have used the medicine over many years?

The Long and Short of Side Effects

Side effects can also be judged by timing and duration. Short-term side effects are transient. Sasha's doctor hoped that her headaches were short-term and would disappear in a few days.

Sometimes the phrase "short-term" is used to designate side effects that begin shortly after the medicine is started. Sasha's doctor knew that if Dexedrine was to cause a headache, it usually would do so at the beginning of treatment, not 2 years later. However, just because a side effect begins soon after the initiation of treatment, it isn't necessarily benign.

Hugh is 12. He is depressed and suicidal, agitated and irritable. He requires little sleep. His mother has bipolar disorder and Hugh's physician believes Hugh does too. He has not responded to Depakote or lithium, so Hugh's parents and psychiatrist discuss a trial of Lamictal. Though Lamictal is FDA-approved for the treatment of bipolar disorder in adults, it is not approved for children with this disorder. Of greater concern is the very slight risk of Stevens-Johnson syndrome, which is characterized by a sometimes-fatal rash. It is thought that the risk of this very serious side effect is greater if the dose of the medicine is initially increased too quickly.

Hugh's doctor increases the dose very slowly.

Long-term side effects generally begin after the patient has been taking the medicine for a long time. They can be a reflection of the cumulative dose the patient has taken over the years or of the number of years the medicine was taken, or they can simply show up years later. In children, they might reflect the developmental stage during which the medicine was taken. Physicians are reluctant, for example, to prescribe medicine to pregnant women out of concern that the developing fetus will be affected in ways that may show up at birth or emerge years later.

If parents give their child medicine, they want an assurance that nothing bad will happen in the long term. How long is the long term? One year? Three years? Twenty years? Parents need only hear one or two very dramatic stories of medicines causing problems 20 years later to overturn their decision to medicate their child. Unfortunately, doctors don't always have the reassuring answers that parents are looking for.

There are many reasons for this lack of answers. Many of the medicines used in children have not been prescribed over long periods. For example, 30 years ago, Ritalin was often discontinued before adolescence because doctors believed that children outgrew ADHD. When it was discovered that many children did not, physicians continued their use of medicine into adolescence. Also, because many of the medicines currently prescribed have not been on the market for more than 20 years, a longer follow-up is impossible.

Medicines are first studied in other mammals, such as mice. Giving medicine to mice allows researchers to give higher-than-normal doses to many generations of mice to see if there is an increased risk of side effects. The FDA will only approve medicine for research in humans if there is no indication of a significant problem. Therefore, unless there is an earlier indication, doctors would probably not be looking for the problem to develop. That is not to say that a problem could not be discovered 20 years later, only that there is no reason to expect it.

The longer doctors prescribe a medicine, the more information is available. A medicine is only approved for use by the FDA after it has been tested in many, perhaps hundreds, of patients. From these trials, a side effect profile is developed. Once the medicine is FDA-approved and doctors begin to prescribe it, many, perhaps thousands, more patients take it. A side effect that develops rarely—let's say less than 1 in 1000—might not be picked up after trials in a few hundred patients. It might only be recognized after a few thousand patients take the medicine.

A study by Lasser, Allen, Woolhandler, Himmelstein, Wolfe, and Bor (2002) showed that approximately 10% of medicines approved by the FDA between 1975 and 1999 developed significant warnings or were withdrawn from the market over the next 25 years. Dangerous problems can occur rarely and not be discovered until a medicine is widely used.

Another difficulty in determining long-term side effects is that for definitive research, one would like to study a large group of patients with the same diagnosis who took a standard dose for a standard time. In children, it would also be helpful if they took the medicine during the same developmental period.

That goal is very difficult to accomplish in the real world, especially the relatively young world of child psychopharmacology. Children start and stop different doses of medicine at different ages for lots of reasons. Doses frequently change, and children simultaneously take other medicines. The children also have a variety of diagnoses and other medical issues that can affect the possibility of side effects. Because the medicines have not been around for long, it is difficult to find a group who has used a given medicine for years. It is very difficult to obtain follow-up on these children 20 years later, and even if you did, you'd have a tough time interpreting the results. If a better medicine is developed in the meantime, then the results are of no practical value.

In short, parents should not be scared off by a list of possible side effects. Without knowing the likelihood and seriousness of the side effect, one cannot evaluate whether the risk is worth the benefit offered by the medicine.

CHAPTER 12

Subtle Psychological Side Effects

||||||||||||||||||||||||||||||||||||||||||||||||||||||||||||||||||||

Proving Biology But Retaining Responsibility

Dramatic physical side effects overshadow medicine's more insidious consequences. As medicines with fewer perilous side effects are developed, subtler psychological and social side effects should come to the fore. Whether labeled as side effects or consequences, they are part of the cost, and sometimes the benefit, of taking medicine.

A dysthymic disorder causes Ron to feel cranky and impatient. His irritability and chronically cantankerous behavior reflect an underlying, if subtle, mood disorder, not a contentious upbringing. His successful treatment with Prozac helps him understand that for years his persona has been affected by an unrecognized illness. Medicine offers the opportunity to shed his disorder and see himself in a new light. Ron can relinquish the guilt hoisted upon him by a society that until recently has seen people as the sole masters of their destinies and had turned its back on the biological roots of psychiatric illness.

The fact that medicine's effectiveness confirms the importance of biology is a welcome relief. Perhaps we are all equal, but we are not all the same. The biological river against which our willpower has to paddle is different for each of us.

Ritalin's benefit is not only to diminish a child's activity level but also to implicitly confirm that the problem is biological. Ideally, a greater appreciation of the struggle others endure is the result. People are responsible for their behavior, but in acknowledging the importance of biological predisposition, we realize that others battle difficulties very different from our own. Psychiatric medicine prescribed for psychiatric disorders should confirm to society that our biological differences are real. The message is: "Don't take it personally. You're just wired differently."

The regrettable other side of this coin is that patients, convinced of the biological roots of their disorder, ignore its psychological roots and the role of personal responsibility. Instead of accepting the demanding responsibility of having an illness, one can blame the illness or the inability to find the effective medicine. An adolescent says, "I storm around the house because I'm bipolar." Instead of understanding the need to manage his impulsivity, a child says, "I pushed Jimmy because of my ADHD." The disorder becomes an outside force controlled only by medicine, not personal responsibility. Biology, proven by the expectation of effective medicine, becomes destiny.

Saving Psychology

Because we are aware of the multiple factors determining behavior, it is unusual for medicine to be the only intervention a psychiatrist wants to make. And because psychiatric difficulties are often the result of environmental and biological factors, sometimes a child psychiatrist recommends a change in the child's environment in addition to medicine—for example, a change in parenting style. When a medicine is dramatically effective, parents can feel less compelled to address their parenting.

Kenny is a hellion. His impulsivity constantly disrupts the house and gets him kicked out of summer camp. He is the perennial visitor to the principal's office for cursing. Kenny responds to Ritalin by becoming less impulsive and less hyperactive. This is a great relief to Kenny's parents. However, Kenny's father now feels less compelled to examine his parenting and continues to curse at and humiliate Kenny when he misbehaves.

Kenny did not experience a physical side effect like diarrhea. However, the consequence of taking medicine has been to allow his parents to avoid addressing their own behavior.

Elise is 7. Vyvanse controls her symptoms of ADHD, but she remains as defiant as the most rebellious teenager. Her parents want to know which medicine will help control Elise's disobedience.

Elise's psychiatrist resists the temptation to try another medicine and sees Elise and her parents in therapy. He notes that when Elise demands, her father threatens. Inevitably, he acquiesces. Elise's mother is no different. Both parents have drinking problems, and neither can tolerate the discomfort of Elise's inevitable tantrums. They have convinced themselves that indulging Elise is the best way of forming a quality relationship with her.

Elise's parents do not understand the purpose of being seen with their daughter. They can't understand why their doctor won't simply give them another medicine to help control Elise's disobedience. They do not see the relationship between their parenting and their daughter's defiance.

Medicine has solved some of Elise's symptoms. Its effectiveness, however, has given her parents hope that pharmacology is the answer to all Elise's problems and this becomes a rationale to deny the influence of their parenting on Elise.

Maria's parents are in the midst of a protracted and ugly divorce. At age 14, Maria is subjected to her parents' ongoing threats and accusations and is regularly coerced into playing her mother's confidant and her father's spy. Maria begins getting into trouble in school for talking back to her teachers. She is brought in for evaluation because the school thinks she is depressed. Maria's mother is on Wellbutrin for depression and thinks Maria should be too. She agrees that she and her husband should decrease the tension in the house, but she does not think this is likely. When the doctor recommends regular psychotherapy meetings for Maria, her mother leaves to find a doctor who will immediately prescribe Wellbutrin.

The possibility of intervention with medicine allows Maria's parents to ignore their need to properly manage their divorce. When medicine is even potentially effective in treating targeted symptoms, the need for other interventions, such as individual psychotherapy and family therapy, may be ignored. The child's difficulties are reduced to a biologically understood diagnosis, while a coexisting psychological understanding of the child is not considered.

Am I Damaged?

Our tools highlight our deficits. By definition, they bring attention to what we are unable to do without them. For the person with the broken leg, crutches symbolize disability. Although the person appreciates that they help her move across the room, the crutches are also a painful reminder of the person's inability to walk and her dependence on a tool to do what others do independently. Because crutches are usually a temporary solution to a temporary problem, they do not become a permanent part of identity.

Eyeglasses are more permanent and do become a part of how we are recognized. They are an ingrained and accepted part of our culture and solve a problem that is usually not integral to how we think of ourselves or how others think of us. Glasses solve the problem and become one minor aspect of our superficial presentation to the world. Some of us even use them to tell the world that we are funky or intellectual, flamboyant or understated.

The tools used to treat brain dysfunction, namely psychiatric medicine, are often seen differently. They treat disorders that are frequently not temporary and that are often seen as reflecting identity. For example, the child with separation anxiety who will not attend school is known for her anxiety. The oppositional child who adamantly refuses to obey is known for his defiance.

If psychiatric dysfunction is seen as emanating from the brain, the organ that runs neurological functioning, then medicine is seen as a reassuring tool. On the other hand, if psychiatric dysfunction is seen as a reflection of mind, the center of identity, then medicine is seen as reflecting personal inadequacies, and sense of self is more vulnerable. It is less threatening to have a sick neuron than a sick mind.

Difficulty moving one's left hand due to a problem on the right side of the brain would be seen as a neurological dysfunction. Similarly, trouble remembering might be due to a problem in a part of the brain called the hippocampus. In either case, a tool that would fix these neurological problems would be viewed favorably.

However, a depressed mood, despite also having a biological foundation, is viewed as a problem of mind and more reflective of identity. Although this view is slowly changing, the tools that help fix this type of problem, namely medicine, are still laden with implications.

Some children are exquisitely sensitive about how their problem and the tools used to treat it reflect who they are. Because they are being taken to the doctor for their behavior, they feel as if the prescribed medicine highlights a personal deficit, not a neurological diagnosis. They misbehave and therefore have to go to the doctor. They refuse to leave their mother and therefore have to go to the doctor. They do poorly in school and therefore have to go to the doctor. These children see medicine as bringing attention to their problem and an affront to their self-esteem. Medicine can be a daily reminder that they are damaged.

This is particularly true when a parent administers the medicine as a punishment or clearly associates the taking of medicine with the dysfunction. "Stop kicking your sister! Did you take your medicine this morning?" Parents who present medicine as a remedy for misbehavior risk causing a psychological side effect. The child might feel that the medicine is the enemy, the confirmation of his problem.

Even when parents present the medicine without such a bias, the medicine can be ongoing proof to the child that he or she is damaged. Children have difficulty separating their disorder from their identity. Although some symptoms, such as inattention, are more easily explained to a child as neurological, even these can be seen as insulting. Young adolescents can be particularly sensitive.

Marc is 15, and his schoolwork has always been average. He could do better, but focusing has consistently been a problem. His father was no different and did not feel comfortable with himself until he flourished at a job in sales after college.

After first battling his parents about taking medicine, Marc is started on Adderall to help him focus. His parents believe it helps. After 4 months, Marc realizes that his grades have improved, but he assumes this response to medicine means he is damaged and not really as smart as his peers. He struggles with whether to continue taking medicine.

Medicine for mood and behavior can cut more quickly to the desperate desire to leave the past behind.

Lana is 17. As a younger teenager she suffered with profound irritability and tantrums. Her fits of rage brought the police to her house on more than one occasion. She was eventually hospitalized, diagnosed with bipolar disorder, started on Depakote and Seroquel, and then transferred to a special school.

Over the next few years, Lana slowly but steadily improved. At 17, she has now returned to the regular public high school. She is getting along much better with her family and peers and doing her schoolwork diligently. She begins lobbying hard to get off her medicine. It is a harsh reminder of terrible times. She sees herself as beyond that now.

Finding Yourself

As a tool of change, medicine challenges parents to decide whose demands their child should meet. When is it better to conform to the demands of society, and when is it better to accept one's self as is?

Antoine is 13, a pleasant young man who never has much to say. He has good visual-spatial skills and can focus on visually based tasks. He also has a language disorder and tends to be unfocused in class. He attains mediocre grades. Antoine is diagnosed with ADHD, inattentive type. Antoine's parents and doctor decide to treat him with Adderall, which he only takes on schooldays. Antoine's grades climb a notch, but they don't skyrocket. Though he is never convinced taking medicine is a real benefit, Antoine complies with his mother's wish for him to stick with the Adderall. When he graduates from high school, Antoine goes off to college, where he decides to stop the medicine. He majors in video technology and does well.

On Adderall, Antoine is more focused and gets better grades. Though he appreciates his slightly improved grades, in school he still feels like a fish out of water. The medicine does not change his inherent discomfort in trying to succeed at a curriculum that stresses reading and writing. Antoine does not feel value in doing what he's good at until college.

Medicine has helped Antoine navigate an academic system that, with its great emphasis on language-based skills, points out his deficiencies. Medicine has become a tool to help carve him into an achieving student. This use of medicine can paradoxically convince a youngster that he is, at best, a weak student and, at worst, dumb. With so much emphasis on succeeding at what is difficult, these children sometimes feel like their strengths are ignored. Antoine might conclude that his parents see him as falling short.

If the school system had recognized Antoine's talents, he might then see medicine as a reasonable means to circumvent his weaknesses. He might learn to take pride in his success. The system within which medicine is used is crucial to determining its consequences for self-esteem.

I'm a Believer

Despite their initial fears and reluctance, many parents come to appreciate the positive effect of medicine. Some of these parents, originally dead set against medicine, become medicine zealots. They encourage their friends to consider medicine and become casual about its use. If other problems develop, they now immediately want to try a different medicine or combination of medicines, overlooking the lack of scientific research regarding efficacy and side effects. In these cases, the beneficial effects of medicine ironically cause the side effect of becoming cavalier.

This is a potentially dangerous side effect because of the relative lack of knowledge about many of the medicines, individually or in combination with one another. If the child experiences no significant side effects, some parents begin to resist coming in for follow-up appointments. The medicine seems easy enough to use; why not simply send prescriptions in the mail? Besides, life is busy, appointments are expensive, and the insurance company doesn't reimburse.

Jason is 8 and has been on Focalin for about 2 years. He has been doing well and so is only seen every few months. Jason's mom begins canceling appointments. Some scheduling conflict always arises. I am beginning to wonder if I would recognize Jason if I saw him in the supermarket.

One day, Jason's mother calls with a question. Jason has been having trouble getting to sleep. She's not sure why. How about trying some Catapres at bedtime? We briefly discuss the possible causes of insomnia and some suggestions about bedtime routines. She's tried them all. She repeats, how about some Catapres? I see Jason and his mom to discuss the possible side effects of Catapres, whether it would interact with Focalin, and the need to monitor his pulse and blood pressure. We decide to give it a try.

Over the next few months, getting Jason in for appointments again becomes a struggle. In June, I receive a frantic phone call from Jason's mother. Jason has been a little dizzy lately; could his medicines be causing this? "When did this begin?" I inquire. About 3 weeks ago, she answers. Why don't you bring him in this afternoon so I can take his blood pressure? He has baseball practice until 7 P.M. Are you still in the office then? I sigh.

If some parents become cavalier, some physicians also become very casual in their use of multiple medicines. Pushed by the need to help the patient who has not responded to more usual treatments or faced with the challenge of treating a complex patient with multiple disorders, some physicians will add on a variety of medicines. In fact, a few studies have found that about a third to a half of children taking psychiatric medicine were taking two or more psychiatric medicines (dosReis, Zito, Safer, Gardner, Puccia, & Owens, 2005; Duffy et al., 2005; Staller, Wade, & Baker, 2005). In general, there is minimal scientific data supporting this practice of polypharmacy in children. So although sometimes it must be done, it must always be done cautiously. One should never be cavalier.

The Holy Grail

Perhaps the most pernicious consequence of taking medicine is that it can prevent parents from learning to accept their child as he or she is. Medicine can be a great help to many children. However, some of the patients treated by child psychiatrists have malignant disorders that do not respond to medicine. These children have illnesses that doctors do not understand well and are helpless to control. Parents of these children are in the unenviable position of desperately wanting to find a medicine to help their ill child when such medicine is not available.

Some of these children would do better in the structured, supportive setting of a residential school. This is expensive and beyond the means of most parents; these children's parents must convince their school district or another government agency to foot the bill. Some of these children will do poorly even at a residential school. Medicine can seem like a hopeful alternative, but it is sometimes a false hope.

Perhaps their child will improve with time, but for now and for the foreseeable future, he or she suffers with a malignant disorder. Parents must accept that. The hope that there is a possibility of finding the right medicine from the right doctor prevents them from accepting their child's plight.

Mr. and Mrs. Potts do not know what to do with 16-year-old Troy. He has had innumerable psychiatric symptoms for many years. As a young child, he was inattentive and fidgety and was given Ritalin and Dexedrine. In middle school, he was depressed and phobic and treated with Lexapro and Zoloft. In high school, Troy has started sniffing glue and smoking marijuana. He has been possibly delusional and treated

149

with Risperdal and Zyprexa; he has arguably suffered with bipolar disorder and been treated with lithium and Depakote.

Troy is completely dysfunctional. He has been evaluated by numerous doctors who, after numerous trials of medicines, have recommended a number of special residential and day programs. Mr. and Mrs. Potts cling to the belief that the next consultant will be the one to find the correct medicine, and so they spend the bulk of Troy's childhood and their savings going from consultant to consultant, trying medicine after medicine.

Assessing Subtleties

Before starting a medicine, all side effects must be considered. We begin with the obvious side effects. Will my child be sedated? Will he develop a rash? Will the medicine affect her growth? Then the subtle side effects must be evaluated—the consequences that are less obvious but just as important. Will medicine affect my child's view of himself? Will he see himself as damaged or as freed from disability? Is my child's use of medicine allowing me to avoid dealing with my marital conflict? By treating my child, am I ignoring my own depression?

Though these questions are often difficult to answer, they must be considered. The obvious difficulty is that, whereas the risk of a headache can be estimated, it is difficult to gauge the more subtle psychological consequences of taking medicine.

CHAPTER 13

Concealed Consequences

||||||||||||||||||||||||||||||||||||||||||||||||||||||||||||||||||||

I am sitting at my computer desperately trying to complete this book. I've been struggling for weeks over how to wrap it up. I'm frustrated. I can't concentrate. I've lost sight of the goal. What was my main point? I can't remember. Instead, my mind wanders to Mr. Hunter, my junior-high-school English teacher. He's talking about topic sentences. What does Mr. Hunter have to do with psychiatric medicine? Why am I thinking about Mr. Hunter when I should be focused on finishing this book?

The phone rings and interferes with my waning attention span. I try to ignore it. That's why God invented answering machines. Technology to the rescue. In vain I try to organize my scattered thoughts.

A minute later, I find myself staring out the window. I'm stuck on a leaf as it whips back and forth in the wind. I wonder if it will hang on. It reminds me of an O. Henry story I read in Mr. Hunter's class. Or was it Mrs. Samberg's class? My mind has left my writing. At this rate, I'll be on Social Security before I finish this chapter.

I have a weird thought. What would happen if I took Ritalin? Would I promptly organize my thoughts and get back on track? That would be fantastic. My mind wanders further. How would I get some Ritalin? Ask a patient to lend me a few? Write myself a small prescription? What are the ethics? What would the pharmacist say? What would my wife say?

The seductive power of medicine has surreptitiously slid into my daydreams.

This is the understated but powerful consequence of increasingly available and effective medicine. It affects the individual and, collectively, the tenor of society. It screams, "I am here! Use me!"

All major inventions affect our view of the world. The wheel changed our ideas about time and space, making possible carts, then wagons, and then trains. The car changed the world further, making possible quick visits to Grandma and long trips cross-country.

Similarly, medicine influences how people manage their lives. For example, medicine has changed the way people evaluate risk and experience pain. Knowing antibiotics are available affects one's willingness to risk infection. After all, antibiotics are always available. Knowing pain medicine exists lowers our tolerance for any discomfort. Why suffer at all when Tylenol is always accessible?

In years to come, will psychiatric medicine also become commonplace? Will the decision to extend attention span be as trivial as the decision to take Tylenol? In 30 years, when I write my next book, will Ritalin be the savior in my daydream or just another staple in my medicine cabinet?

Medicine has become a part of life and often the obvious solution. The desperate parent no longer asks, "Doctor, can you help her?" Rather, the confident parent asks, "What medicine are you going to give her?" with the expectation that the problem will be solved. Medicine can be so ubiquitous, whether through the testimonials of friends, the recommendations of physicians, or the advertisements on television, that we often allow ourselves to slip past the fear about long-term side effects. Slowly, adversity is tolerated less. When people are faced with discomfort, medicine becomes the answer.

What is the consequence of being so confident that medicine will be helpful? As effective medicine becomes the available tool to control life, some part of personal responsibility and accomplishment is lost. Treatment is done to the patient, rather than coming from the patient. We expect that an answer will be provided and grow impatient with solutions that require sustained effort.

This is not to suggest that we should reduce psychiatric treatment to "Just snap out of it!" or an arduous long-term psychotherapy. Medicine is often highly effective and has its rightful place in the treatment plan of debilitating symptoms that all the effort in the world could not change. Many psychiatric disorders mandate the use of medicine. Nevertheless, with this benefit we must also acknowledge that medicine is a tool that changes our mindset about life.

Quick Is Convincing

Medicines that must be taken repeatedly and have an immediate and dramatic effect seem more essential than medicines that work gradually and less perceptibly. When patients associate the medicines with their immediate clinical effect, they risk falling prey to the belief that treatment is only about biology.

Larry is 12 and has mild ADHD—or maybe he's just relatively inattentive. In either case, his difficulty focusing interferes with his schoolwork. Larry takes Ritalin twice a day. He understands that 30 minutes after taking Ritalin, he is focused in class and remembers to write down his assignments. However, because Ritalin is effective, Larry ignores some of the advice his psychologist has given him. Similarly, his parents ignore the psychologist's advice to check his homework each night. Instead, they give Larry Ritalin and figure his homework will get done. When Larry forgets to write down his homework, his parents call the psychiatrist wondering if the dose needs adjusting, rather than trying to understand if they are following the psychologist's advice in the most effective way.

Ritalin helps Larry focus. In doing so, Ritalin is given the responsibility for managing Larry's behavior. Larry learns that medicine, rather than his psychologist's advice, helps him remember his homework.

Children who take stimulants are not addicted to stimulants, but some learn to rely on medicine, not themselves, to effect change. Whereas many children with ADHD could not do their homework without medicine, some with borderline ADHD ultimately benefit from the struggle to succeed without medicine. They learn to take frequent breaks and divide long assignments into many shorter ones, and they learn that certain fields of study are not for them.

This same principle is true of fast-acting antianxiety medicines like Xanax and Klonopin. Children whose anxiety disorder clearly responds to these medicines are sometimes loath to part with them, and they resist the need to learn to confront the anxiety-provoking stimulus. They are not too lazy to engage in self-help. Rather, they are correctly convinced that this medicine prevents their excruciating anxiety. The dramatic effectiveness of medicine is compelling. The slow progress of behavioral interventions, though empowering in the long run, is frustrating and easy to avoid.

Children need to learn that they can effect change and that they can handle the adversity dealt them. Medicine can be allowed to promote dependence, or it can be used to remedy uncontrollable symptoms so that the patient can then master what is within his or her control.

Arlene is 11 years old and suffers with the immobilizing anxiety of panic attacks. She responds to the Klonopin prescribed by Dr. Rein. After a few weeks, when Dr. Rein suggests stopping the Klonopin, Arlene begins feeling mildly anxious. She is unsure if she can manage this anxiety without the medicine. She looks at her mother with imploring eyes that say, "Don't do this to me. I can't make it without the Klonopin."

This story reflects a child's knowledge that medicine has helped. If Dr. Rein and Arlene's mother agree that Arlene is not ready to stop the medicine, then the medicine should be continued. If, however, they feel that Arlene can be gently pushed to learn that she can endure and cope with mild anxiety, they will help Arlene feel more competent by stopping the medicine. Finding this balance is a delicate art.

When to Make the Call

Medicine is a tool of change and, as such, a tool to control outcome. This is not bad. In fact, it is reassuring. Medicine can control debilitating symptoms and ameliorate dysfunction. It is an effective intervention.

Deciding when to intervene becomes the challenge. Knowing *how* to intervene in brain functioning forces us to decide *when* to intervene.

A parent asked me if I had a medicine for whining. Although she was kidding, this question offers an interesting example of the difficulties of weighing dysfunction against intervention. If the whining is not excessive, but the mother is depressed and unable to hear the whining without smacking her child, should the whining be stopped? Or is it simply reasonable for a parent to want to stop a child's whining because it will improve the atmosphere of the household?

On the other hand, what would be the consequences of a medicine that decreased whining? Physical side effects aside, what are the implications of making whining disappear with the pop of a pill? How smooth should a childhood be? How easy should parenting be? When do we learn from trying to manage adversity? Although these are unanswerable questions, they demand consideration.

Do we want to control sadness? Not temporarily obliterate it, as many try to do by getting drunk, but plainly and cleanly end it. If it were simple and without significant physical side effects, would we take a pill after our favorite team lost the World Series? Would we give our child medicine to help him or her deal with the college rejection letter? How controlled do we want our experience of life to be?

If at the beginning of this book we questioned when we should change our bodies with our rapidly advancing technology, we must now decide when not to. With the ubiquity of medicine, what should be left to chance? What are the consequences of excessive control?

Every parent seeks the sensitive balance between accepting his or her child and changing the child. Parents' obligation to teach their child is an obligation to change the child, to mold him or her into a functional adult. Change is the essence of pushing yourself when you're shy and resisting your video games when you're tempted. Change is the essence of finishing chores to completion and controlling explosive tantrums. Parents simultaneously accept their child while molding their child. It is the essential task of parenting. Medicine quickens the ability to mold the child, and because it does so, the process of change is lost. Children may grow up without the sense of effectiveness that comes with having managed adversity.

How Much Control?

Assessing what to control will be very difficult. Gutsy decisions will have to be made.

Pathology begs to be controlled. No adolescent should experience a depression that could result in suicide. But how about the demoralization and transient suicidal thoughts that result from being jilted by a boyfriend? A large number of teens experience these symptoms, and although they are painful, the overwhelming majority survive them. Most gain a perspective on life that helps them in the future. If a medicine could inoculate children against these suicidal thoughts, however, parents would surely have their child vaccinated. The uses of adversity might be sweet, but that doesn't mean we should go looking for trouble.

Lisi is an intelligent, pleasant young woman who was the target of teasing during her middle-school years. In seventh grade, she became despondent and had thoughts that the world would be better off without her. She never acted on these thoughts.

Now Lisi is 16 years old and doing well. She looks back at her middle-school years, recalling her suicidal thoughts with a new perspective. She realizes that in years past she would overreact. She still gets sad but knows it will pass. She appreciates that problems are not solved by suicide.

Had Lisi been inoculated against suicidal thoughts, she would have missed what became a life-altering realization. As we move away from the life-threatening and extremely painful, we come to the uncomfortable. However, perhaps what was once tolerably uncomfortable is now seen as truly painful. Advances in technology change our perspective. The more we can control, the more we expect to control.

If a child slips and falls on the ice, he or she learns to walk slowly and carefully on ice. What if a pill was available to convey the information? Take the pill, and you're inoculated. Without ever having fallen, you know not to run on ice. You diminish the risk of falling and hurting yourself, but you miss the opportunity to learn. When the process by which the child learns is changed, life lessons are lost. And the pleasure of success is forfeited.

I am still struggling to focus on my writing. Ritalin would probably help—success in the form of a pill. But my wife and pharmacist need not worry. I am not going to take Ritalin. I do not have a disorder. I am laboring but not dysfunctional. I am not going to relinquish life's surmountable struggles to medicine. Something would be lost. Instead, I will continue to type and delete and type and delete.

And what do I get for my efforts? A lot of trial and error. Paragraphs begun and often deleted. Spacing out and coffee breaks. In the short run, a heap of frustration. In the long run, I hope, a manuscript.

Suddenly, I get an idea, and I'm off and running, with any luck, in the right direction. I've smacked my knees on these hurdles many times before. Each time, I've ultimately met the challenge. Some solutions have been better than others. My mother was right: persistence will be rewarded.

In the end, I might not accomplish everything I want. I might finish this task battled and bruised. I might have to accept that my name will not go down in the hallowed halls of American literature or of American medicine. Ritalin would certainly not change that. What if it would? Never mind. I am going forward without medicine but with a certain satisfaction. I am adapting and learning, and I am going to finish this book.

CHAPTER 14

Medicine's Competition

||||||||||||||||||||||||||||||||||||||||||||||||||||||||||||||||||||

The Showroom

You need to buy a car. It's your first car, so you're an inexperienced buyer. You go to the showroom to see what's available. The new Cabraro looks cool. Sporty, powerful engine, bucket seats, but big price tag. Maybe the Chaufferator minivan. Plenty of seats for the carpool, room to lug all that garbage you've been accumulating, modest price tag. Maybe the Cheapita. Cute, a trillion miles per gallon, fits into any parking space, costs next to nothing. Or perhaps forget the car, and stick with the bus.

You take some brochures. Over the next few days you consider each car's benefits and drawbacks. You come to a decision and take the plunge.

It isn't enough to weigh the risks and benefits of any treatment. In a world that offers so many competing alternatives, and with so much at stake, a parent must weigh the risks and benefits of one treatment against the others. Psychiatric medicine is only one treatment. There are others. Psychoanalytic psychotherapy, family therapy, cognitive-behavioral therapy, supportive therapy, parent counseling, acupuncture, special diets, herbs, vitamins, vision training, tutors, residential schools, special classes—the list goes on and on. And then there's doing nothing at all.

Which of these will be considered obviously depends on the nature of the problem. It also depends on where you live and who is available to administer the therapy. The goal of this chapter is to highlight some of the general issues and to acknowledge that every choice, including the decision not to treat, has a cost and a benefit.

Buyer Beware

What are the chances any treatment will work? In comparing treatments, we look to scientific research to assess the probability of success. In the absence of research, parental instinct and professional guidance must suffice. Nevertheless, research should be the starting point of comparisons.

As we've seen, the scientific literature offers information about the various medicines. For example, the stimulants improve attention span and decrease activity levels. The SSRIs are effective in diminishing the obsessions and compulsions of those with OCD. Both of these have been proven in scientifically sound studies published in professional journals.

However, the scientific literature on the effects of some other categories of medicine is less comprehensive. Some of the existing research is well done but not yet replicated. A portion of our knowledge of the effects of psychiatric medicine in children is simply extrapolated from what is known about its effects on adults, a dangerous assumption.

Another problem is the information that doctors and patients don't see. Only since 2007 have drug companies been obligated to post their drug trials on an FDA website. Prior to that, they were not legally bound to share all their data with professional journals or the public. If a company funded two studies investigating the use of a medicine and the results of one study were positive and the results of the other study were negative, the company might have submitted only the positive study for publication in a professional journal. With the FDA's mandate for greater transparency, companies must share the negative results with the scientific community and the public on the website, although not necessarily in professional journals. Doctors, however, generally get their information from professional journals. How many check the website to see whether unpublished drug trials are positive or negative is unknown. As a result, doctors often want to read about positive results from more than one study done at more than one setting. This does not mean that negative results do not exist, but it improves the possibility that the medicine has been shown to be effective. That said, although the scientific literature is an important source of information, it does not necessarily contain all the information.

There is often even less scientifically validated information for psychotherapies. Some, such as cognitive-behavioral therapy, have been proven effective in certain disorders. And recently more research on these interventions is being done. The efficacy of some types of psychotherapy, however, can be difficult to study, much less prove. Intuitively they often make sense, and many patients will attest to having benefited. For example, individuals often report benefits from the insights gleaned from individual therapy. Standardizing that psychotherapy in order to prove it effective in treating a particular disorder, however, is more difficult to accomplish.

Vitamins, herbs, and other "natural" substances are not legally defined as medicines and are sold without prescription, often without having been proven effective by scientific studies. They may be touted by certain practitioners and appeal to a parent's desire for an organic, nonsynthetic solution to a child's problem. Their efficacy is often unproven to the satisfaction of the broad scientific community. Because these substances are sold over the counter, side effects are assumed to be negligible, which is another dangerous assumption. It is always worth remembering that caffeine and nicotine are "natural" substances with significant side effects. Any substance that can offer a benefit can also cause a side effect or potentially interact with other medicines being taken.

In short, parents must ask whether a treatment has been proven effective and, if so, to what standard. Sometimes the scientific evidence will support a combination of treatment approaches, such as medicine with a form of psychotherapy. Ultimately, most parents will need to trust their consultant, who should be experienced and able to objectively present sound evidence for the recommended treatment or at least acknowledge that his or her opinion is based on experience rather than objective data.

Parents will sometimes find themselves caught between experts, and then they must base their decision on the persuasiveness of one over the other. Or they might be convinced by a friend's glowing testimonial or alarming personal tale. When they do respond this way, parents should acknowledge that they are deciding without scientifically based data.

Names and Numbers

In evaluating treatments, parents can be unwittingly misled by a treatment's name or description. They can misunderstand what the treatment does and whether it will reliably accomplish that task. Maybe the Chaufferator, in fact, only has room for five passengers. Or maybe it has room for seven, but they all must be under 4'6" tall and weigh less than 65 pounds. Parents might assume that mood stabilizers stabilize mood. One mother called me requesting her child be started on a mood stabilizer because her moods were unstable. Sounds like a logical request, but it isn't. She didn't know that mood stabilizers are the class of medicines used to treat bipolar disorder. They stabilize the moods of patients with that disorder, not just anyone who takes them.

In addition, parents assume that the medicine's name conveys a certainty that it will be effective. If the child is depressed, give him an antidepressant to fix his depression. As we have seen, a medicine is given a certain label, but that does not mean the medicine will always work. Most effective treatments are only seen as effective because they are more effective than placebo. It might be a statistically significant difference when medicine helps 60% of the patients and placebo helps 35% of the patients. It might be enough of a difference to allow the FDA to approve the medicine for the treatment of that disorder. But it also means that 40% of the patients taking medicine did not improve.

The 60% figure can also be deceiving because it reflects the improvement of a chosen group, namely those patients who fit certain rigorous criteria to be admitted as subjects into a study of that drug. If you do not fit those criteria, the 60% rate of improvement might not be terribly relevant. In the real world, doctors treat patients with a wide variety of problems, not highly selected research subjects. This is not to fault the research, but it demonstrates the leap of faith we must sometimes make when extrapolating from research to the real world.

Money, Money, Money

How crass to raise the issue of money when considering the emotional health and treatment of a child! Nonetheless, when one compares treatment approaches, money can often be a highly significant factor.

The cost of many medicines is considerable. We have all walked away from the pharmacy counter bug-eyed and incredulous as we consider what we have just spent on the small bottle of magic pills. Generic brands and mail-order pharmacies have offered less expensive routes. Relative to psychotherapy, however, medicine generally is an inexpensive alternative. In the minds of the parents deciding what to do to help their child, psychotherapy can seem like a daunting expense. If medicine is not cheap, it is at least cheaper.

Although medicine and psychotherapy are not equivalent, a

parent can logically conclude that if minimizing the child's symptoms is the goal, why not go the less expensive route? The effectiveness of medicine can be a very persuasive argument for saving money on therapy. Why spend money to talk about a biologically based disorder? When my child's shoulder hurts, I don't send him to a psychotherapist to talk the pain away. Why should he need to talk just because his serotonin levels are a bit out of sync?

This logic can be very sound or seriously flawed. Some children have biologically based difficulties that respond quickly to medicine. They are otherwise happy and well-adjusted children. They and their parents need to be educated about their disorder the way an asthmatic needs to understand her lung disorder. Trying to control their symptoms by talking can be a use of money better spent on a family vacation.

On the other hand, some children have difficulties that require protracted psychotherapy, which can sometimes seem tedious and, yes, very expensive. It is often difficult to predict who will respond to this treatment, but it cannot be overlooked as one of the most powerful interventions a psychiatrist can make. Parents who search for the magical medicine that will quickly solve a problem that would be better treated by therapy do not understand the underlying problem. Parents who understand this but do not have the money to invest in psychotherapy are caught in the frustrating predicament of obtaining unaffordable treatment. Whereas expensive surgery is paid for by medical insurance, psychotherapy, which can be protracted in length and uncertain in outcome, is often not. For many, the expense mandates the choice of intervention.

Who Pays?

Money can also pit parents against their school district, ultimately bringing very sticky questions of financial responsibility into the decision of choosing a treatment.

Mrs. Ames is 39 years old. She is not a patient. She is a third-grade teacher who often feels as if she needs to be a patient. Mrs. Ames has been a successful teacher for the past 15 years. All the parents pray that their child will pull the lucky straw at the end of second grade and end up in Mrs. Ames's class for third grade. Mrs. Ames is such a natural talent that the principal regularly gives her more than her share of difficult children.

This year, Arthur, Gillian, Eric, and Roberto all pulled Mrs. Ames. In addition, they each have a 504 plan. A "504 plan" refers to the accommodations for people with disabilities mandated by Section 504 of the Rehabilitation Act of 1973. These four children were all issued preferential seating, which means they all sit in the front row, right in front of Mrs. Ames. How fortunate! Arthur, Gillian, and Eric were given a 504 plan because of their ADHD, for which they each take medicine. Roberto was given a 504 plan because he is hard of hearing.

Then there's Phil. Phil is disorganized and forgetful. He doesn't write down homework assignments and leaves his math book in his desk instead of taking it home. Phil's mother goes in to talk to the ever-patient Mrs. Ames. Can she sit Phil in the front row the way Phil's psychologist requested? Can she spend 5 minutes with Phil at the end of the day to make sure he has written down his assignments and remembered to put his math book in his backpack? In short, can she offer Phil accommodations, or should Mom go with Phil's psychologist to the school district to get Phil a 504 plan because of his ADHD?

Mrs. Ames is feeling guilty. She's doing her best, but she has no more front row seats available, and she's already spending 5 minutes each with Arthur, Gillian, and Eric. She has 20 other children in the room who also need their teacher at the end of the day. In years gone by, Mrs. Ames ended each day reading a few pages of Mark Twain to the class. The children loved the characters and got a feel for 19th-century America. Now her time is spent dealing with children's special needs. She's not sure what to tell Phil's mother, and she's frustrated that Phil's mother will not consider using Ritalin, which would help him focus and might solve some of these problems. In short, Mrs. Ames is spent.

Schools are mandated to provide an appropriate education to children. And parents rightfully expect them to do so. A school district is faced with the dilemma of how much money its residents are willing to pay in taxes and how to apportion the money collected. There are limited resources and competing interests. Increasingly, schools are being mandated to refrain from recommending medicine. Simultaneously, they are being mandated to provide more and more services. Are parents obligated to consider medicine? If so, are they obligated to do it to help get the school district off the hook, or should they do it to help their child manage when the school can offer no more?

In addressing these problems, schools have a vested and practical interest in the question of medicine. Their advice is usually intended to be in the child's best interest but can seem self-serving. One parent reported that school personnel repeatedly told her that if her child would take Ritalin, he would probably be able to move out of the self-contained classroom. This might have been true, and it might have been the best outcome for the child, but it struck the parent as a suggestion made by the school in the school's interest. If a child takes medicine, he or she is less likely to require as high a level of service from the teacher. This allows the teacher more time for other students, or it allows the school district to spend less money on extra support staff to help that child stay organized and on task.

This may seem callous. However, there are real-world implications that must be faced. How much money do we as a society want to spend on maximizing the educational experience of each child? If medicine can help the more dysfunctional, should it be encouraged?

Time, the Limited Resource

If money can be tight, time can be even tighter. You can win money in the lottery, but you can never expand time. Especially in an age of the overprogrammed child, treatments that take time are taking time away from other pursuits, like seeing friends and doing homework. These are not subtle costs. If a child is having social or emotional difficulty, often the last thing you want to do is take a bite out of time with friends. If he or she is already taking too long to do homework, taking up after-school hours with therapy better be worth it.

Obviously, if treatment is effective, the time is wisely spent. If not, the time spent cramming different treatments into an already overstuffed schedule can cause tension and discord that are incongruent with the parents' goals for their child.

Ray is 8 years old and has always seemed immature and anxious. As an infant he reached all his milestones on the late side. Now he is seen weekly in occupational therapy to help improve his fine-motor skills, weekly by a physical therapist to help develop his gross-motor skills, and twice a week by a language therapist to work on his word-finding and writing skills. In addition, he plays soccer after school on Thursdays. Although he is not the star of the team, his parents want him to be a part of the social scene.

Ray has also demonstrated all the signs and symptoms of ADHD. His parents have resisted the use of medicine. Ray's mother sees a story on the news about the use of biofeedback to help children with ADHD learn to focus. She makes an appointment at the biofeedback center that is featured on TV.

She learns that this is a time-consuming procedure—a few afternoons each week for maybe 6 months. She hasn't a clue when she'll fit this into Ray's already overbooked schedule. Each therapist makes a great case for the importance of what he or she is doing, but

Ray's mother feels like she's trying to fit nine slices of pizza onto an eight-slice pan.

When the school psychologist recommends psychotherapy, Ray's mother is overwhelmed by guilt.

"But when?" Ray's mother asks.

Somehow Ray's mother fits it in. Psychotherapy will be Tuesdays at 7 P.M. Ray finishes language therapy at 6:15. He and Mom can grab a slice of pizza to eat in the car as they hustle over to the therapist's office for psychotherapy. In the meantime, the housekeeper has dinner and plays with Ray's little sister until Ray and Mom get home at about 8:15.

Ray's father, who gets home from work at about 9 P.M., thinks this schedule is nuts. "When does he get to play?" he wants to know.

The time any therapy takes is a hidden cost. Some therapies, such as biofeedback, take a greater bite out of the weekly schedule. On the other hand, in terms of the human psyche, some interventions take a long time, and if you want their benefit, you have to invest the time. This can demand a patience not generally fostered in today's fast-paced world of instant gratification. In a world of medicines, such as Ritalin and Adderall, that work within a half hour, having the patience to wait 3 weeks for Strattera, much less 8 or 10 weeks for an SSRI to be effective, can seem like forever. If SSRIs seem slow moving, some psychotherapies can appear to be glacial in speed. Though ultimately powerful, psychotherapy with a young person can be as plodding as a turtle. This can seem like an expensive waste of precious time. When effective, however, psychotherapy can offer a life-altering relationship.

Chris's father dies when he is 12 years old. Shortly thereafter, he and his mother move to a new town. Chris is angry at home and begins to put off his schoolwork. He feels isolated in his new school. Though Chris's mother wonders if Chris should be on an antidepressant, Chris is seen in psychotherapy by a child psychiatrist. After some initial rockiness, he develops a warm relationship with the child psychiatrist, whom he continues to see for 2 years. He makes some friends and begins to understand his anger. Before going off to college, Chris drops in on his doctor one afternoon just to say "thanks."

Patience, Patience, Patience

In a world of instant gratification, patience can be as hard to come by as time and money. Some children's easily precipitated frustration can also strain a parent's patience.

Derek is 14 and loves his computer. He's no computer whiz, but he is an expert when it comes to spending time on Facebook with his friends for hours every night. During the school year this interferes with getting homework done. During the summer, he is on the computer until the early hours of the morning, conversing with people from Duluth to Dublin in a variety of chat rooms. His parents can only guess what other stimulating websites keep him occupied. They know he isn't getting much sleep—at least not at night.

Most days, Derek doesn't get out of bed until 2 P.M. At night he complains that he can't fall asleep, and it's back to the Internet.

Derek's mother calls Dr. Berman because Derek has requested Ambien, a sleep medicine. Dr. Berman suggests a host of interventions to help Derek regain control of his bedtime. For example, she recommends that Derek shut the computer down by 10 P.M. His mother knows this makes sense, but Derek has a fit. Why can't Dr. Berman simply give him some Ambien so that he can fall asleep on the nights he wants to get to sleep earlier?

Some treatments take time or money or both, but some also take patience, effort, and a willingness to endure frustration until the plan works. Derek's mother must decide if Derek can endure the demands of Dr. Berman's program and if she can endure Derek's tantrums. Treatment approaches can differ in the amount they demand from the patient and the patient's family.

When Doing Nothing Is Doing Something

Then there's doing nothing at all. In considering treatment options, one always considers the possibility of doing nothing, of not treating. Although this seems like a simple alternative, it can be laden with meaning. Parents who take a child with a problem to a child psychiatrist have often crossed a crucial threshold before they make the appointment. They have consulted their friends or the Internet and have already wrestled with the option of treatment. When they pick up the phone to make the appointment, they expect that something will be done. Although many patients welcome the doctor's opinion that the patient's complaint is not a problem that requires treatment, others are disappointed or angry and consider going elsewhere for the treatment they feel they need. Convincing these parents that nothing need be done is a challenge.

Doctors want to please the patient, to confirm that they feel the patient's pain and want to help. It is not easy to do nothing. The patient is in pain, and the doctor has a tool to alleviate the pain. Even when the doctor's judgment is that nothing should be done and that the pain will go away on its own, there is an inclination to do something to satisfy the patient. Especially in child psychiatry, with medicines that are often effective for disorders that don't exactly fit *DSM-IV* criteria, the doctor can have the grandiose dream that the medicine will lead to a wonderful outcome for which the parents will be forever thankful. If potential side effects are not too dangerous, then "Who knows? This medicine just might help" becomes all the encouragement needed to write the prescription. It takes great willpower to pass up the chance to make what appears to be a life-altering intervention.

Then there are parents who call for an appointment begrudgingly, having already decided that no problem exists. Perhaps they call at the teacher's incessant urging or to quiet the little voice from within that nags them to satisfy the pediatrician's concern. After the evaluation, they choose the alternative of not treating to avoid facing the problem. They convince themselves that the problem is just part of growing up and assume the child will outgrow it. Doing nothing becomes a confirmation that no problem exists.

What Is Your Goal?

For others, deciding not to treat can actually be a well-thought-out plan, agreed upon by doctor and patient, a result of considering the risks and benefits of the alternatives. Like any treatment, the decision not to treat has its own risks and benefits. Doing nothing arguably saves time and money, though untreated disorders can also cost both time and money. More indirectly, the option of not treating forces us to confront the goals of treatment and demands that we ask ourselves whether refraining from treatment will help us accomplish them.

What *is* the goal of treatment? Is it to minimize current pain? Is it to improve long-term outcome? Some treatments help in the short run but not in the long run, whereas other treatments might do both. Does not treating do either?

All medicines used in child psychiatry have an immediate effect in that they decrease symptoms in the here and now. Medicines improve focus, ease depression, lessen anxiety, and diminish agitation. If one chooses not to treat, one is obviously forgoing this benefit, and one has to decide if that matters. Neither all medicines nor other treatments necessarily affect prognosis. Therefore, in the long run, it is not known whether specific treatments have an advantage over the option of not treating.

The long-term effect of stimulants on the course of ADHD is unclear, for example. Certainly, they have an effect in the short term. They have been shown in a multitude of studies to improve attention span and diminish activity level. But do children who have taken stimulants function better as adults? Do stimulants affect prognosis? An 8-year follow-up of a National Institute of Mental Health study of children with ADHD suggests that they might not (Molina et al., 2009). In this study, adolescents who continued to take medicine as prescribed by their local physician (not by the researchers) generally did no better than those who did not.

Another question is whether the results are different for children with ADHD, predominantly inattentive type—children who are disorganized and inattentive but not hyperactive. One would think that stimulants would help these children do better in school. That should help their long-term outcome. But maybe they'd ultimately do as well in life without medicine. Perhaps, depending on lots of other variables, some would benefit from medicine, and some would benefit from being left alone to figure out how to organize their belongings and plan their schedules. Again, this is unknown.

Although it cannot be assumed that medicines help in the long run, neither can we be sure that psychiatric disorders left alone will simply go away. As we'll discuss in Chapter 17 in more detail, this is a dangerous and incorrect assumption, as proven by a mounting pile of evidence.

Depressed children are at greater risk for depression as adolescents and adults (Garber, Kriss, Koch, & Lindholm, 1988; Harrington, Fudge, Rutter, Pickles, & Hill, 1990). Anxious children often outgrow their anxiety, but a significant number of them will develop other anxiety disorders (Pine, Cohen, Gurley, Brook, & Ma, 1998).

Kay had been an irritable child, but at 13 she began feeling hopeless and worthless. Her parents declined the pediatrician's ongoing recommendation that Kay be evaluated by a psychiatrist. Now, at 19, Kay is a good student at a very competitive university. She tends to be withdrawn and unhappy and has a few friends who are also gloomy and morose. She does not see her many assets and has a chronically critical, pessimistic view of the world. She periodically considers whether life is worth the trouble. Her friends are worried, and on occasion they have found Kay drinking by herself. She is mildly depressed and at risk for more severe depression, with the associated dangers of suicidal thoughts and drug and alcohol problems.

In short, although there are no assurances that any treatment will affect the future, children with untreated psychiatric disorders are at risk for a host of difficulties, some life-threatening. Children do outgrow some problems, and most psychiatric disorders do not inevitably progress into adulthood. Parents, not knowing which course their child will take, try to predict the impact of treating their child. Some parents will get away with the prediction of "he'll probably outgrow it." However, research is confronting us with the fact that often he will not. The choice of not treating also has its risks.

Getting at the Root of the Problem

In choosing among the many available treatments, parents are guided by an understanding that reflects the science of the day. For centuries the cause of psychiatric illness had been reduced to nature or nurture. One had to choose between these two apparent rivals. Having it both ways was not an option. The dominant theory of the era determined most patients' treatment course. There was little choice. Life was simple.

When I was in training 30 years ago, my colleagues and I would joke that we knew the treatment before the patient walked in the door. Psychotherapy. Our joke reflected the final years of an era in which psychopathology was almost always seen as the result of psychological influences, and psychotherapy was therefore the core of any treatment.

This understanding would be tempered and ultimately expanded by the surge in knowledge about brain biology. Nonetheless, this thinking dominated the bulk of the 20th century and continues to influence many parents' choice of treatment. These parents see only the alleged psychological roots of a problem and overly rely on psychotherapy to solve the problem. They consider medicine to offer symptomatic relief and therefore bring their child to talk to the therapist in order to get at "what's really bothering him." It is as if the only way to remove the weed is to pull it up from the root, a view based on the assumption that the weed and root are indeed connected.

Psychotherapy has its place. It illuminates the origins of some people's troubles and helps others deal with the consequences of their disorder. But what if some psychological difficulties do not have their roots in life experience? Then nurture as the cause falls short, and psychotherapy, although possibly supportive, ceases to be the answer.

Some behaviors inherently reflect faulty neurochemistry, not early experience, and the goal of treatment becomes changing the brain's chemistry. This is accomplished by medicine—or, in the future, if studies prove their efficacy, by herbs or vitamins or some other biological intervention. Are you for nurture as the cause and psychotherapy as the cure, or for nature as the cause and medicine as the cure?

These simple dichotomies are proving to be the fallacy of yesteryear. What if psychotherapy changes the brain's chemistry? In other words, what if talking to the patient results in the same changes in brain chemistry as prescribing medicine? Then, regardless of cause, medicine and psychotherapy would be seen not as two different treatment approaches but rather as two different means to the same end. Perhaps the talking would be about one's early experiences, or perhaps it would emphasize learning techniques to avoid rages or reduce pessimism. The result would still be changed chemistry and a loss of symptoms for the patient.

Is this a credible possibility or an incredible fantasy? Research is beginning to show that traumatic life experience changes brain chemistry. For example, in a small but fascinating study of rats, Roth, Lubin, Funk, and Sweatt (2009) showed that rat pups who were handled roughly by their mothers in the first week of life expressed a gene that is responsible for making a protein used in brain development differently than rat pups who were handled tenderly by their mothers. In other words, experience influenced how genes were expressed and subsequent brain development. In short, nurture affected nature. In a still more interesting outcome of this study, when these rat pups became mothers themselves they mistreated their own offspring, and these offspring had the same changed gene as their mothers. In a final intriguing twist, according to researcher Michael Meaney, pharmacological intervention in rats can reverse the way this gene is expressed (Levin, 2009).

Research in humans is also demonstrating that the environment—for example, post-traumatic stress—can affect brain morphology and functioning. The extent to which these results apply to different events in the life of a developing child remains to be proven. Another question: What level of environmental stress affects brain function? And which brain functions does it affect, at what age, and toward what end? It is reasonable to conjecture that smaller life experiences might change brain chemistry, albeit in an unknown manner, in a vulnerable individual.

Drake, 7, is a pessimistic, anxious young man. His mother reports, however, that over the past 6 months Drake has been particularly irritable and gloomy. Drake's grandfather was treated for depression. Does Drake have depression too?

A careful history reveals that Drake's irritability coincides with his father's working long hours, often not getting home until 11 P.M. or midnight. On weekends, Drake's father sleeps late to catch up. Drake has barely seen his father for months. The psychiatrist suggests that Drake might improve—regardless of whether he has depression—when his father's workload eases over the upcoming weeks. In fact, he does.

Presumably, the absence of his father affects Drake's brain chemistry, resulting in greater irritability. A change in environment causes or is associated with a change in brain chemistry and results in a symptom. If that is so, Drake's parents would want to know when changing the environment can return his biology to its former state, thereby curing the symptom. If this could not be done, should Drake then take medicine?

This is not a proven cause-and-effect phenomenon but conjecture about the direction in which psychiatry seems headed. As parents struggle to choose a therapy approach, this is the model on the distant horizon, a model in which life experience and neurochemistry are connected. In this model, life experiences cause biological changes, perhaps more so in individuals who are somehow prone to these changes. These biological changes result in symptoms that are then reduced by helping the body return to its former biological state. Helping the body might come in the form of medicine or psychotherapy. For example, as discussed earlier, Baxter and colleagues (1992) demonstrated that the brain functioning of patients with OCD changed similarly whether they were treated with medicine or cognitive-behavioral therapy.

A study by Aylward and associates (2003) also showed changes in brain function caused by nonpharmacological treatment. Ten children with dyslexia and 11 children without dyslexia performed certain reading tasks during functional MRI scanning. This scan measures the brain's use of oxygen. Before receiving a 3-week reading treatment program, children with dyslexia showed low oxygen use in certain areas of the brain. After the reading treatment, these children had improved reading scores and increased use of oxygen so that their scans resembled those of the non-dyslexic children. Again, noninvasive learning leads to modification of the brain.

Before getting carried away, let's acknowledge that these are small studies of people with particular disorders and that there are probably myriad factors that influence this relationship between environmental changes and biology.

Then, let's extrapolate a bit. The child's prewired and developing brain is constantly affected by a multitude of life experiences vis-à-vis parents and peers, television and video games. Each experience affects the brain. Let's go one short step further to acknowledge that the child's moods and actions have an impact on those around him or her, and these in turn have an impact on the child. Life is a continuous interaction between the person and his or her environment. Experience affects brain chemistry, and brain chemistry affects the environment.

For the parent choosing a therapy for his or her child today, this is of minimal practical importance. It suggests that a child's experiences influence his brain but gives no practical assistance in choosing a therapy. The point is that we live in an age of changing landscapes, an age in which understanding the problems of human experience and the best means of solving those problems is changing.

The Choice Is Yours

To parents, choosing a treatment for their child's psychiatric difficulty must seem like flipping through an enticing catalogue in which everything looks potentially helpful. Confronted with an abundance of treatments and a shortage of long-term studies, parents struggle to find a trusted individual to assess the current and future impact of treating and not treating. So much is at stake with so little information.

Regardless of treatment choice, parents must be ever-mindful of their goal. Is treatment intended to solve today's problem or improve tomorrow's prognosis? Parents must remember that every treatment carries risks. Although side effects are most often associated with medicine, all treatments cost time and money and potentially affect the child's self-image and the family's functioning. Parents must weigh these costs against their goals for treatment.

CHAPTER 15

Oh, To Be a Parent!

|||||||||||||||||||||||||||||||||||||||||||||||||||||||||||||||||||

The Pressure of Parental Emotion

Assess the benefits; calculate the risks: Sounds so simple. So mechanical. If only deciding to medicate were that easy. There is an incalculable pressure that drives or halts the process. That pressure comes from parents and is deeply rooted within the complicated emotions that come with being a parent.

Rarely is this pressure the arm-twisting of hysterical parents. More often, it is the quiet pressure of the conscientious parents, anxiously scanning their child's future for life's pitfalls, wanting to intervene without causing harm. It is the push from the parents who want every possible advantage for their child, yet minimal risk. This pressure is usually influenced by the deep feelings that underlie parents' concerns for their child.

The vigilance of parents is sustained by hopes and dreams, worries and fears. With so much emotional investment and no crystal ball, assessing which hurdles of your child's life are truly insurmountable and which are simply challenging is vexing. Parents can rush to treat transient, situational sadness as depression or age-appropriate inattention as ADHD. They can overestimate a medicine's risks or its power to heal. Decisions can be based in reason but propelled by emotion.

Jack is 4 years old and does not speak. Well, that's not *exactly* true. He speaks at home. In fact, he's a regular motor-mouth at home. But at nursery school and other public places, he does not speak—at all. Not a grunt. Outside of the house, Jack is either clinging to his mother or, if without her, on constant alert, his eyes wide open and scanning for threats, his face expressionless, his mouth closed.

Jack is diagnosed with selective mutism. A course of behavioral therapy involving parents and teachers is minimally helpful. Eventually, at the age of 5, Jack's father's insistence trumps his mother's reluctance, and Jack is started on Prozac. He does remarkably better. He is less anxious and more at ease and begins to talk in school.

Over the next year, Jack's mother, a research scientist, continuously raises the possibility of discontinuing the medicine. Finally, Jack's mother can accept it no longer. She insists the medicine be stopped. "I don't care if he goes back to not talking. I can't tolerate having my child on a medicine for which there is so little long-term information."

One can certainly appreciate how Jack's mother feels. She is weighing the unknown risks against the benefits and arriving at a decision. Nevertheless, the anxiety that underlies her decision is unmistakable. Despite her acknowledgment of the importance of speech in the life of a 5-year-old, her decision is propelled by the fear of the possibility that the medicine will someday harm her son. There is no evidence for this fear, and as a scientist she realizes this. But there is only minimal evidence to contradict this fear.

Although parents fear unknown side effects, they also are in pain over their child's discomfort. This pain, rather than halting treatment, can propel the search for treatment. Parents who live with the hurt and frustration of their socially rejected child look for a solution. Medicine is not the obvious solution, but if the difficulty can be seen as a symptom of a disorder, certainly there must be a medicine with which to treat it. Again, the parent is acting rationally, albeit driven by emotion

It's 4 P.M. and I'm trying to finish my paperwork so that I can leave the office early. My son's soccer team has a tournament out of state and a few of his friends and their fathers are leaving tonight to drive to the tournament. The tournament is supposed to be fiercely competitive, but win or lose, going away with your child and a bunch of his friends is fun for everyone.

I'm stalled when the phone rings. Brett's mother calls in tears. She says it's almost an emergency. I know her from a few years earlier, but she reintroduces Brett to refresh my memory. Now 11 years old, Brett is obviously bright but often daydreams. He is doing only adequately in school. He "should" be doing better. In second grade, the school psychologist suggested that Brett might benefit from medicine to help treat ADHD. His parents consulted me, but resisted medication. Brett seemed happy, if a bit quirky. Did he have Asperger's? I'm growing impatient. Why the tears? Can't we talk about Brett's school performance when I return? How is this an emergency?

Now, in fifth grade, Brett enjoys talking to adults about the wars of ancient Rome. Unfortunately Brett's peers don't find Brett stimulating company. They find him weird. They are bored by the wars with Carthage. Feeling hurt and looking for any kind of attention, Brett forces goofy jokes that fall flat. All this further repels his peers.

Now the emergency. Through her tears, Brett's mother tells me that Brett is the butt of daily playground teasing and is becoming more and more dejected. After school, he comes home glum and not wanting to go to religious school where he is in class with those who torture him. His parents have lived with his peculiarities, but seeing their son as a lonely social reject is ripping their hearts out.

Brett's mother cries that she only wants Brett to have a friend or two. She remembers that I told her that sometimes children on ADHD medicine get along better with their peers. She wonders if it could help Brett's social difficulties.

I am anxious to get going. My son and his friends are waiting. This is not a psychiatric emergency. Then I consider the satisfaction I'm going to have watching my son and his friends. I think about Brett's mother wanting her son to have just one friend on the playground at recess. The disparity is glaring. We make an appointment to revisit medicine and its possibilities.

Reaching for the Gold

In contrast to parents who want to end their child's pain, many parents are motivated to seek treatment to quell other concerns about their child. Some want to help their child reach his or her potential. This goal, however, conceals the parents' fear that the child will fall short in life. Perhaps it masks the parents' need for the child to appear successful to others. Perhaps the parents worry that their child will endure the same difficulties they endured while growing up. Perhaps they fear that, without treatment, their child will feel "like a bad kid" because of his or her behavior problem. Parents are capable of a multitude of worries, and any one worry can serve as a motivation to medicate.

The need for one's child to reach his or her potential also reflects parents' desire for their child to have every advantage, to extend his or her reach, to pluck as much of life's fruit as the child desires. The possibilities offered by medicine expand the expectations of parents. If medicine can remove one of life's hurdles, how much more is possible? Parents feel an obligation to consider reasonable treatment courses, particularly if recommended by a trusted professional.

It would be unfair to say that many parents turn to medicine to enhance their child's abilities or to make a child what he or she is not. Most parents have the good sense to accept their child as he or she is and only want to vanquish a symptom of a disorder.

As medicine becomes an accepted part of life, however, it can be difficult to distinguish symptom from characteristic and to resist considering the possibilities medicine offers.

It is a wonderful thing to amble through life. Not much makes you crazy. You take adversity in stride. You observe life without the raging determination to tackle it. This is a wonderful trait, but it can make a parent nuts.

My son Jeff always showed evidence of being bright. He'd ask thoughtful questions. He'd construct imaginative projects. Learning to read and write was never an issue. Teachers liked him. Kids liked him. So what's the problem?

Jeff ambled. He didn't seem driven to do his schoolwork. Although he needed prodding to get started on his homework, he was always quick to reassure us that everything was under control, that his homework was always finished. We had no reason not to believe him. His grades were usually fine. How was it that his older sister and younger brother were up until all hours doing homework and Jeff was always ahead of the game, homework completed, TV remote in hand?

Well, maybe he wasn't quite as far ahead of the game as it seemed. In middle school, with its need for increased organization, he had a few missing assignments. Some remained missing in action, and others, done with a minimum of zest, were ultimately recovered from the depths of a book bag.

Raised in a culture that put a premium on education, Jeff knew that we, his parents, thought schoolwork was important. But whereas he hustled on the ball field, he rarely seemed terribly motivated in the classroom. He was simply happy and unperturbed.

A host of half-read books were always scattered around Jeff's room. Having lost interest in one, he was on to another. A talented catcher on his baseball team, this position was both a blessing and a curse. Catchers have a hard time losing focus. They're in the game on every pitch. On the other hand, they have a ton of equipment, every piece capable of being left at the field. To increase the chances that

Jeff would return from every practice with both shin guards, the chest protector, the mask, the catcher's glove, the regular glove, both cleats, the hat, and everything else, he and I wrote a supply list for him to check after each practice. Truth be told, I felt better, but I doubt Jeff ever actually used the list.

Jeff was happy and content, without caring much about organization or pursuits that did not catch his interest.

Actually, this story is not about Jeff. It is about me. It is about a parent worried about his child. I began to wonder if other children were more goal-directed than Jeff. I questioned why Jeff's life seemed more about procrastination than planning. He seemed smart enough, but in a community of achievers I feared he would see himself as unsuccessful.

Was Jeff your run-of-the-mill middle schooler? Or was he more unfocused than his peers? For all the children I treated with attention-deficit hyperactivity disorder, was I missing the diagnosis in my own child? Should he be tested? Should Jeff be on Ritalin? Was the shoemaker's son walking around barefoot?

I got my bearings. Jeff was fine. Perhaps he was not especially motivated to give schoolwork his utmost effort at that stage of life. Perhaps as a seventh grader, he was not as aware as his parents that college was right around the corner. Perhaps he needed a little more parental intervention at that age. On the other hand, Jeff was happy. His grades were certainly good enough. He was developing, not disordered.

As it turns out, I don't think I missed a thing. Jeff ended up doing very well at a very competitive university. He might not be as obsessive as I am, but he has found a pursuit that excites and motivates him. He reads big, fat, boring books to completion and is organized enough to care for himself in the most remote parts of the world.

If Jeff developed through that period, so did I. I learned something about parenting and about myself through this experience, and I gained an appreciation for the emotions that drive parents into the office of a child psychiatrist.

How well does a child have to perform for parents, who want

the best for their child, to be satisfied? "Up to their potential" is the typical answer. What is a child's potential? Does it exist in a pure, absolute form, uninfluenced by outside forces? If it can only be reached when the child is influenced by medicine, is it still the child's potential? If growth hormone influences height, what is a child's potential height? If supplements influence muscle mass, how massive is a child's potential musculature? If Ritalin improves attention span, how focused can a child become?

Though a parent weighs risk and benefit, his or her decision cannot be reduced to such objective criteria. Benefit is not measured in absolute units. It is strongly influenced by the parent's desire to settle for nothing less than full potential.

Meredith is 12 years old and has a history of debilitating depression. After a trial of psychotherapy, Meredith's parents reluctantly agree to a trial of Zoloft. At a low dose, Meredith does very well.

A year later, in the throes of middle school, Meredith is noted to be highly distractible. Although depression may have played a significant role in her inattention in the past, this is no longer the case. A careful evaluation reveals that in addition to depression, Meredith has subclinical ADHD, predominantly inattentive type. That is, she doesn't quite fit the rigorous criteria for this diagnosis, but she is far more distractible than her peers. Her parents and I decide against the use of a stimulant medicine to treat Meredith's inattention. She is doing well enough.

A few months later, I get an interesting call from Meredith's mother. Meredith is a nationally ranked gymnast. Not number one, but nothing to sneeze at. Meredith's mother has noticed that Meredith looks at all the girls warming up when she should be concentrating on her routine. She does well based on her athletic ability but loses points when her inattention causes a break in her routine. During practice her coach is constantly bringing her back to the lesson at hand. What would happen, her mother asks, if Meredith took Ritalin for gymnastics?

I tell her that Ritalin would probably improve Meredith's attention span, but I see where this is going, and I am getting uneasy.

Although I might think Meredith's gymnastics ranking is unimportant, her mother wants her child to have every advantage. She wants Meredith to be the best gymnast she can be. Why? Maybe for a college scholarship. Maybe to improve self-esteem. Conquering your inattention and climbing a few notches on the ladder would feel pretty good. Maybe it has to do with the mother's own issues, or maybe she just wants the best for her child and doesn't want to let even the slightest disability get in the way.

Medicine expands the horizon of change, offering the possibility of changing a disorder's symptoms, as well as a person's characteristics. The line can be very blurry. No parent wants his or her child to suffer with the symptoms and risks of a disorder. But parents also have hopes and dreams for their children and medicine can seem like a way to reach them.

Just as confronting the possibility of a rare side effect when considering the use of medicine takes courage, resisting the temptation to overstep one's bounds as a parent takes courage. Rarely are the answers simple or clear. It takes courage to consider the alternative. What would happen without using medicine?

Doran is in her junior year of high school in an upper-middle class, academically oriented community in which virtually everyone goes to college. Doran is a happy, pleasant, very busy young woman who volunteers in her church's youth group and heads the youth corps of the local nursery school for the underprivileged. Although this will all look splendid on her college application, Doran is a caring soul who truly believes in her work and would do it even without applications looming.

Doran has always needed to work harder than others to stay organized and manage her time. She can focus in class but is easily distracted while trying to do homework at night. Perhaps, with all she does, she's simply spent by the end of the day. Perhaps the lure of

Facebook is too much to overcome. Yet even when Facebook is off, she finds a hundred reasons not to get started on homework. She'll finally get started at 7 P.M., but the homework that most of her friends complete in 2 hours takes 6 for Doran. Doran usually goes to sleep at 1 or 2 A.M. She's up at 6:30 the next morning for school. She powernaps when she can to get through the day.

Doran tells her parents that she thinks Adderall would help her stay focused at night. Her parents have also been wondering about this. Her doctor thinks she probably has long-standing "borderline" ADHD, but he wonders about the role of her recent sleep deprivation. He also questions how much her community's emphasis on academics is just a poor fit for Doran. Doran is taking three AP classes and Honors English. She is intellectually capable of these classes, but the evening demands are too much.

Doran's parents struggle with what to do. They love their community and are not moving to another. They are not about to start a crusade to change the educational system. Doran refuses to transfer from the AP classes, preferring to be sleep deprived instead. Her parents want Doran to go to a college that she is intellectually capable of attending. In college, she'll have more latitude with her schedule and will be able to manage better.

Yet they worry that medication, even with its minimal side effects, would be tinkering with Doran's personality. They wonder if they should simply allow Doran to do adequately. Perhaps this will serve as a lesson for the rest of her life. But the question "what if?" looms large. Doran's parents don't ever want to have said, "We should have. . . ." They never want their error to negatively affect their daughter's life. They struggle with their decision.

How will Doran's life turn out with or without medication? I suspect that, given her native intellect, social charm, and happy disposition, Doran will not know the difference 20 years from now. But her parents want her to have every advantage in life. At a more competitive university, she'll associate with peers who are more academically driven and take classes that are more challenging.

To turn down medication, Doran's parents would need the courage to allow their child to fail, if not in absolute terms, then in relative terms. They would need the courage to risk allowing their child's life to flow without intervention. In an age of college ranking, they need the courage to ask themselves how much Doran's college choice will affect her future. They also need the courage to allow Doran to suffer, and hopefully grow from, the pains of her mistakes, such as overextending her schedule and taking too many challenging classes.

Many psychiatric symptoms are too costly, too painful, to endure in the hope that someday one will have benefited from having experienced them. But what a parent sees as a "symptom" may simply be a child's characteristic or the interaction of a characteristic with the demands of the environment. Sometimes this mismatch leads to the experience of failure. If they are unable to change the environmental demands, parents are in the unenviable position of deciding whether to seek treatment for their child or to simply offer parental guidance and the privilege of marinating in the consequences of one's decisions.

How is a parent to know? Which failure catapults the child to greater long-term success and which failure drags the child like a cement block into the abyss of further failure? An experienced clinician can offer the guidance offered by research. In the end, however, the burden of deciding rests on the shoulders of the parent.

A Parent's Struggle

The boat is in her hands, but Marilyn is torn by indecision. The first mate shouts, "Right! Away from the rocks!" The navigator screams, "Left! Away from the reef!" Rain pours down in buckets. The wind howls. She can't hear. She can barely think. Fog is everywhere. It is dark. The sea tosses her little boat. Is she heading into rocks or into a reef? Right or left? Left or right? The boat is at stake, but she can't decide which way to turn. She just can't decide.

Marilyn awakens with a start. She is in a sweat. She feels spent. She is at home, safe in bed. She lies there exhausted, looking up at the ceiling. That plaguing question strikes again. Does Brad really need to take medicine?

In the middle of the storm, the parent stands at the helm, having to decide if his or her child needs medicine. For some parents, the fear of medicine outweighs their need to control. For others, the potential benefits are too enticing. In either case the parent faces the formidable struggle of deciding.

CHAPTER 16

The Pressures on
the Prescriber

||||||||||||||||||||||||||||||||||||||||||||||||||||||||||||||||||

Lots of factors can send a baseball over the fence for a home run. The powerful swing of the bat certainly helps, but the speed of the pitched ball, where the ball hits the bat, the wind acting as help or hindrance, and even the humidity influence where the ball lands.

Similarly, many factors influence the writing of a prescription. It's not simply a parent's drive to assure his or her child's happiness or a doctor's need to help the patient. Subtle and not-so-subtle factors influence the prescription process.

The Marketing of Medicine

Ours is a society bathed in advertising. With direct-to-consumer advertising, the public is advised to "ask your doctor if Superdrug is right for you." These advertisements make medicine appear to solve almost any problem. More than once, children educated by ads have told me that they identified with the socially anxious person on TV and asked if they could have a trial of a particular SSRI. Or they were impressed that Strattera only needs to be taken once a day and asked me if they could give it a try for their ADHD.

Doctors are also flooded with advertisements for medicine. The professional journals that doctors read every month to keep up with medical research are awash in ads that sing the praises of medicine. They cover the pages of the numerous free periodicals physicians receive in the mail every week, extolling medicine's many benefits.

Drug company salespeople who frequent the doctor's waiting room sometimes bring useful information about their medicine. They also bring articles proving their medicine's efficacy. Other times they bring money-saving coupons or a variety of educational kits to be given to patients. In their most agreeably presented view, medicine is always a consideration.

The articles and original research reported in psychiatric journals are dominated by biological psychiatry. These articles and reports often focus on the biological roots of psychiatric illness or the actual efficacy of medicine. Especially in the many free monthly newspapers and magazines, articles review one physician's series of cases or one physician's learned opinion. This sharing of experience is terrific for generating ideas for future research and lets clinicians know what others are doing. But the effect of being constantly bombarded by these findings and opinions is that it makes the results seem more valid, more proven. Doctors are liable to lower their scientific guard and forget that a particular medicine has not been proven effective by rigorous testing. Positive effects of medicine, both proven and alleged, are ubiquitous. Therefore, medicine becomes standard care.

Nonpsychiatric MDs

Psychiatrists are not alone in perusing medical journals and newspapers covered in advertisements for medicine. Pediatricians, general practitioners, and neurologists are all immersed in the same culture. Psychiatrists come from a tradition, developed through most of the 20th century, of treating patients by listening. Only over recent decades have psychiatrists become more comfortable writing prescriptions. Other physicians come from a longer tradition of treating with medicine and are perhaps more prone to think pharmacologically. They also write prescriptions for psychiatric medicines. In fact, in one study of children enrolled in two Medicaid programs, approximately half to three-quarters of children receiving antidepressants were receiving them from nonpsychiatric physicians (Zito et al., 2002).

A few factors drive the high rate of nonpsychiatric MDs prescribing psychiatric medicine. First, nonpsychiatric MDs are often more available than child psychiatrists. Try to get an appointment with a child psychiatrist. It isn't easy. As the public has become more aware of child psychiatric problems, child psychiatrists have become very busy. Waiting a few months for an appointment with a child psychiatrist is very frustrating, especially when the referring doctor can write a prescription that the patient can start in the meantime.

Second, some medicines used by child psychiatrists are effective for symptoms as well as disorders. For example, as we've seen, stimulants are effective for ADHD, but they also improve the focus of those without ADHD. This gives the busy pediatrician leeway to prescribe a medicine that will probably help, even if the child is in the diagnostic gray zone. Other medicines, like the SSRIs and atypical antipsychotics, are used for many disorders, such as various anxiety and depressive disorders and agitation of different causes. This gives the prescriber some diagnostic wiggle room, allowing him or her to prescribe a medicine that has a good chance of helping regardless of what the patient's exact diagnosis is. A placebo response rate of around 30% or 40% also helps cover some diagnostic uncertainty.

Third, the relative safety of psychiatric medicines makes it easier for nonpsychiatric MDs to write prescriptions with less concern. Of course, when this safety is called into question, both physician and patient get understandably uncomfortable. For example, the controversy regarding antidepressants causing suicidal thoughts has given many physicians pause about whether they have the time to monitor this important, if unlikely, possibility.

Whether or not nonpsychiatric MDs should be writing these prescriptions is each physician's individual decision. However, like psychiatrists, nonpsychiatric physicians should make sure that they are prescribing with all due care. That means knowing the many factors, including psychological and educational, that affect the child. It means diligently assessing the use of medicine and its side effects on an ongoing basis.

The Insurance Nightmare

Another powerful gust of wind pushing the prescribing of psychiatric medicine into the bleachers is the patient's insurance coverage, or lack thereof. The goal of insurance companies is to turn a profit. Like all companies, they attempt to do so by minimizing costs. Psychiatric medicine seems like an ideal tool to accomplish this. Fostering a split between the psychological and biological understanding of psychiatric disorders, the insurance system encourages less expensive professionals, such as psychologists and social workers, to do the more time-intensive treatment of the psychological causes, and the more expensive professionals, namely psychiatrists, to do the seemingly quick and easy pharmacological treatment of the biological causes. Medicine is the preferred treatment when indicated after a thorough evaluation. However, it also often becomes the treatment of choice for virtually any psychological problem that might seem responsive to it after a cursory evaluation. This has numerous implications.

Patients see psychiatrists as busy prescription writers who do not necessarily get to know the intimate details of the patient's life. Instead, during the short visits allotted to them, patients may feel as if the doctor only has time for "any guilt, appetite changes, or suicidal thoughts? Stay at 20 milligrams, and I'll see you in 2 months." The ignored patient feels as if he or she is getting the bum's rush through the doctor's medicine mill. Although this can confirm to the patient that he or she has "only" a biological disorder, even patients with biological disorders have a need to be listened to by their physician.

For psychiatrists, this system redefines their job description. This fact was driven home to me in a phone conversation with an insurance-company claims processor who was questioning me about the treatment of one of my patients. I explained to him that I was monitoring the patient's medicine. He then asked me whom the patient was seeing for psychotherapy. When I reported that I was also seeing the patient for regularly scheduled psychotherapy, the perplexed claims processor responded, "But I thought you were a psychiatrist!"

In truth, psychiatrists have mixed feelings about being so closely associated with pharmacological treatment, feelings that reflect their historical search for a proper place among other physicians. Although psychiatrists often resent being pigeonholed as prescription writers who do not need to understand the patient psychologically, being identified with medicine also serves to bolster the psychiatrist's identity as physician, a coveted label.

Through the psychologically oriented mid-20th century, psychiatrists began blending in with other mental-health professionals, whose only contact with patients was through talking and listening. Psychiatrists were teased about forgetting how to use a stethoscope and were sometimes referred to as therapists instead of doctors. In discussions with fellow mental-health professionals, to the chagrin of the psychiatrist, patients were sometimes referred to as "clients." Now, with the advent of medicine and the power of writing the prescription, psychiatrists once again have a way to distinguish themselves as physicians.

The drive toward more pharmacological treatment also affects primary-care physicians. The profit-minded insurance system redefines them as the work-horse and dumps any possible responsibility on them. Prescription writing done by a pediatrician is even less expensive than that done by an infrequently seen psychiatrist. Of course, this puts more pressure on the pediatrician to master another medical problem and to carefully evaluate another patient. It also shunts the patient away from the appropriate professional.

I have been treating Jordan for ADHD for 4 years. Jordan is fairly typical of children with ADHD. He is occasionally disruptive in school, has difficulty with some aspects of learning, and at home requires constant minding by his mother. But Jordan's mom is on top of the situation. She works with the school to assure that Jordan's teacher uses effective teaching techniques. Although she admits her imperfections, she is always mindful of how she parents Jordan.

I see Jordan about every 3 months. Between appointments Jordan's mom occasionally calls with questions about parenting, worries about Jordan's mood, and expresses concerns about his social relationships.

One morning, I receive a call from Dr. Finch, the psychiatrist who reviews treatment plans for Jordan's insurance company. Dr. Finch is an adult psychiatrist who is not board-certified in child psychiatry. He wants to know why I am the physician prescribing Jordan's Ritalin. Why isn't this being done by Jordan's pediatrician?

After peeling myself off the ceiling, I explain to Dr. Finch that as a board-certified child psychiatrist I am more knowledgeable about ADHD and its treatment than the pediatrician. I remind Dr. Finch that ADHD is not a benign condition of childhood. Jordan should be treated by the physician most knowledgeable about his disorder—a child psychiatrist.

The insurance company for whom Dr. Finch works reduces the treatment of ADHD to prescribing medicine and puts the responsibility on the back of the already overworked pediatrician. Sometimes treatment is reduced to the doctor's secretary writing out prescriptions, which are quickly reviewed and signed by the busy doctor. A secretary writing a prescription is even less expensive than a pediatrician writing one. The meaning of each prescription is minimized, and more prescriptions are written.

The Collaboration Quagmire

Even without pressure from insurance companies, the undersupply of child psychiatrists makes split treatment a modern-day reality for many patients. Usually the psychiatrist monitors medicine, and the social worker or psychologist sees the patient in therapy.

In the best of all worlds, this collaboration between different treating professionals benefits the patient, as the treatment group can share ideas and differing points of view. This requires the psychiatrist and therapist to have a good working relationship. It means that each professional must understand and respect the perspective of the other, and this takes lots of time and lots of communication.

Minnie is 9 and has ADHD, for which she has been successfully treated with Concerta by Dr. Fenton. Dr. Fenton sees Minnie and her mother about every 6 months for roughly 20 minutes. During that time, Minnie is usually quiet. This is in contrast to the impulsivity she often displays at home.

Minnie's parents are in the midst of a messy divorce, and Minnie is in weekly treatment with Ms. Prada, a social worker. Ms. Prada is a supportive and compassionate woman with insight into Minnie's feelings and behavior.

Recently, Minnie has been more impulsive and angry. She's not finishing her homework. Although Ms. Prada continues to offer good parenting suggestions, Minnie's behavior is not improving. Ms. Prada recommends that Minnie's mother call Dr. Fenton.

After explaining to Dr. Fenton's secretary her reason for calling, Minnie's mother gets Dr. Fenton on the phone. She explains the reasons she's worried about Minnie. Dr. Fenton listens for a minute or two. He hears about the increase in impulsivity and that Minnie is no longer completing her homework and suggests that the dose of Concerta be increased. If that does not work, Minnie should come in for an appointment in about a month.

A month later, Minnie is not improved and comes in to see Dr. Fenton. During the half-hour appointment, Dr. Fenton hears that the higher dose of Concerta is ineffective. He ascertains that Minnie is not sleeping well these days and that she's been acting in a slightly sexually provocative manner. She has also taken to having meltdowns, sometimes crying herself to sleep. Given Minnie's grandmother's history of bipolar disorder, Dr. Fenton suggests that Minnie might have bipolar disorder, and he gives Minnie's mother a prescription for Depakote. Minnie's mother feels upset about the diagnosis of bipolar disorder, angry that Dr. Fenton made such a hefty diagnosis so quickly, and confused about what she's going to do.

Dr. Fenton knows that Minnie's parents are divorcing, but he has not assessed the impact this has had on Minnie. He does not know that Minnie's father has moved into his girlfriend's apartment and that Minnie sleeps there every other weekend with the girlfriend's ill-mannered children. He has not considered the effect on poor Minnie of being asked by her mother to spy on her father. He does not know his patient.

Ms. Prada and Dr. Fenton have no significant communication. Dr. Fenton sees himself solely as a psychopharmacologist. He is quick with his pen but hasn't left enough time to find out from the patient or her therapist what is going on. In this case, the collaboration is more like parallel play: Neither professional knows what the other has learned.

Parents also must appreciate the nuances of collaboration and the potential pitfalls. In doing so, they can prevent the entire system from collapsing into a poorly implemented, ineffective, and superficial treatment of a serious problem. Their understanding also promotes the responsible use of medicine as a plan to treat a disorder or symptom, instead of a gamble with high hopes and unrealistic expectations.

Ms. Molloy, a social worker, has been seeing Tracy, an 18-year-old recent high-school graduate, in psychotherapy for the past 3 months. Tracy will be leaving for college in 4 weeks and is not improving. Ms. Molloy feels medication is in order. After tirelessly calling a number of unavailable psychiatrists, she calls Dr. Shilling, an adolescent psychiatrist, who, her colleagues tell her, is very busy but very competent.

On the phone, Ms. Molloy tells Dr. Shilling that Tracy needs to be medicated for depression. Dr. Shilling is irritated that the treatment has been decided before he has even seen the patient, and he does not know if he has time to see Tracy. "Can't you just squeeze her in?" begs Ms. Molloy. "She only needs to be started on meds before she goes off to college." A reluctant Dr. Shilling consents.

Tracy's mother accompanies Tracy to her first appointment and thanks Dr. Shilling profusely for fitting her daughter into his schedule. She knows Tracy will benefit from medicine, just as she has. After talking with Tracy, Dr. Shilling agrees that she is mildly depressed and might benefit from medicine. Tracy seems like a reliable young woman, but her weekend drinking troubles Dr. Shilling. Tracy's tumultuous relationship with her boyfriend also gnaws at him. Does Tracy have depression, or is she going through the angst of leaving for college? Nevertheless, he starts an antidepressant. He then sees Tracy 3 weeks later, 2 days before she leaves for college 6 hours away. No improvement is noted.

Tracy is supposed to see Dr. Shilling when she comes home for a weekend in October, but it's Homecoming and she decides to stay at school. She next sees Dr. Shilling over Thanksgiving break, this time not accompanied by her mother. Tracy thinks that maybe she's feeling a little better. She's not sure. College is stressful. She's broken up with her high-school boyfriend, but it's tough to keep up with schoolwork while partying every weekend, starting on Thursday. Dr. Shilling groans. Tracy tells Dr. Shilling that her parents wanted her to stop therapy with Ms. Molloy when she left for college, so the therapist is out of the picture.

Dr. Shilling is frustrated. He has put himself in the position of treating a young woman with whom he does not have and cannot develop a suitable doctor-patient relationship. He is reduced to monitoring her medicine on a "catch as catch can" basis and has lost his only outside source of information, Ms. Molloy. Ms. Molloy is frustrated because she has lost complete contact with her depressed patient. Tracy's parents are frustrated because Tracy is not improving on medicine. She doesn't seem depressed, but she's still irresponsible. What's this medicine supposed to be doing anyway?

Tracy's treatment has certainly been complicated by timing. Beginning a treatment that requires monitoring when you're on your way to college is difficult at best. Collaborations take time to develop. Tracy's parents also had no clear understanding of the goal of treatment and no appreciation of the need for an ongoing team effort to help Tracy, while respecting her need for independence and confidentiality.

A good collaboration is a challenge for all concerned. Hurdles of time and money stand in the way, as does the need for each professional to establish his or her own working relationship with the patient. Although psychiatrists want to treat people in an effective and financially efficient manner, they do not want to be reduced to being the hand that writes the scrip. For the therapist, finding an available psychiatrist whom you trust, to whom you can adequately communicate your assessment, and from whom you can possibly get medicine for your patient is not easy. Parents want problems solved so their child can develop happily and healthily.

Despite these difficulties, when the collaboration works, it can work very well.

Cheryl is 15 years old and has had a long and complex psychiatric history. She has been plagued by depression and was sexually abused by a camp counselor as a young girl. Cheryl has often strongly resisted therapy but eventually consents to seeing Dr. Sloan, a child psychologist who also sees one of Cheryl's friends.

Dr. Sloan is able to connect with Cheryl, and after about a year, she thinks Cheryl would benefit from psychiatric medicine. Cheryl's depression is out of control, and all the adults suspect she is more than a little involved in abusing drugs. Cheryl's parents bring her to Dr. Ames, a child psychiatrist recommended by their pediatrician. Dr. Ames evaluates Cheryl and agrees that medicine is indicated. He feels, however, that he should have fairly regular meetings with Cheryl so that he can keep a close eye on her drug use and monitor the effect of the medicine. He appreciates Cheryl's working relationship with Dr. Sloan, whom he knows, and he feels that this therapy should also continue.

Everyone, including Cheryl, agree that weekly meetings with Dr. Sloan will continue and that every few weeks Cheryl will check in with Dr. Ames. Although this is a time-consuming and financially burdensome endeavor, all feel it is the best treatment approach.

After about 6 months, Cheryl's parents become involved in a contentious divorce. Nevertheless, each is able to maintain some civility around Cheryl's psychiatric treatment. At one point, when Cheryl's sexual acting out leads to consideration of a therapeutic boarding school, her mother thinks that family meetings, with both Drs. Ames and Sloan present, would be beneficial. These meetings allow for efficient communication and minimize Cheryl's opportunities to misinterpret what others have said in an attempt to divide and conquer her parents.

In this example, Dr. Ames is able to provide a medication consult and still maintain an appropriate doctor-patient relationship with Cheryl and her parents. He is aware of the nuances of their family's dynamics, has an ongoing working relationship with Cheryl, and frequently communicates with Dr. Sloan. Both Drs. Ames and Sloan have invested great effort in trying to help Cheryl. Though they are not wealthy, Cheryl's parents are able to and insist upon paying both doctors for their time spent. This is respectful. This is equitable. This is also highly unusual.

Cheryl's treatment is being carefully planned. It is unlikely that medicine will be abruptly tossed into the mix without careful consideration. A system with sufficient resources minimizes the risk of prescriptions being hastily and inappropriately written.

Rating-Scale Simplicity

Since the advent of *DSM-III*, psychiatry has defined disorders with lists of empirically tested, observable signs and symptoms. Although this has been a major advance in standardizing diagnoses, society has grabbed onto these lists of symptoms as being the whole truth and nothing but the truth. Diagnosis is reduced to a simple task that one can do on one's own with the help of the proper checklist. The proper number of check marks leads to the expectation of treatment with medicine. Sometimes parents read the checklists of the *DSM* without paying attention to the criterion that the symptoms cause clinically significant dysfunction. Other times, parents quickly put stock in a list of symptoms before it is accepted by the scientific community.

Mr. and Mrs. Brooks are looking for answers. Their 12-year-old daughter, Bonnie, is a handful. She is moody and often irritable. In the most recent issue of their weekly news magazine, there is a story about bipolar disorder in children. The article lists symptoms compiled by a physician, Dr. Marowitz, who has written a book on the subject. If you check off a certain number of characteristics on the list, the article advises you to consult your physician.

Bonnie's parents take out their pen and start checking. Talks too fast? Check. Trouble sleeping? Check. Poor handwriting? Check. Bedwetting? Check. By the time they have finished checking, they feel relieved that they have a diagnosis. They are ready to start Bonnie on lithium, a medicine used to treat patients with bipolar disorder.

Much is wrong with this picture. Though Dr. Marowitz is a respected physician and entitled to his opinions, the diagnosis of bipolar disorder in children is the focus of a lively debate, and many child psychiatrists do not accept Dr. Marowitz's checklist as a valid tool by which to make this diagnosis. They see the diagnostic criteria for bipolar disorder in children to be evolving but still very uncertain. Dr. Marowitz's list is inclusive of many types of troubled children.

Though they are perceptive parents, Mr. and Mrs. Brooks are not sure of the clinically relevant threshold of some of the symptoms. Like most desperate parents, they ignore the fine print suggesting they consult their physician and use the list to do their own diagnosing.

In the age of information, everybody's an expert. A mass of information is readily available to a public hungry for answers. A well-read public becomes highly vigilant, but the public is in danger of believing everything they read without a critical eye.

As long as people understand diagnosis as simply checking off lists of symptoms, they will try to do it themselves. Every medical student learns, however, to treat the patient, not the lab result. The depth of this admonition is often missing in the cursory evaluation by parents who feel compelled to treat the child based on the results of only a checklist. Ultimately this leads to unreasonable expectations and overprescription of medicines.

Should the Prescription Be Written?

The number of prescriptions for psychiatric medicines has certainly risen dramatically, the result of numerous factors. But the underlying question that fuels the debate about the overprescription or underprescription of psychiatric medicines is whether a particular prescription should be written at all.

CHAPTER 17

Too Many Prescriptions?

|||||||||||||||||||||||||||||||||||||||||||||||||||||||||||||

What is the emotion that bubbles up in you when you discover that your neighbor's child is taking a psychiatric medicine? Do you feel sorry for the poor child? He was always a bit peculiar. Are you wondering which crazy child psychiatrist diagnosed a psychiatric disorder in a child who seems so normal? Are you feeling a bit paranoid, maybe a bit competitive? "Martha loves Josh to have the edge. She's always been controlling, but I never thought she'd go this far."

Because people's views on the subject are fueled by strong emotion, psychiatric medicine always seems overprescribed, never underprescribed. Headlines describing the "soaring increase in prescriptions" certainly imply that prescribing is out of control. But is it?

Let's bring some reason to this cauldron of emotion. When do "many" become "too many"?

It's Sunday morning, and Mr. and Mrs. Peterson prepare for the weekend routine. Mr. Peterson, his cup of steaming coffee in hand, sits down with his bagel and newspaper. Mrs. Peterson has her tea and a book. Mr. Peterson unfolds the paper to the headline "Psych Meds

Skyrocket in Kids." He sips his coffee and shakes his head in disbelief. "Honey, will you look at this headline? They're saying that more and more kids are being given psychiatric medicine. This is crazy! What's the world coming to?" Mrs. Peterson shakes her head in agreement. "You're right, dear, these medicines are prescribed much too much. Those prescriptions shouldn't be written."

Let's join Mr. and Mrs. Peterson in the family room and ask them about their disbelief.

"Good morning, Mr. and Mrs. Peterson. May we pull up a few chairs and join you? We're a group of parents trying to understand people's fears about psychiatric medicine. You were pretty upset by that headline."

"You bet. When our kids were growing up, and they're now 40 and 43, no kids were taking this kind of medicine. It's nuts, I'm telling you."

"I'm actually a child psychiatrist and prescribe a lot of this medicine to children."

"Oh, my!" says Mrs. Peterson. "We didn't mean to insult you."

"No offense taken, Mrs. Peterson. Would it be okay if you told me what leads you to believe that medicine is overprescribed? I suspect there are a lot of fallacies around."

Mrs. Peterson jumps right in. "Well, first off, these medicines are dangerous. They cause cancer and seizures, and kids get addicted to them."

"Mrs. Peterson, that just isn't so. They definitely cause side effects, but these are almost always manageable. More information is certainly needed about treating children for many years with medicine. In the short run, though, most of the medicines we prescribe do not cause irreversible or dangerous side effects. And children do not get addicted to psychiatric medicines. Far more often, parents have to convince their children to take the medicine. That's not addiction. Some teenagers do abuse some psychiatric medicines. They also abuse rubber cement and over-the-counter cough medicine."

Now Mr. Peterson chimes in. "They're overprescribed by parents who are trying to give their kids an edge over other kids. Our daughter told us about a mother who got her daughter Ritalin just in time for the SATs. That's just not fair."

"Mr. Peterson, you're probably right that some parents try to use certain types of psychiatric medicine to give their child the advantage. But I practice in a fairly affluent, competitive community, and I rarely see that. I often see parents use medicine to help their child reach his or her potential but rarely to gain an unfair advantage."

Mrs. Peterson has been looking thoughtful and finally says, "Excuse me, Dr. Kalikow. I've been thinking about what you said. I guess I'm not really concerned about children getting addicted. But people are just too reliant on medicine. People aren't solving their own problems anymore. They run to medicine. And the drug manufacturers are only too happy to encourage them."

"Mrs. Peterson, drug companies must be thrilled about their sales, and they market to beat the band. But if people have psychiatric disorders that were not previously understood or recognized, shouldn't they take medicine? You'd be very happy if someone with a liver disorder could suddenly cure it by taking medicine. You wouldn't expect them to solve their problem themselves."

Mr. Peterson jumps to his wife's defense. "Doc, I'm willing to grant you that science marches forward and that, as we understand more about the brain, we'll define some difficulties as disorders that we'll treat with medicine. But the brain is not the liver. There's an element of willpower in what the brain does and, as far as I know, no willpower for the liver." Mr. Peterson is on a roll. "Do you let people try to work out their symptoms before you prescribe medicine? If you're too quick on the draw, well, that's not doing them a favor. People need to use their willpower to solve some of these so-called symptoms."

"I have to agree with you, Mr. Peterson. Some people will always use medicine to diminish their symptoms. Maybe you're right that people run to medicine too quickly, but it's hard to decide who should take medicine. The brain is not the liver, but it too has plenty of symptoms that can't be solved by willpower. Some symptoms cause a lot of distress and can't simply be willed away."

"Well, young man, you make some good points. But now, if you'll excuse us, my wife and I will be taking our morning walk. You're invited to come along. Otherwise, it's been nice talking to you."

"We'll be leaving, Mr. Peterson. Thanks for taking the time to talk."

Mr. Peterson puts on his jacket and before walking out the door, takes a pill from a small bottle.

"Mr. Peterson, if you don't mind me asking, what kind of medicine are you taking?" I ask.

"It's just a little anti-inflammatory something or other I got at the supermarket. I take it before our walk. The exercise is good for my heart, but I need the medicine to help me keep the old hip quiet. The doctor says I could use some physical therapy—you know, stretching and the like. But to tell you the truth, this is much easier."

"Oh, you mean some quick pharmacological relief to help you through the day?"

Mr. Peterson smiles.

There is no question that the number of psychiatric medicine prescriptions for children has skyrocketed. Studies have documented that from the late 1980s into the late 1990s the number of prescriptions written for stimulants and antidepressants more than tripled (Olfson, Marcus, Weissman, & Jensen, 2002; Zito et al., 2002). This kind of statistic makes for dramatic headlines. But are the numbers too high? Are these medicines overprescribed? By what criteria do we decide who *should* take medicine? Let's look at a few possible answers to this question and then use the numbers we know to see if medicines are over- or underprescribed.

Treating Disorders

Perhaps only people with a disorder—and all people with that disorder—should be given medicine. Then one could survey a city, discover the number of people with different disorders for which medicine is available, and, presto, know the number of people who should receive medicine. Life, however, is not that simple.

There are a few problems with that approach. The first is that ascertaining the prevalence of a given diagnosis is difficult. For example, the prevalence of ADHD in the United States used to be given as between 3% and 5%. The studies establishing this range focused on children who were impulsive, hyperactive, and inattentive—what is currently known as ADHD, combined type. As the criteria changed over the years and those for ADHD, predominantly inattentive type, were better defined, an entire new group was diagnosed with ADHD, and the total prevalence was sometimes seen as being about 8%. The change in criteria essentially doubled the prevalence.

For other disorders, such as bipolar disorder in children, the criteria for diagnosis have been hotly debated and are only beginning to be agreed upon. Establishing the prevalence is therefore currently difficult, as is the ability to use diagnosis to determine whether the medicines that treat that disorder should have been prescribed.

Another Problem with Disorders

The second and more important difficulty with using a diagnosed disorder as a prerequisite for taking medicine is that it supposes that everyone with a disorder for which there is medicine should take medicine. This assumption needs to be proven, and we ought to have evidence that medicine is the most effective treatment for those with the disorder.

What about that word "effective"? To be considered effective, how many and which symptoms have to improve and to what degree? Does "effective" imply that medicine is helpful in the short run, or does the person have to show improvement 20 years later?

Prospective studies that follow children whose disorders have been treated with different types of therapy are only beginning to show that sometimes medicine provides the most effective treatment over a protracted period of time, and then perhaps only for some symptoms. Meanwhile, other evidence shows that nonpharmacological treatments are equally effective in the short run for some disorders. These mixed results imply that the medicine *could* be given, not that it *should* be given.

In order to make the latter case, we need to prove that of all the treatments available, including no treatment at all, medicine is the most effective, relative to its side effects, over many years. That very demanding level of evidence is simply not available in child psychiatry.

Probably the closest that research has come to attaining this level is the Multimodal Treatment Study of Children with Attention-Deficit/Hyperactivity Disorder, also known as the MTA study (MTA Cooperative Group, 1999). Begun in the late 1990s, it has provided an ongoing prospective follow-up of children with ADHD. Because the data from other studies so clearly established the effectiveness of medicine in the short run, this study did not initially include an untreated control group to prove the medicine's short-term efficacy. For the purposes of comparing long-term outcome, however, a comparison group was eventually added.

In this elaborate, groundbreaking study involving six research sites, 579 children, all of whom met strict criteria for ADHD, combined type, were divided into four treatment groups. The first group was treated with intensive behavioral therapy and stimulant medicine prescribed by physicians on the research team. These children were followed very closely with regular monthly visits. The second group received stimulant medicine prescribed by doctors on the research team in the same closely supervised manner as group one, but no behavioral treatment. The third group received very intense behavioral therapy, but no medicine. And the fourth group was cared for by local community mental-health professionals.

Of note, the behavior therapy used by groups one and three was well beyond the intensity of treatment typically received by the overwhelming majority of children with ADHD. It included parent training in both individual and group sessions and ongoing consultation for the children's teachers by a behavioral specialist. Each child also worked for 12 weeks with a part-time, behaviorally trained aide in the classroom. In addition, the children attended an 8-week, 45-hour-per-week summer program specializing in the treatment of ADHD, including behavior-modification treatment and social-skills training. In short, the behavioral treatment was as multilayered and as close to full time as possible.

Also of note, it turns out that the patients in group four, treated by community physicians, were seen by the physicians much less frequently than the patients in groups one and two. Although about two-thirds were prescribed stimulants, the doses were less frequent and much lower, sometimes even ineffective.

At the first examination point of this study, after 14 months of treatment, the researchers found that well-supervised treatment with medicine was clearly superior to both behavior therapy and to medicine treatment infrequently supervised by a local physician. All four groups had a percentage of children who improved over 14 months; however, groups one and two clearly had the larger subgroups of improved children. Though in some respects group one did better than group two, overall these two groups did far better than the other two groups. Ongoing follow-up of these different groups has also been done, although after the first 14 months, everyone was free to choose whatever treatment they wanted. Thus, the study became a follow-up study of a large group of children with ADHD, with the original groups no longer receiving specifically different treatment from one another. Information about long-term prognosis of the different treatment groups will, therefore, be limited.

The point is that for children who have ADHD, combined type, that is well defined enough and severe enough to land them in a research study, medicine given in a well-supervised manner is an integral part of treatment in the short term. The MTA's results are corroborated by another study that has followed children for 2 years (Abikoff et al., 2004).

Unfortunately the MTA's 8-year follow-up is less optimistic (Molina et al., 2009). It shows that those who had been treated with medicine for 14 months no longer maintained the benefits 8 years later. Initial prognosis was not predicted by whether the child had taken medicine. Rather it was better estimated by characteristics, such as the child's intellect, the severity of the child's ADHD symptoms, and whether the child had conduct problems. Perhaps this lack of long-term effect reflects the need for medicine to be taken on an ongoing basis. However, those who did continue to take a stimulant medicine, at a higher dose but not as prescribed by the research team, generally did not seem to be doing better than their peers who were not taking medicine. Other studies have looked at the long-term functioning of patients with ADHD, but these patients did not receive standardized treatment. These studies have shown some long-term benefits to stimulants, but other long-term outcomes remained unchanged (Hechtman, Weiss, & Perlman, 1984). Thus, although the efficacy of medicine is well proven in the short run, its long-term efficacy is debatable. This does not prove that those with ADHD should take medicine in the long run.

Who Takes Stimulants?

Despite the lack of consistent proof for the long-term efficacy of medicine, we could posit that those who are diagnosed with ADHD, combined type, using strict criteria, *should* get medicine in the short run. If we say that everyone with a particular disorder should receive medicine and we accept the most commonly cited prevalence of ADHD as about 8% of children, then about 8% percent of children should be on medicine for ADHD. Is this so?

During the first half of 1992, Jensen and colleagues (1999) surveyed 1,285 children from 9 to 17 years old living in four different communities: Atlanta, Georgia; suburban New York City; New Haven, Connecticut; and San Juan, Puerto Rico. They discovered that though approximately 5% of children were diagnosed with ADHD, only about 12% of the children with this diagnosis were prescribed a stimulant medicine. In other words, if having the disorder of ADHD implies that one should be medicated with a stimulant, then stimulants were woefully underprescribed—88% of children with ADHD were not being medicated. The researchers also found that half of the children treated with a stimulant medicine did not meet research criteria for having ADHD. These children had many symptoms of ADHD, but they did not meet the full criteria for the disorder. If having the disorder, as strictly defined by the criteria of *DSM-III-R* (the revised *DSM* in use at that time), was the prerequisite for being medicated with a stimulant, then the stimulants were also overprescribed.

However, another study found different results. Angold, Erkanli, Egger, and Costello (2000) examined the use of stimulants among 4,500 children between 9 and 16 years old in the Great Smoky Mountains of western North Carolina. They diagnosed ADHD in 3.4% of the children and ADHD, NOS ("not otherwise specified")—that is, children thought to have ADHD without meeting explicit criteria—in another 2.7%. About 7% of the 4,500 children, however, received stimulants. In other words, more children were taking stimulants than were diagnosed with ADHD. About 75% of children with ADHD had taken medicine. So if a child was diagnosed with ADHD, there was a fairly good chance he or she was treated with a stimulant. Of course that also means that 25% of children with ADHD were not receiving medicine. However, when the researchers looked more closely at all the children who had taken stimulants, only about 40% of them had any diagnosis of ADHD, and almost 60% "never had parent-reported impairing ADHD symptoms of any sort."

If having a disorder is the criterion for treatment with medicine, this study found that stimulants were slightly underprescribed, in that only 75% of children with ADHD received stimulants, *and* greatly overprescribed, in that almost 60% of children receiving stimulants did not meet criteria for ADHD, though their teachers did report observing low-level, if not impairing, symptoms of ADHD.

Interestingly, stimulants were prescribed to about two-thirds of the children with ADHD, NOS, who also met criteria for a diagnosis of oppositional defiant disorder. This suggests that these children were being treated for a symptomatic disorder, probably oppositional defiant disorder, albeit not strictly defined ADHD.

More recent research supports these general findings. In a Missouri-based study of 1,610 children Reich, Huang, and Todd (2006) found that about half of the youngsters diagnosed with ADHD were receiving stimulant medication, but that about a third of those who received medicine did not meet criteria for ADHD. These patients, however, did have many symptoms of ADHD. Looking at nationally representative samples, Froehlich, Lanphear, Epstein, Barbaresi, Katusic, and Kahn (2007) and Visser, Lesesne, and Perou (2007) found that only about a third to a half of children meeting criteria for ADHD were treated with stimulants.

There are a host of technical problems in doing large studies such as these. Taking the statistics offered by any study as an absolute reflection of reality is a mistake, as findings depend on the particulars of any study, including what state or region the statistics come from. The point, however, is that not all children with ADHD receive stimulant medicines and not all children who receive stimulant medicines have ADHD. If one uses having a disorder as the sole criterion for receiving a stimulant, medicine will seem both overprescribed and underprescribed.

And How about Depression?

The task of deciding whether medicine is overprescribed or under-prescribed is even more difficult when one considers psychiatric disorders other than ADHD. For these disorders, there is less data examining how many children take medicine, whether they have a disorder, and whether medicine is clearly the most effective treatment.

Treatment studies of depression can be confusing and inconclusive, making it difficult to conclude that all depressed children and adolescents *should* be on medicine. The most impressive study has been the Treatment for Adolescents with Depression Study, or TADS, a 12-week study of 439 adolescents with major depressive disorder done at 13 sites and reported in the *Journal of the American Medical Association* in 2004 (March et al., 2004). This study divided the teenagers into four groups. The first group received Prozac and cognitive-behavioral therapy (CBT), a talking/doing therapy. The second group received only Prozac. The third group received only CBT. And the fourth group received only placebo.

The first group did best, with about 70% of patients responding to treatment. The Prozac-only group did second best, with about 60% of patients responding. About 43% of the CBT-only group responded, and about 35% of the placebo group responded. As noted in previous chapters, in addition to the TADS, a few other short-term studies, involving fewer patients and lasting weeks to months, have shown that some SSRIs are more effective than placebo for children and adolescents with depression who fit criteria severe enough to land them in a research study (Emslie et al., 1997; Emslie et al., 2004; Keller et al., 2001).

These conclusions, while proving that medicine is more effective than placebo in the short run, can leave the doctor unsettled and uncertain that a particular patient *should* be on medicine. As previously discussed, in these studies, usually 30% to 50% of the placebo group improves. These studies also focus on patients with a clear diagnosis of major depression. Often doctors treat patients with borderline or mild levels of depression or with a host of other difficulties that might have kept them out of a research study. Also, disconcerting evidence has come to light that drug companies had previously withheld the results of studies showing that some anti-depressant medicines are no better than placebo (Meier, 2004). Last, these positive studies are short-term, lasting a few months, not long-term, lasting years. The short-term nature of these studies makes it a bit more difficult to say that all depressed children should take antidepressants.

The 5-year follow-up study of the TADS participants does not help prove that all depressed youth should take an antidepressant. In following up with almost half of the adolescents in the original study, Curry and colleagues (2011) found that nearly everyone in this group of moderately to severely depressed adolescents recovered from the initial depression. Unfortunately, about half of those who recovered had a recurrence within those 5 years, but the data do not allow us to conclude that medicine affected that outcome.

These concerns questioning whether antidepressants are mandatory must be balanced, however, by studies showing major depression to be a serious, potentially malignant, often chronic disorder (Ferro, Carlson, Grayson, & Klein, 1994; Kovacs, Feinberg, Crouse-Novak, Paulauskas, & Finkelstein, 1984; Kovacs, Feinberg, Crouse-Novak, Paulauskas, Pollack, & Finkelstein, 1984) and by our knowledge that depressed children are at much greater risk for developing suicidal thoughts and suicidal behavior (Kovacs, Goldston, & Gatsonis, 1993). For example, Maria Kovacs, a leading researcher in childhood depression, found in one study that about two-thirds of depressed children, with an average age of 11, experienced suicidal thoughts; approximately 10% had made a suicide attempt; the number attempting suicide would double over the subsequent 6 to 9 years; and approximately three-fourths of these attempts were made during an episode of depression or dysthymic disorder (Kovacs et al., 1993). If medicine decreased the symptoms of an acute depression, we might conjecture that it would lower the chance of a suicide attempt.

Based on our modest information, it cannot be said that all depressed children and adolescents *should* take medicine, although one could arguably conclude that adolescents with moderate to severe depression should do so. Medicine must reasonably be considered for any particular patient. On the other hand, to start with the prevalence of depression, both milder and in more complex forms, and extrapolate to the number of children and adolescents who *should* take medicine is a stretch.

How many children and adolescents do take antidepressants? Studies by Olfson and associates showed that, between 1996 and 1999, approximately 0.5% to 1% of children under 18 took an antidepressant (Olfson, et al., 2002; Olfson, Gameroff, Marcus, & Waslick, 2003). Vitiello, Zuvekas, and Norquist (2006) found that fewer than 2% of youth took an antidepressant, representing an increase from 1997 to 2002. This increase reflects greater use among adolescents, with just under 4% of that group taking an antidepressant. The number of children taking antidepressants is less than the number of children and adolescents with depression, which has been cited as ranging from about 2% to 8% (or even higher, depending on the age group studied and the procedure used for the study). Another study, by Rushton and Whitmire (2001), found that SSRI antidepressants were used by 1.5% of 6- to 14-year-old Medicaid recipients in North Carolina in 1998. This study is fairly consistent with the findings of Olfson and of Vitiello and shows that these medicines are being used by fewer children than the number that have depression.

The problem is that Olfson, Gameroff, and colleagues found "little evidence that antidepressant treatment is linked to clinical severity" (2003, p. 1241). In other words, even though fewer patients are taking antidepressants than have depression, antidepressants are not being reserved for the most serious cases, as the American Academy of Child and Adolescent Psychiatry recommends. Also, the fact that antidepressants are being used to treat 2- to 4-year-olds (albeit only 3.2 in 1000 insurance-plan enrollees) with virtually no significant research supporting this use is troubling (Zito et al., 2000).

In short, although it has been shown that antidepressants are effective and should be considered as a treatment option for adolescents with depression, it has not been established that all children and adolescents with depression *should* take antidepressants. Like stimulants, antidepressants are probably both overprescribed and underprescribed: underprescribed to some patients with moderate to severe depression and overprescribed to others with less severe depression or in age groups or diagnostic categories for whom its benefit has not been proven.

And the Others

How about disorders beyond ADHD and depression? Are these patients being overmedicated? Determining whether a child with obsessive-compulsive disorder *should* be treated with medicine provides a different kind of problem. Cognitive-behavioral therapy (CBT) has been shown to be as, or perhaps even more, effective than medicine, with the combination of CBT and medicine shown to be more effective than either alone (Pediatric OCD Treatment Study Team, 2004). However, although OCD is a debilitating and often chronic illness, there are no long-term studies showing that children who take medicine do better than those who do not. Though short-term studies indicate that medicine should certainly be considered in the treatment of this often-incapacitating disorder, extrapolating from the prevalence of OCD to conclude that all these children *should* take medicine goes beyond the available data.

Given the lack of specific information regarding the number of children with OCD who take SSRIs, it cannot be concluded that children with OCD are being overmedicated. It's more likely that

215

many children and adolescents with OCD are both undermedicated and undertreated with CBT.

Even less information is available on the effective treatments of other serious psychiatric disorders. Mood stabilizers are frequently used for children diagnosed with bipolar disorder, as we've seen, but the prevalence of this disorder is currently difficult to determine, and the effectiveness of these medicines is uncertain. Although Hunkeler and colleagues (2005) documented a clear increase in the use of medicine, finding that antidepressant and anticonvulsant use roughly doubled between 1994 and 2003, it would be hard to determine if these prescriptions should or should not have been written. It should be noted that even after this substantial increase, the proportion of children and adolescents taking anticonvulsants was still much less than 1 in 100. Also, the evidence that lithium treatment of adults with bipolar disorder appears to lower their suicide rate (Gibbons et al., 2005) creates a compelling argument that some teens with bipolar disorder should take medicine.

Similarly, although the number of prescriptions for atypical antipsychotics increased dramatically between 1996 and 2001, with the medicines being prescribed to approximately 1% of children and adolescents (Patel et al., 2005), the diagnoses of the patients for whom medicine was prescribed are unknown. Therefore, it cannot be said that these medications are overprescribed, because it is not known whether the number of prescriptions exceeds the number of people with a disorder.

As we have seen, "having a disorder" is not a simple way to decide who should take medicine. There is simply not enough evidence to show that every person with any disorder should take medicine in the long run, though for some disorders there is increasing evidence that medicine should be used, or at least considered, in the short run. In the real world of treating patients, having a well-defined disorder is simply too high a standard by which to decide who *should* take medicine. Sometimes the doctor is providing symptomatic relief for an ill-defined or presumptive diagnosis, not for a well-defined disorder. This fact brings us to our next possible criterion for who should take medicine.

Treating Symptoms

Dr. Jensen's (1999) study found that half the children taking stimulants did not meet criteria for ADHD. Dr. Angold's (2000) study found that one group of patients with loosely defined ADHD might have been treated for their extreme defiance. Dr. Patel's (2005) study found that atypical antipsychotic medicines were being prescribed to children, although evidence for their efficacy and safety in children is limited. Dr. Zito's (2000) study found that antidepressants were being prescribed to 2- to 4-year-olds. What were all those prescribing doctors thinking?

Perhaps these doctors were trying to treat patients early in the course of what the doctor thought could be a long-term illness, hoping to change the prognosis of a serious disorder. More probably, many of them thought that these children had symptoms that might respond to medicine in the short run—not disorders, but symptoms. *Should* these symptomatic patients have received medicine? Do these children represent the overprescribing of psychiatric medicines?

Andy is 10 and has Asperger's disorder. He has a hard time relating to those around him, which is understandable because Andy usually alienates his playmates by droning on about snails and their eating habits. Andy is quite bright and easily focuses on reading about sea animals. But in school Andy is disorganized and inattentive. He does not meet criteria for ADHD, but his doctor thinks a stimulant might help Andy focus in school. He prescribes a trial of Concerta.

On medicine, Andy is more focused. He is still socially odd but better able to complete his schoolwork.

Should Andy be treated with a stimulant? Although he does

not have ADHD, he is symptomatic and improves on medicine. Because Andy does have another diagnosable disorder—Asperger's, a disorder sometimes comorbid with ADHD—many would say Andy should get medicine. He has a problem of some sort, so why not just give him the medicine? There is only modest research on using stimulants to treat the inattention of children with Asperger's. The benefits outweigh the risks, however, so it's certainly worth a try.

What if Andy did not have Asperger's or ADHD? Let's say he was able to relate to people easily but was relatively inattentive and forgetful. Should he be treated with a stimulant? He is symptomatic. Is that sufficient reason to medicate? How about the child who doesn't quite fit criteria for ADHD, but whose symptomatic impulsivity is helped by stimulant medicine so that she is more socially accepted by her classmates? Or the college student who can work harder and longer at his homework to overcome relative inattention but can't focus well enough to complete the final exam in the allotted 2 hours? The possibilities are endless.

Doctors seem split on handling such decisions. Although doctors are taught that diagnosis should lead treatment, a study from Great Britain and Northern Ireland, traditionally countries in which ADHD has been rarely diagnosed, shows a different way of deciding treatment. McKenzie and Wurr (2004) showed that of child psychiatrists and pediatricians who routinely treat children with attention difficulties, more than 60% of child psychiatrists and more than 70% of pediatricians would prescribe a stimulant without having made a formal diagnosis of ADHD. In fact, only 13% of pediatricians applied the diagnostic criteria for ADHD in a "tight" manner. In short, symptoms are often treated without the patient necessarily suffering from a disorder.

Although stimulants receive the most media coverage, the possibility of using medicine for the treatment of symptoms is not limited to this one class of medications. Antidepressants, antianxiety medicines, atypical antipsychotics, and others are all used to treat the symptoms of children who do not have a clear-cut, *DSM-IV*–defined disorder or symptoms proven to be responsive to medicine. In documenting an explosive increase in the use of antipsychotic medicines, Olfson, Blanco, Liu, Moreno, and Laje (2006) reported that from 2000 to 2002 over a third of those for whom the medicine was prescribed had a diagnosis of a disruptive behavior disorder and just under a third had a diagnosis of a mood disorder—this at a time when no great body of research supported these indications for antipsychotic medicine. One clearly senses that, although many of those treated might have been symptomatic, they were not diagnosed with a disorder for which these medicines were proven treatments.

Manny is 5 years old and very disruptive. He is often anxious and has frequent explosions. He doesn't fit criteria for ADHD or bipolar disorder or any other particular diagnosis. Perhaps Manny has some kind of intermittent explosive disorder, but there's no high-quality data on treating someone with that diagnosis.

Dr. Henriquez has been trying valiantly to help Manny's parents cope with Manny's behavior so that he can remain in the classroom. Finally, he decides to treat Manny with a low dose of Risperdal. This is a medicine with potentially significant side effects, but Dr. Henriquez believes the potential benefit outweighs the risk, at least in the short run. On .25 milligrams of Risperdal, Manny does better.

Psychiatric medicines have become indispensable in treating the symptoms of children struggling with disorders such as bipolar disorder, schizophrenia, autism, and anxiety disorders, not because their efficacy is proven by the most sophisticated studies, but because less rigorous studies or simply clinical lore has found them to be effective in lessening these symptoms. In fact, a few studies have shown that many children are on more than one psychiatric medicine, despite a lack of scientific evidence proving the effectiveness of these combination treatments (dosReis et al.,

2005; Duffy et al., 2005; Staller et al., 2005). When children have difficulties that are beyond the reach of our fledgling diagnostic nomenclature or when symptoms are not at a level that merit a diagnosis, these medicines are often prescribed anyway. And they often successfully treat symptoms.

Should these children be treated with medicine? Defining a symptom is by definition subjective, and, therefore, so is the decision to use medicine.

Pushing the Limits?

College students have a way of cutting straight to the practical.

Hallie is a college freshman. Throughout high school she was treated with Lexapro for her anxiety disorder. She was a competent though not highly diligent student, and any inattention in class was seen as the result of Hallie's anxiety. She had never been seen as having ADHD, predominantly inattentive type.

Hallie calls me one day from college. "Dr. Kalikow," she says, "I took one of my friend's Adderalls, and it was unbelievable. I became more focused. I took great notes and became really interested in the class discussion. Astronomy was suddenly fascinating. My friends say I'm always spacing out. They're all sure I have ADD. I think they're right because sometimes during class I'm thinking of other stuff. And even in the library I sometimes find myself staring out the window."

I silently groan. I know where this conversation is going. I'm glad that Hallie feels comfortable calling me with the big news, but I see her request on the horizon.

Why so glum, Dr. Kalikow? A little Adderall isn't going to hurt Hallie. She's fairly responsible—for a college freshman. She's not going to mix it with Ecstasy or cocaine. She's not going to sell it to her friends. Loosen up, Dr. K! By graduation Hallie's use of Adderall will be ancient history. She's just treating a symptom. She'll do better in school. She'll be happy. She'll feel good about herself.

My visceral discomfort tells me I'm struggling within. Did I miss the diagnosis of ADHD when Hallie was younger? Did I miss a diagnosis that even a group of college kids picked up on?

I admit that I would find it very comforting to be convinced that Hallie has bona fide ADHD. But no way—I'm not second-guessing myself. I've been through all the *DSM-IV* criteria with Hallie and with her parents. Did Hallie have some symptoms of ADHD? Sure. But a diagnosis of ADHD, inattentive type? No. If I treat Hallie with Adderall, I'll be treating a symptom, not a disorder.

Treating symptoms without a clearly diagnosed disorder can be disconcerting. Lessening a patient's pain is pretty clear. Drying up someone's runny nose is pretty clear. But helping someone who successfully graduated from high school focus better in college? This is tricky.

A student from a highly competitive college program pointed out to me that many of his peers who do not have ADHD take stimulants to enhance studying. Because all tests at his school are graded on a curve, many students recognize that abstaining from stimulants puts one at a disadvantage. Provocative college students argue, "What's the problem? We're treating the symptoms caused by our program." Symptoms can be very dependent on one's values.

We value life. Therefore, taking medicine to decrease the symptom of suicidal thoughts seems justified. We value freedom from pain, both physical and emotional. Therefore, taking medicine to lessen the symptom of pain seems justifiable. We value the ability to function. Therefore, it seems justifiable for a psychiatrist to take a medicine that will improve his hearing or a house painter to take a medicine that will improve his arm's range of motion. As more value is placed on academic success, it seems more justifiable to use medicine to improve a child's school performance. Inattention, which interferes with school performance, becomes a symptom, not simply a characteristic. When does a characteristic become a symptom?

221

My puny biceps are one of my endearing characteristics. They are not symptoms. However, if I lived in the world of bodybuilders, a world in which massive and well-defined biceps are highly valued, indeed the goal of their work, then my puny biceps would be symptomatic of dysfunction, and steroids would become symptom reducers. We can criticize the bodybuilder's values. But within his or her value system, if the benefits outweighed the risks, steroids could be justified.

It is comforting to know that other fields of medicine struggle with the same question. Others also tread the fuzzy line between treating a symptom and enhancing a characteristic.

Marnie is 12 and has always been one of the shortest children in her grade. Her parents are of average height. After an X-ray, the pediatrician says that Marnie will probably max out at 5'2". Her mother worries that Marnie will struggle with a social disadvantage, that she'll have a harder time attracting boys. She'll always be seen as younger than her peers and will be the mascot, instead of an equal. Marnie's mother sees Marnie's height as a symptom and would like to consult a pediatric endocrinologist about prescribing growth hormone while there's still time.

Marnie's father disagrees. He argues that his own mother has been short her entire life and that didn't prevent her from being a social dynamo as a teenager or from getting married and having children. Besides, he says, 5'2" is not that short.

They consult the endocrinologist, who reviews the risks and benefits of growth hormone. She then explains that whether Marnie's relatively short stature is seen as a symptom is subjective. The endocrinologist herself is struggling with whether she would be medicating a symptom or enhancing a trait. What if everyone wanted to increase his or her height in an effort to improve functioning? Would she be treating symptoms or characteristics? *Should* Marnie be medicated, or would this represent the overprescribing of growth hormone?

The Value of Values

Who *should* take medicine? The prevalence of a disorder doesn't really indicate who should take medicine. The patient's symptoms are no objective guide. The question is inherently subjective. It is also subtly deceptive. The deeper question is: "What does one value?"

Medicine is simply a tool around which our various values compete. As values change, for an individual or a society, so does the answer to whether one should take medicine. We value life, freedom from pain, the ability to function. If medicine brings us closer to these goals with minimal risk, it seems justified and, in our own mind, a compelling *should*. The scarcer the evidence that medicine will bring us what we value and the greater the evidence that it will bring risk, the more it seems like it *could*—but not should—be prescribed.

Values are played out in many possible scenarios. The values surrounding a single, working-class mother being able to function at work to support her three children is compelling. The values surrounding a 28-year-old man with a shoulder on the mend who would like to be able to play golf three times a week instead of just once are less compelling.

So we come to the values that underlie the prescribing of psychiatric medicine to children. Preventing the death of a suicidal adolescent demonstrates a compelling, agreed-upon value. Preventing an extremely disruptive, volatile child from regularly threatening his family demonstrates the value of safety and the compelling need to keep a child living at home, if possible. Allowing a child to reach his or her academic potential is becoming an increasingly compelling value in a world that places a premium on academic achievement.

Although all agree that virtually anything should be done to save a life, how much should be done in the pursuit of educational success is debated. The prescription of stimulants is continuously questioned because it forces us to confront the level at which we value a child's educational success and what we will do to help a child reach his or her potential. This is success defined not necessarily by the quality of learning but by the quality of the grades achieved. Whereas college students might value high grades because they are essential to successfully compete for a limited number of jobs, some parents see grades as necessary for self-esteem or as a way to expand their child's opportunities.

Our educational system has a largely "one size fits all" approach, and many children do not succeed for a variety of reasons: They may struggle with attention issues; they may have a harder time in class because they are better at building, fixing, and designing and possess strong visual rather than listening skills; they may have trouble staying focused while reading and therefore avoid it. For all these children who have great difficulty adapting to an educational system that places a premium on reading, writing, and sitting quietly, stimulants frequently can help. If the parents of these children feel a strong need for them to succeed in school, they will consider the use of stimulants.

In deciding who should take medicine, we bare our values, the values that often reflect the importance of what is at stake. When a child's future is at stake, for some parents the benefit of medicine soars, but for others the risks of medicine loom large.

The question we face is not whether medicine is overprescribed or underprescribed. Until we confront our values in an attempt to establish who should receive medicine, and unless we confront our fears to decide if they are rational, that question is impossible to answer.

Mr. Peterson's Return

"Well, young man, I've given some thought to what you said." Mr. Peterson has returned from his walk, and the group of us are still hanging out on his lawn arguing about who should take medicine.

"What did you come up with?" I ask.

Mr. Peterson replies, "The benefit of taking my little pill clearly outweighs the risks. I take my walk every day, and if my hip gave me pain, I probably wouldn't walk. That walk is good for my heart, and that, I hope, prolongs my life, which Mrs. Peterson and I value dearly. I don't seem to get any short-term physical side effects, and long-term side effects seem unlikely—and at my age, well, who cares? But my most important realization is that what I value is my life, and if that little pill helps me hold onto it for another month or another year, well then, I *should* be taking it."

Mr. Peterson isn't finished. "As for all those parents who give their kids psychiatric medicines, sure, they have to weigh risks and benefits. But most important, they have to ask themselves what their goal is. If they're trying to make their own lives easier or they're trying to get a leg up on getting their kid into some Ivy League school that the kid doesn't belong in anyway, those are values for which I have no respect. I don't think those kids should be taking medicine. But if their kids are overwhelmed by life and medicine makes their way easier, well, I still think they have to be careful not to depend on medicine, but if it were my child struggling, I might just do the same."

CHAPTER 18

Rosie

|||||||||||||||||||||||||||||||||||||||||||||||||||||||||||||||||||

In the previous chapter Mr. Peterson struggles with whether psychiatric medicines are overprescribed. Parents on the front line struggle not with philosophy but with the actual decision of whether to medicate their child. Let's put philosophical issues aside and spend a school year with Mr. and Mrs. Parker, who must determine how best to help their daughter, Rosie.

CHAPTER 1

Every first phone call holds a surprise.

"Hello, this is Dr. Kalikow. Is Mrs. Parker at home?"

"Oh, Dr. Kalikow, thank you so much for taking the time to call back. Dr. Rice, our pediatrician, gave us your name. My daughter, Rosie, is a patient of his. Rosie's been having some problems. I've never done this before—I mean, called a psychiatrist. What should I do? Do I just make an appointment or what?"

"Why don't you tell me in a sentence or two about the kind of difficulty Rosie's been having?"

"Sure thing. Rosie is 8. She's driving us crazy. Dr. Rice thought you could help."

"How is she driving you crazy?"

"She's been refusing to go to school. In the morning, she screams that she's not going to that 'f-ing' school. I didn't even know she knew that word. She grabs the leg of this heavy chair in the dining room and doesn't let go. I had to pry her hands off it. All the while she's cursing and screaming that she hates my guts."

Mrs. Parker was at wits' end.

"When I finally get her walking to the car and I'm dragging my poor 5-year-old along, who only wants to finish his Pop Tart, she takes off down the street. And now I've got my 5-year-old crying, and I can't leave him alone in the car, but I can't let Rosie run down the street. And so I am chasing her past the neighbor's house wearing just my nightgown and slippers and my husband's raincoat that I threw on just to take her to school. She's running like a car thief, and I'm tripping down the street trying to keep the slippers on my feet and hoping nobody sees me. And meanwhile my husband's at work, and I can't get him on his cell phone, and I don't know what to do."

Actually, Mrs. Parker was not at wits' end—she was downright desperate. Without ever having met the woman, I felt obligated to try to help her out of this mess.

After she caught her breath, she went on, "Dr. Rice said you'd be able to help us. He said that you'd know what to do."

I explained to Mrs. Parker that although I greatly appreciated Dr. Rice's vote of confidence, these problems are sometimes difficult to solve. Let's keep the expectations reasonable and avoid the inevitable disappointment when Rosie is not skipping to school by Friday.

"Can I bring Rosie in tomorrow morning, Dr. Kalikow?"

I told Mrs. Parker that my soonest appointment was the following Monday morning at 9 A.M. and that I would like to see her and her husband first. We would discuss Rosie's difficulties going to school and take a complete history. I wanted to understand how she does in school, how she does with friends and family, how she eats and sleeps, whether she has any medical problems, and so on. I explained that this would take about two hours. Then we'd set up an appointment for Rosie.

227

"I'm not sure what there will be to talk about for two hours, Dr. Kalikow. But I know you know what you're doing because Dr. Rice said so. Besides, you sound nice, and I really appreciate your talking to me on the phone this late at night. I mean, you don't even know me."

Truth be told, I was eyeing my clock as Mrs. Parker was talking. I had been on the phone for about 10 minutes, and I still had two calls to return before I left the office. I had done my job for the first phone call. I had been supportive and set up a first appointment. It was time to move on.

"Mrs. Parker, I'll see you and your husband next Monday morning."

"Okay, Dr. Kalikow. But one last question?"

"Sure."

"Does my husband have to come? He's an electrician with his own business, and he's really busy in the morning. Is it okay if I come alone? I mean, he's usually not home in the morning when Rosie goes to school anyway."

Beware of "one last question." It often tells the tale.

"If at all possible, it's pretty important for your husband to come in. He'll be able to tell me his view of Rosie. It will also be important to have him here to discuss our plan for treating Rosie."

"Well, that's just it, Dr. Kalikow. Pete doesn't really believe in psychiatry. He grew up in a pretty old-fashioned house where every problem was solved by a slap on the head. He thinks that Rosie just needs a whack to straighten her out. But I won't let him do that. Pete says that he doesn't want any daughter of his seeing a shrink—I'm sorry, Dr. Kalikow, I mean psychiatrist—for the next 10 years. He says that too many kids are being given medicine, and he won't have any of that. You wouldn't use medicine, would you, Dr. Kalikow?"

Ah, just "one last question."

"Mrs. Parker, that's an important question, and I think it would be better to discuss that when you and your husband are here in the office, after I've taken a more complete history. I do have patients who take medicine, but I also have patients who don't. We need to evaluate Rosie and see what's best for her. There will be plenty of time to talk about medicine if we think it might be of help.

"But tell your husband that I would never and could never start Rosie on medicine unless the two of you agreed that we should."

I was still eyeballing the clock, but I was also realizing that these last questions needed to be dealt with in a sensitive and patient way right now. Patients expect their fears and opinions to be heard respectfully, and despite Dr. Rice's superlative recommendation, if I had any hope of fostering a working relationship with these parents, I had to take a minute to help quell their anxieties.

"Well, okay, Dr. Kalikow. I'll tell all this to Pete. He really cares about his daughter more than anything in the world and would do anything for her. He's just a little thick-headed and stubborn, but he's got a heart of gold and . . . "

"Then I'll see you both next Monday, Mrs. Parker."

"Okay, Dr. Kalikow. We'll see you then."

CHAPTER 2

Mr. and Mrs. Parker were sitting in my waiting room at 9 A.M. Monday morning.

I ushered them into my office.

"Nice place you got here, Doc," Mr. Parker said, "but they sure did stick you in the back of the building. I hope they gave you a break in the rent."

"Are we sure glad to see you," Mrs. Parker said while entering my office. "I didn't think we'd get here. Rosie gave us a run this morning. Mondays are always the most brutal. So what do you want to know, Dr. Kalikow?"

I had barely introduced myself, but I already felt like I'd known these people for years. Despite their current difficulties, there was an ease about them. Mrs. Parker was forward and uninhibited, pleasant and likable. Though they had a look of skepticism in my being a psychiatrist, they seemed to have an inherent trust in me as a medical doctor.

"Give me a minute to get some basics like Rosie's date of birth and your address, and then we'll talk about what's been happening at home."

After I wrote down their address and phone number, Mrs. Parker jumped right in. "Like I told you on the phone, Dr. Kalikow, she's just been impossible. She's been a real crank. I mean, she's never been easy, but since about Halloween, every morning's been a nightmare. She wakes up angry at the world. Barking at her brothers. Sometimes I can't get her out of bed. She won't wash her face or brush her teeth. I'll tell you, Dr. Kalikow—"

"Patti, she's not that bad. You're making her sound like a nutcase or something. Why don't you tell Doc about how she loves to draw cartoons and about the painting she surprised you with on Mother's Day? She's a great artist, Doc—"

"Peter, get real! You don't know. You're not home in the morning. I am! I'm the one who's trying to get her out of bed, trying to get her teeth brushed, trying to get her washed up, trying to get her off to school. I can't take it anymore. My mornings have been hell. And I've got other kids to care for."

All of a sudden, the affability was gone, and I was getting a hard glimpse into the inner tensions of their marriage. Mr. Parker sat quietly. He couldn't deny that he just wasn't home much in the morning. There was an air of vulnerability about him. He seemed hurt, angry, perhaps a bit guilty, and certainly scared.

Then he shot back, "You just coddle her too much. You never put your foot down. You let her walk all over you, just like your brother walked all over your mother."

"I don't coddle her. I've just learned that with Rosie you can't simply be telling her what to do all the time. She's not like the other kids. You have to give her a little room to breathe."

Mr. Parker responded with a dismissive wave of his hand and a slow, judgmental shake of his head.

I quickly jumped in.

"Why don't you tell me when you noticed a change in Rosie?"

Mrs. Parker began, "Well, you see, Dr. Kalikow, Rosie's complicated. It's hard to pin this down to an exact day. As I said, Rosie's never been easy. Her brothers are easy. Chris is 12. He does his homework without my asking, does whatever I tell him to do. He's the most popular kid in the class and the goalie of his soccer team. Before Rosie, I thought Chris was a great kid because I was such a great mother. Then, 4 years later, Rosie comes along, and I'm not so sure what kind of mother I am."

"Patti, Doc was asking when all this started," Pete said, having regained his composure.

"I'm sorry. It's just that this has been real hard, Dr. Kalikow. I'm a stay-at-home mom. I think that's best for my kids. So I give being a mom all I've got, but sometimes it's just not enough." Mrs. Parker was getting teary and reached for a tissue. "Anyway, about 2 weeks before school started, my mother died fairly suddenly. She had some medical problems, but nobody expected it so soon.

"I guess you never expect your parent to die. It's always a shock. Rosie and her grandmother had been real close before her grandmother moved to South Carolina. They used to crochet together. My mother was the only one who understood Rosie. Rosie took it pretty hard."

"Tell me what it's like in the morning before school," I said, appreciating the importance of this information but trying to refocus Mrs. Parker on Rosie's recent behavior.

"So school started about 2 months ago, and Rosie started the year giving us a problem just like she does every year. But this year things were worse. She was even more adamant about not going. She was cursing every morning. Her brothers thought she was crazy, even the little one. I tried coaxing her, bribing her, threatening her. I wanted to talk to the teacher to get her help, but my husband over here thought this was family business and that we don't need to be airing our dirty laundry in public. Of course, he wasn't home to help in the morning, either."

Mr. Parker didn't respond but looked at his wife, shaking his head and running his fingers through his wavy black hair.

The Parkers went on to give me the details of getting Rosie to school and all the other difficulties they'd had, starting with her hating to be left at preschool. I asked what Rosie was like at home.

Mr. Parker jumped in first, "She's tough, Doc. I know I'm not home and that a lot of this falls on Patti here and that I give Patti a hard time. But I also know that Rosie's tough. She isn't like the boys. She's always irritable or angry. She can be a royal pain in the ass.

"With Rosie we're always walking on eggshells. You never know who's coming down the stairs, Dr. Jekyll or Mr. Hyde. She's a pistol, all right, Doc." Mr. Parker couldn't seem to decide if he was emotionally drained and in harmony with his wife's frustration or if he was just a little proud of his daughter with whom the world would one day have to reckon.

Mrs. Parker added, "Rosie's a worrier. She's always thinking about what's coming around the bend. She anticipates and frets. She's cautious. She doesn't jump right into things. Making decisions can be a nightmare because she's afraid she'll make the wrong choice, even if there is no wrong choice. So she has a hard time getting going.

"She also gets real embarrassed. When she was little, she hated when we'd compliment her. Like we'd tell her she did a beautiful drawing, you know, the way you tell a child even though it's not the *Mona Lisa* or anything. Rosie would always look down at the floor, get real intense, and say, 'Don't say that!' It was like she was embarrassed to get the attention."

"What is she like when she meets new people? Does she get embarrassed then?"

Mrs. Parker went on, "She clings to me like a piece of Saran Wrap. She won't say anything for the longest time. When she was younger, I'd take her to the playground, and all the kids would be running and laughing, while Rosie would be sitting on my lap demanding that we go home."

"You said she's a worrier. Do you think she worries about the two of you, in particular?" I asked.

"How do you mean?"

"Do you think Rosie worries about the two of you when she's not with you? For example, if you're late getting home, does she worry? Does she say she worries about the two of you dying? Does she follow you around the house because she needs to be with you? Is she ever afraid of losing you in the mall?"

232

"Are you kidding, Doc?" Mr. Parker answered. "If it was up to Rosie, we could stay out all Saturday night. And she goes all over the house. Lots of times, she doesn't want us anywhere near her. But now that you mention it, sometimes she wants Patti to be in her room at bedtime more than the boys ever did. Not always, but sometimes."

The Parkers went on to describe that Rosie had no difficulty separating from them other than for school. She went on sleepovers and was up and down the block going to her friends' houses. Rosie was well liked and popular, though she had difficulty initiating relationships with peers. She was known as a good cartoonist, and all her friends wanted a crazy cartoon done by Rosie hanging on their bedroom wall. Once she was comfortable, she was also quite a comedian, and sharing jokes was something she and her father enjoyed together.

Rosie's temper, though, was legendary. She was known to hit her brothers, kick at her mother, and call her father an "asshole." She could be as sweet as sugar one minute, then in a fury the next. When pushed, her parents admitted that most of the time she was pleasant, but the abruptness of her rage and their need to walk on eggshells was a constant challenge.

Transitions were often difficult. Rosie liked the world to be as she expected and didn't deal well with adapting to change. She became easily frustrated by the unexpected. That's when she usually had an emotional meltdown.

"Does she ever have these meltdowns in school?" I asked.

"That's just it, Dr. Kalikow. Until this year Rosie's always been pretty much the ideal child in school. She had a little trouble getting to school, but, over the past few years, the teacher never knew it. She really focuses on her work when she's there, and she never does anything to get herself in trouble."

Mrs. Parker went on to tell me that Rosie was very bright. She read very well for a third grader and was a storehouse of information about anything you could possibly want to know. Her handwriting, however, was a bit awkward, and sometimes Rosie would get so frustrated keeping her homework within the lines that she'd just throw her pencil across the room.

Medically, Rosie had always been a healthy child. The Parkers recalled that when she was about 6 years old, she occasionally had tension headaches, but she had never had surgery or been hospitalized or lost consciousness or had a seizure. She took no medications and had a good appetite. She slept well but often needed her mother upstairs at bedtime.

Discussing bedtime reminded Mrs. Parker about Rosie's difficulty with her pajamas. When Rosie put on her pajama top, she always had to make sure the sleeves were straight, not twisted. She went on to say that Rosie was very finicky about how her socks felt, that the thread near the toe had to be just so and the socks always had to be pulled up and not flopping around her ankles. Rosie was finicky about the way most clothing felt and would wear the same sweat pants over and over.

She was also very particular about the taste of food. Ketchup had to be Heinz, and pizza had to be Elio's. Whenever the family went to visit Aunt Selma, whose apartment looked like a time warp back to 1963 with old *National Geographics* and Dean Martin records gathering dust, Rosie would always pull her mother aside and whisper, "I don't like the way this place smells, Mommy."

I asked Mr. and Mrs. Parker if any of Rosie's blood relatives had had psychiatric problems such as depression, anxiety, alcohol or drug problems, and the like. Mr. Parker looked at his wife and smiled.

"You don't have enough paper in that pad of yours to write all we've got to tell, Doc."

They went on to tell me about Mrs. Parker's mother, who had suffered from depression her whole life and had been treated with lithium for many years. Mrs. Parker's brother was a chronic worrier. Mr. Parker then told me about his father, who had panic attacks starting about the time of his retirement. These attacks prevented him from going to Christmas parties at his sister-in-law's house, causing a bit of a family uproar. Seeming evasive, Mr. Parker reported that his brother had some difficulties, but did not elaborate.

We had been sitting for almost two hours by now, and I was nearing the end of my questions. I was about to give the Parkers some preliminary thoughts about Rosie's diagnosis before we set up a time for me to meet Rosie when Mrs. Parker suddenly said, "So, Dr. Kalikow, I'm still not sure what we should do tomorrow morning when it's time for school. Are you going to tell us what to do now?"

That's what I love about parents, I thought, they never let me enjoy the process of figuring out a diagnosis. They never appreciate the satisfaction of putting all the pieces neatly together. They always want practical advice about what to do with their children.

I punted. "Let's set up an appointment so that I can meet Rosie. Then we'll talk about how you should try to get her to school." I arranged to see Rosie in 2 days.

CHAPTER 3

The next morning the phone rang at 7:55. I was sitting at my desk waiting for my first patient of the day. I used my answering machine to screen the call, not wanting to get involved in a phone call that would cause me to be late for my eight o'clock patient.

At first, I had a tough time figuring out who it was.

"Dr. Kalikow, she's down the street again. Please call me when you get this message. My number is . . . ."

Who's down the street, and why was this woman so distraught?

Then I realized it was Mrs. Parker and she was in tears. I immediately picked up the phone.

"Hello, it's Dr. Kalikow."

"Thank you so much for picking up the phone, Dr. Kalikow. It's Patti Parker. Rosie's running down the street again. She ran out after I told her to go downstairs for breakfast. I just can't go after her. What should I do?"

So much for waiting to meet Rosie.

"What do you think will happen if you don't run after her?" I asked.

"She'll come back in about 10 minutes. She always does," she said, regaining her composure.

"In that case, wait for her to come back. Don't go running down the street. It's demeaning. Besides, I'm sure Rosie's a lot faster than you."

Mrs. Parker chuckled. "That's certainly true. But what should I do when she comes back into the house?"

"Try sitting down with Rosie and calmly but firmly telling her that you know it's difficult but that school is very important and that you need to figure out a way for her to go."

"But she'll just run off again if I try to take her. What if I just give her a day off?"

I heard the door to my waiting room open, and I knew my patient was waiting. I was suddenly feeling the frustration of trying to make a treatment plan for a difficult patient I had not even met, knowing I had to get off this phone call in about 30 seconds.

"If she stays home today, it's not the end of the world. But after I meet Rosie tomorrow, we'll have to come up with a more organized approach because she obviously can't stay home every day."

There was an audible sigh of relief from Mrs. Parker. She had been granted a 24-hour reprieve.

CHAPTER 4

The next morning, I was to meet Rosie at a 10:00 appointment. I disliked having to take Rosie out of school to see me, but it was the only appointment available, and I knew Mrs. Parker would be relieved that she didn't have to get Rosie to school that morning. At 10, I opened my office door and stepped into the waiting room. Mrs. Parker was sitting in a chair. I did not see Rosie.

"Dr. Kalikow," Mrs. Parker said, "Rosie's in the bathroom."

"No problem," I said, "While we're waiting, why don't you give me a quick update?"

"You don't understand, Dr. Kalikow. Rosie's locked herself in that little bathroom out in the hall. She refuses to come in."

Suddenly, I got the picture. Did I think this was going to be easy?

"Let's go out in the hallway and see if we can coax her out," I said.

I had seen this before. Every so often a very reluctant child tries to escape meeting the hoary head of Dr. Kalikow by holing up under a waiting-room chair or locking himself in the car. This bathroom routine, however, might have been a first. I gave Rosie credit for ingenuity.

Usually, a slow, gentle approach lures children out of hiding after they have had a chance to check me out.

I was going to try some nonthreatening conversation with Rosie through the closed bathroom door when the ever-spontaneous Mrs. Parker took matters into her own hands.

"Rosie, come out right now and meet Dr. Kalikow. He's a very nice man."

"Go to hell, you fat ass!" said a small but firm voice from the other side of the door.

No, this was not going to be easy.

"Rosie, I will not have you talk to me that way," Mrs. Parker responded.

"Shut up, you turd."

Suddenly, I heard the whir of a roll of toilet paper, as if someone had just given a quick yank.

A helpless Mrs. Parker looked at me with imploring, tired eyes that begged me to do something. I motioned Mrs. Parker to return to the waiting room. Let's see what I could accomplish on my own.

Rather softly, I offered, "Hi, Rosie. I'm Dr. Kalikow."

Another whir of toilet paper.

"Very effective, Dr. K," I thought. Mrs. Parker had returned to the waiting room, Rosie was locked in the bathroom, and I was standing alone in the hallway talking to a closed door.

For a few minutes, I tried unsuccessfully to make gentle introductions through the closed bathroom door. Each attempt was answered by a whir of toilet paper. Finally, at the risk of upping the ante, I decided to use my imagination and go for broke. I turned on the water at the kitchenette sink in the hallway and started washing the dirty coffee mugs sitting next to the sink.

"I guess I'll just hang out and do some dishes," I said to no one in particular, but hoping Rosie would hear. "You don't happen to have some sponges under the sink in there, do you, Rosie?"

There was no response from the bathroom for a long time. I was beginning to wonder if Rosie had fallen asleep sitting on the toilet or if she was plotting to plug up the sink with all that toilet paper and then open the faucet at full tilt. I kept washing and talking and talking and washing. I turned the water on and off. I hummed and whistled. I didn't know about Rosie, but my coffee mugs were spotless.

After about 20 minutes, while I was getting very animated at the sink, I heard the door knob turn slowly. A little hand emerged with a blue sponge. Rosie opened the door ever so slightly so that she could get a glimpse of what all the excitement was about. I took the sponge.

"Thank you, Rosie."

Over the next few minutes, I used the sponge to continue to wash the dishes. Very gradually the door opened millimeter by millimeter. I could barely see her face. Rosie continued to watch through the crack in the door but said nothing.

Parents always wonder what it is a child psychiatrist talks about when evaluating a child. I always say that I often learn more from watching how the child behaves than I do from the exact content of what he or she says. It was becoming increasingly apparent that Rosie's temperament was characterized by great persistence, that she was slow to warm up to people, and that her mood was probably anxious. In plain talk, Rosie was willful, stubborn, and scared.

Most slow-to-warm children gradually come out of their shell, if you approach them slowly and allow them time to check you out. Rosie was a bit beyond that. She didn't move much more for the rest of the visit. Eventually Mrs. Parker came out into the hallway. I suggested that, before Mr. Parker and she and I sat down again, we should set up another appointment to see if Rosie would come out any further. We set it up for 2 days later.

Mrs. Parker said to the slight opening in the door, "We'll be leaving in just a minute, Rosie. Can I talk to you for a minute, Dr. Kalikow?"

"Sure."

When we got into the office, Mrs. Parker shut the door behind her, looked me in the eye, and whispered desperately the inevitable question, "What am I going to do tomorrow morning, Dr. Kalikow?"

I had forgotten about Mrs. Parker's problem at hand. She had to get Rosie to school. I tried to think quickly and practically, knowing that whatever quick advice I gave would probably not work with a child like Rosie, who was as stubborn as a pit bull.

"When you get home today, if things are pretty calm, I want you to sit down with Rosie and explain to her that you know it's hard for her in the morning, but that after a little while in school she always feels more comfortable. Also, explain to her that this is a problem that you and her dad are going to help her with, but that staying home is not an option."

Mrs. Parker looked at me and said what I had hoped she wouldn't say, "Dr. Kalikow, I've said all that before. It doesn't work."

"But things have been at least a little tense in your house recently. There's been a lot of screaming and threatening. I want you to try what I'm saying, but I want this to be a calm conversation. Rosie might escalate, but I want you to concentrate on keeping your cool. Don't get pulled into any arguments Rosie might offer you."

"Okay, Dr. Kalikow, I'll do my best," said an exasperated Mrs. Parker.

We went back into the hallway. Rosie was still in the bathroom, the door slightly ajar.

Mrs. Parker said, "Come on, Rosie, we're going now. We're going to see Dr. Kalikow again on Friday."

Rosie sprung out of the bathroom, almost knocking her mother to the ground as she flung the door open.

"I hate you!" she said as she ran down the hall and out the building.

Mrs. Parker looked at me with the pained resignation of a bewildered parent.

CHAPTER 5

Two days later, Mrs. Parker showed up with Rosie for a 4 P.M. appointment. When I came into the waiting room, Rosie was curled up on a chair. Mrs. Parker was sitting next to her. I sat down in one of the remaining chairs, across the waiting room from Rosie.

"Hi, Rosie," I said, "It's nice to see you."

Rosie curled her body tighter and looked up at her mother with an angry look that said, "I'm here, but I'm not talking to this creep."

Over the course of the next few minutes, I chatted with Mrs. Parker about the weather, simply trying to keep the interactions pleasant, light, and without a focus on Rosie, who needed plenty of time to check me out.

I was wondering how I was going to slowly bring Rosie into this interaction, when the irrepressible Mrs. Parker smiled and said in her stage voice, "Dr. Kalikow, Rosie made it to school yesterday. We're very proud of her."

Another sudden tightening of a curled-up Rosie, who clearly did not appreciate being the topic of conversation.

Mrs. Parker needed me to respond, and so I did.

"That's terrific," I said, but as I answered, my mind was going through my mental files searching for a way to engage a very reluctant Rosie. I saw the blackboard and was struck by an idea. Within 2 minutes, I had a crude map of the United States and Canada. The incoming cold front was in the news and so I started with that. I pontificated about everything I did not know about the cold fronts from Canada, making silly pictures out of the maps. After a few minutes, I had Rosie's attention.

I finally broached my first dialogue with Rosie since our ill-fated first outing.

"Rosie, do you think I should use pink chalk or blue chalk for the cold front?"

A whispered response, "Blue."

Timing, I thought to myself, is everything. I had scored.

Over the next few minutes, I carefully proceeded to converse with Rosie about the map and color preferences. Within about 20 minutes, she slowly ventured off her chair and over to the board at my invitation to draw in her own warm front in pink. After another 20 minutes, Rosie walked into my office to look at my toys, while her mother and I remained in the waiting room.

While Rosie was in my office, I asked Mrs. Parker, "How did you get her here?"

"I bribed her. I told her we could go to Totally Pizza, her favorite restaurant, for dinner, if she came without a fuss. Even with that, it wasn't easy, but we're here."

I got out of my chair and walked into my office. Rosie was exploring my toys and the children's drawings on my wall. Although conversation was not plentiful, Rosie answered my questions about which pictures she liked. Her answers were brief but articulate, and she demonstrated a keen sense of observation. She was clearly relaxing her defenses.

A few minutes later, Rosie and I walked back into the waiting room. It was about time to leave, but before Mrs. Parker and Rosie walked out, I asked Rosie if I could ask her one more question. She seemed to tense, as if she figured our brief honeymoon was over.

"Do you know any good jokes, Rosie?" I asked.

Rosie smiled coyly and looked up at her mother.

"I know which joke you want to tell," said Mrs. Parker. "It's kind of gross, Rosie, but okay, you can tell Dr. Kalikow."

Rosie looked at me. "What do you do if you get swallowed by an elephant?" she asked.

"I have no idea," I said to Rosie, then looked at Mrs. Parker, who looked embarrassed by the joke but relieved that Rosie's cold front was beginning to thaw.

"Run around until you're all pooped out," said Rosie, her smile broadening.

"It's time to go, Rosie," Mrs. Parker said. Then she added, "Thank you, Dr. Kalikow," in a kind but definitively parental voice that said, *Do what I do.*

"Thank you, Dr. Kalikow," Rosie said.

"See you, Rosie," I answered, as Mrs. Parker and Rosie turned to leave.

CHAPTER 6

Mr. and Mrs. Parker came in the following week so that I could review my findings and arrive at a treatment plan. Mrs. Parker jumped right in as she was taking her seat.

"Well, Dr. Kalikow, Rosie's been to school three of the past five days. I think we may have turned a corner. I stopped chasing her down the street, and she doesn't seem to be running away as much any more. But it's still real tough once we get her to school. She's cursing at—"

"Hold on, Mrs. Parker," I said. "Let's set an agenda for today's visit. First, I want to tell you a little bit about what I think is going on with Rosie. Then we'll talk about what we're going to do. Is that okay?"

Mr. Parker chimed in, "Yeah, Patti, let the man talk. For the money we're paying him, I want to know what he thinks. I get your opinions at home, and it doesn't cost me a dime." Mr. Parker turned to me with a knowing, devilish smile and motioned me to go on. He had thrown me a barb about my fees, thrown his wife a barb about her uninhibited talking, and come across as a willing participant in just a few sentences. All this with an absolutely winning charm.

I proceeded to tell the Parkers my impressions thus far.

"We need to understand Rosie on a few different levels. First, let's look at Rosie's temperament. She—"

"She always had a wicked temper," Mrs. Parker offered.

"I didn't say she had a temper, Mrs. Parker. I said temperament. Those are two different things. Temperament is something we all have. Like skin color. The traits a child is born with. Rosie has always been a child who took a while to feel comfortable in a new situation. She's guarded and cautious and carefully observes any new situation before she joins in. That's why she doesn't bounce right into the fray when she goes to her friends' birthday parties. She was probably born with that trait."

"I don't know, Doc, Patti's been staying at birthday parties with Rosie forever. Rosie expects her to stay and has a fit if her mom says she's leaving. I just think, and I'm not getting on you here, Pat, I just think that if Patti would have been tougher, we'd have a happier little girl."

Mr. Parker did not intend it, but Mrs. Parker was hurt.

"Peter, what Dr. Kalikow is saying is right. You never took her to birthday parties. You never had to deal with watching all the kids running and laughing and playing while your kid was wrapped around your leg like a pair of tight jeans. The boys aren't that way. I didn't do this, Peter."

"I think I can explain how you are both right, but give me a minute to go on before we put it all together. I think there are certain traits with which Rosie was born and that she showed within her first couple of years. In addition to being slow to warm, Rosie's reactions to the world around her have usually been intense."

"Always intense," said Mr. Parker, now shaking his head in agreement.

"It's as if some children are born without a dimmer switch," I said. "Either they don't respond much, or they respond with the intensity of a police searchlight. They have a tough time modulating their responses. Rosie has also been someone who did not adapt well to the unexpected. She needs routine, predictability. It seems to me that many of her eruptions have occurred when she was suddenly faced with the unexpected."

Mrs. Parker seemed mesmerized by the idea that children could be born with certain traits that become part of their personality.

"You know, Dr. Kalikow, this is making so much sense. Chris, our oldest, was always smiling and cheerful. He never fussed much, loved to be cuddled, ate what I fed him, and slept through the night. Then Rosie came along, and after a while I thought, 'What am I doing wrong?' She was just so . . ." Mrs. Parker stopped to grab a tissue and blow her nose, ". . . difficult. For a while I didn't want to have any more kids. You're telling me that I'm not the reason Chris is so wonderful, and I'm not the reason Rosie's so difficult."

"I'm not saying that your parenting is not important. It's very important. You've had a lot to do with making all three of your children wonderful people. But there's a difference between wonderful and easy. Rosie is giving and considerate and funny, but she's not easy. I'm simply saying that each child comes with some biological traits and that parents need to tailor their parenting to each child."

I seemed to have Mr. Parker's attention, so I went on, "Let me put it another way. I have an aunt who used to be a sculptor. She once explained to me that she doesn't simply take the next piece of marble and sculpt whatever she wants. First, she examines the stone. She sees where the stone's natural lines and cracks are. Then she tries to sculpt the stone according to its makeup. As she sculpts it, she uncovers other fault lines and grains, and she adapts her sculpting to what she has learned.

"It's the same way with children. We have certain basic rules of parenting that we use for all our children, but we also adapt our parenting to the inborn characteristics of each child. These inborn characteristics are called temperament."

CHAPTER 7

Mr. Parker was stuck and needed, once again, to point the finger at Mrs. Parker. "Doc, I was a bit of a rascal, too, when I was a kid. But if I stepped out of line, my father gave me a crack." He drew his arm back as if he were going to hit someone with the back of his hand. "I learned not to cross my father. Patti, here, spends the day giving in to Rosie. Then, by the time I get home, Patti is ticked off and yelling at every little thing she does. You can't tell me that's any good for her."

Mrs. Parker wasted no time, "How dare you, Peter! You're never home before 8. I'm spent by then. You should try keeping up with three kids, even the easy ones. And with Rosie it's worse."

Mr. Parker shot back, "You should try getting up at 5:30 in the morning to get to a job, only to find out that one of my guys is home with the flu, the contractor wants the job done yesterday, and I'm laying wire in someone's crawl space with you calling me on the cell phone to tell me about Rosie running down the street. Oh, I'm having lots of fun. Just tell me when you want to trade for a day or two."

"I know you work hard, Peter, but so do I. Just because you're tired when you come home doesn't give you the right to contradict me in front of her—"

"I've got to stop you both. I'm sure this is all very important to each of you, but I want to stay focused on Rosie."

"I'm sorry, Dr. Kalikow. We don't need to make this into Tuesday afternoon with Jerry Springer. Things just get a little hot around our house sometimes."

"It seems like they do. But without taking sides in a conflict that I'm sure predates your seeing me, let me make a few comments about what just happened because it answers the point you raised a few minutes ago, Mr. Parker."

Mr. Parker looked puzzled. I'm not sure he remembered the point he had made.

I continued, "Children learn in lots of ways. When you were talking about the way your father handled you as a kid, Mr. Parker, you were making the point that children are influenced not only by their temperament but also by the environment in which they grow up. Relationships with the important people in our lives are a powerful part of that environment.

"The threat of getting smacked in the head was just one part of your relationship with your dad. You were also influenced by all the positive emotions you had for him. You also learned by seeing the consequences of what you did. If your mom gave in every time you whined, you'd learn to whine. Yet another way kids learn is by watching their parents. Kids are like sponges; they soak up what they see and hear without even knowing it."

I stopped to catch my breath.

"Another subtle but deep influence on children is the atmosphere parents create with each other."

Mrs. Parker was becoming teary again. "Dr. Kalikow, Pete and I go back quite a ways. Maybe that's part of the problem. We've known each other so long. We dated in high school. Before we knew it, we were married and had kids. We were just kids ourselves. We love each other. But Rosie adds a big tension. I think the stress brings all the skeletons out of the closet."

Mr. Parker put his hardened hand gently on his wife's. His eyes were moist.

"Doc, I don't want you to think we're always like this or that we're one of those couples who's off talking to the lawyers. We're going to do whatever you tell us is best for Rosie. We both love her. I don't know if we can change this temperament thing, but if we can be better parents, we're going to try."

I responded, "For now, all I want you to do is keep the house a little less emotional. Rosie brings enough emotion for an entire neighborhood. You two can bring some humor and affection, but try to check the tension at the door. When the time is right, if we need to, we'll talk about all those underlying issues."

I continued, "Also, try to focus on being supportive of each other in front of Rosie. I don't want her to think she can divide and conquer. I almost don't care what the two of you decide on any particular issue. I trust your judgment. But present a united front to Rosie."

CHAPTER 8

The Parkers put the tension aside and were ready to let me continue my lecture. Explaining the multitude of factors underlying a child's behavior in a simple, straightforward manner to parents who want to understand, but want more to fix, was no easy task.

"Sometimes a child presents with an array of characteristics that are clearly interfering in their ability to function. In that case, the characteristics aren't just characteristics of temperament, they become symptoms. And if doctors have seen that combination of symptoms before, we might identify it as a disorder.

"In Rosie's case, her chronic worrying is what is known as generalized anxiety disorder. In fact, if you look closely, I think you'll find that when Rosie is irritable, she's often simply worried.

"Many kids with generalized anxiety disorder present as clingy or whiney, or they ask lots of questions looking for reassurance. They want to know why their parents aren't home from the movies yet, whether there's too much lead in the wall paint, what will happen if they fail next year's statewide math test even though they're the best math student in their class. But Rosie isn't always so obvious about what's bothering her, and her anxiety often presents not as whining but as meltdowns or blowups or that short-tempered, prickly quality.

Mr. Parker stopped me. "I know Rosie has always been a worrier, but I guess I was always more caught up in the force of her personality. I don't know if I'd prefer her to be whiney and clingy or if I'm proud that she's such a pistol."

"I'm not sure you have much of a choice, Mr. Parker."

"I guess I don't. But what makes her one way and not the other?"

"I think that these disorders, like generalized anxiety disorder, look different in different children in part because their underlying temperaments are different. It's like red paint looking different depending on what type of wood you're painting. Rosie's temperament is highly intense, not very adaptable, easily frustrated, and so on, and so her anxiety comes out as a meltdown.

"So let's get back to Rosie and her anxiety," I continued. "What worries Rosie about going to school? Perhaps she's worried that her labored writing will prevent her from keeping up with the class. Perhaps she's worried about who her new teacher will be. It's hard to know what precipitates Rosie's anxiety. She's not the kind of child who comes right out and tells you."

"You're telling me," said Mr. Parker.

"But Rosie does have a few characteristic areas of worry. One of them is being away from you. You see this at the beginning of every school year. It isn't clear that being away from you is the only cause of her worries each September, but it's clear that she clings desperately to you both, and especially Mrs. Parker, to help her deal with her anxiety."

Mrs. Parker suddenly jumped in. "Dr. Kalikow, the last issue of *Woman's Day* had an article about kids who won't go to school. It said they had something called separation anxiety disorder. And Rhoda, down the street, had the hardest time getting Jeremy on the bus. She said her psychologist said Jeremy has separation anxiety, and Rhoda thinks Rosie has it too."

I said, "Mrs. Parker, Rhoda's right in that Rosie's symptom of resisting school is similar to what is seen in children with separation anxiety disorder. So is her mild reluctance to be alone at bedtime. But I think that Rosie's difficulties separating are not pervasive enough to diagnose separation anxiety disorder. Kids with separation anxiety disorder are usually very fearful of being away from their parents. They shadow them around the house, won't let them go out on Saturday night. That's not quite Rosie. Let's just say she has some traits of this disorder."

I knew this was getting complicated, and I debated about whether to go on.

"Rosie's extreme shyness when meeting people is also not quite captured by a diagnosis of generalized anxiety disorder. We might see this as a function of Rosie's slow-to-warm temperament, or it might be the start of social anxiety disorder, which is characterized by an extreme fear of being observed, feeling scrutinized by others. People with this disorder are exquisitely sensitive to embarrassment."

From the corner of my eye, I could see Mrs. Parker nodding her head in agreement.

"For now, though, given Rosie's age and the fact that this does not interfere terribly in her functioning, I think it's simplest to see these as manifestations of Rosie's generalized anxiety disorder.

"But you can see that the thread that runs through all these diagnoses is anxiety. So one simple and accurate way to understand Rosie's difficulties is that she's greatly affected by anxiety."

"Doc, Rosie is difficult. Like you said, she's intense. She takes a while to get used to things and so on and so on. But now you sound like you're diagnosing a disease or something," Mr. Parker said.

"Mr. Parker, I'm not saying Rosie has a disease. With a disease, a doctor can tell you the cause. He can tell you what biological changes are present in the body and maybe the prognosis. For example, tuberculosis. I can tell you what bacteria cause tuberculosis. I can tell you just what happens to the lungs of someone with tuberculosis. And I can tell you what is probably going to happen to the person with tuberculosis.

"If something is called a disorder, we know less about it. We know the standard symptoms, but we don't really know what the biological changes are. We can't predict as well what is going to happen."

"I don't know, Doc. I'm an electrician. I find a power source. I run the wires. If there's a problem, I can hunt it down and fix it. I'm glad Rosie doesn't have TB, but I can relate to that. You know just what the problem is and what the solution is. With a disorder, I don't know, it sounds kind of like a bag of problems with nothing linking them together."

"Two comments, Mr. Parker. First, a disorder is a bag of problems. But I wouldn't say nothing links them together. They're a bunch of problems that are often seen together and that we assume have some common origin.

"Second, the problem with disorders of emotions, like generalized anxiety disorder, is that the problem is in the brain and that's a very tough place to study. It's relatively easy for lung doctors to get a biopsy of a lung and put it under a microscope. It's real hard to get a biopsy of a person's brain. People have an aversion to letting doctors cut out a smidgen of their brain to put under a microscope."

"You're telling me Rosie has some kind of brain disorder? Like a chemical imbalance or something?"

"I guess I'm saying that the biological seat of Rosie's difficulty is in her brain, Mr. Parker. I mean her difficulties are not in her heart, her lungs, or her liver. The brain is the organ that houses fears and worries, sadness and anger.

"But you have to appreciate, Mr. Parker, what a young science child psychiatry is. I expect that if we could have this discussion in 100 years, I could better describe the brain of someone who is worrying and the brain of someone who is worrying to excess. Right now, we're just beginning to figure out what's going on. There's lots of research going on, but if I told you anyone really understood this stuff as well as you understand the wiring in a house, I'd be lying to you.

"Also, even if there is something different in the brain of someone with an anxiety disorder, we're not sophisticated enough yet to know if the brain difference caused the anxiety or if some life experience caused the brain difference. In other words, are children with anxiety disorders born with a chemical difference in their brain that manifests as anxiety during their childhood, or do they have some experience in childhood that changes the chemicals in their brain and causes them to be anxious? Or do both of these happen?"

Mrs. Parker had been sitting quietly. She finally spoke.

"Dr. Kalikow, what I'm getting from this discussion is that you think Rosie has a disorder."

"That's right. The diagnosis of generalized anxiety disorder captures the key role anxiety plays in understanding Rosie's behavior. Some might say that Rosie has anxiety disorder, not otherwise specified, but that's just another way of saying her anxiety disorder doesn't fit neatly into any set of criteria. Rosie is complicated, though, and as we proceed, I'll also tell you about oppositional defiant disorder, which fits children who are often irritable and defiant of authority, especially at home. And I'll tell you about severe mood dysregulation, a disorder that is slowly gaining acceptance as a way to incorporate a lot of these symptoms—the anxiety, low frustration tolerance, irritability, and temper outbursts—under one diagnosis."

"Now we're talking about something I can relate to, Doc, the outbursts, the irritability . . ." said Mr. Parker.

"And we can't forget temperament," I added. "I don't want to reduce our understanding of Rosie to just a list of disorders."

Mrs. Parker responded, "Yes, I understand all that about

temperament and the environment. But you're saying that we didn't cause this disorder. I mean, if it is a biological disorder, we didn't do it. Somehow I find that a great relief." She sighed.

"Mrs. Parker, everything you do as a parent has some cumulative effect on your child. Mostly, though, you and Mr. Parker appear to be loving, caring parents. Have you made mistakes? I'm sure you have. I think that the tension in the house has increased Rosie's anxiety, exacerbated the characteristics of her temperament, and made it tough for you and Mr. Parker to work together.

"But Rosie has been different from just about day one. Your parenting didn't do that. I think a difficult Rosie caused parenting to be a really tough job, not that your parenting caused Rosie to be difficult."

"Well, Patti, I'm glad you feel better that Rosie has a bunch of disorders, but I'm not sure I'm crazy about it."

Mr. Parker had a sensitive, vulnerable side, but I was discovering that a wall of sarcasm often surrounded it. I felt angry at him when he spoke that way and couldn't imagine that Mrs. Parker didn't feel that way too.

"I'm not happy she has a disorder. But I feel like I didn't cause Rosie's difficulties, and that's a relief," Mrs. Parker responded sharply. "Besides, I know why you're having such a problem with this."

"I'm not having a problem. I'm just more interested in what we are going to do than in a disorder that may not exist. I'm just figuring we're heading towards medicine, and I'm not going there. Like Uncle Marvin always says, 'If you go to a surgeon, he operates,' and I feel comfortable with you, Doc, but I've gotta tell you, I'm worried about all I'm hearing about medicine in kids."

"I can see that worries you, Mr. Parker. But I didn't say anything about medicine. Let's take it one step at a time."

CHAPTER 9

"Dr. Kalikow, I've only got a few minutes before I have to leave to get the kids off the bus. What am I going to do tomorrow morning?"

"Okay, Mrs. Parker, let's decide what you're going to do. First, just a couple of basic rules to remember—"

"Tell me the rules, Dr. Kalikow, but just remember that I've got to leave in about 5 minutes, and I need to know what to do."

"Fair enough. First, I know it sounds impossible, but stay calm. You need your wits about you in these highly emotional times. If you lose control, and I know you will at some point, try to regain control of your anger and frustration. You'll try again next time. Unfortunately, I'm afraid there will be more than enough opportunity to try again.

"Next, remember that usually Rosie's provocative, obnoxious behavior masks her underlying anxiety and worry. Don't be provoked. Don't let Rosie dump her anxiety onto you by pulling you into the fray. Though you care deeply about Rosie, stay just a tad removed. You're going to be warm and understanding, yet a bit businesslike.

"You're also going to work on supporting each other. This is emotionally wrenching for each of you, and you need to know that the other person is supportive, not critical. When we come up with a plan, you both need to be on board."

"Brief, Doc, brief. We understand what you're saying," Mr. Parker inserted.

"Let's do a few different things," I continued. "Rosie should be seen on a regular basis for a little while, so we can learn more about her. Also, you both should be seen to talk about parenting issues. That's going to be very important."

"Who should we see for that, Dr. Kalikow? My friend Mona takes Sammy to a therapist every week. She says he only goes to the psychiatrist for a few minutes every so often to check his medicine."

Mr. Parker couldn't resist. "That's what I'm talking about, Doc. We're not using medicine. From what Patti tells me, this guy Mona sees takes a look-see for 5 minutes and charges her an arm and a leg."

"And Mona says she can never get him on the phone when she has a question. She tells me she's running the medicine show herself."

I put my hand up to stop the Parkers.

"Hold on a moment. I've got to make a few comments. First, I do

252

see children in therapy and their parents for parental counseling. Thirty years ago, when I was in training, that was almost the only treatment for children. So, yes, psychiatrists are trained to talk with patients. But Mona's right, some psychiatrists are focusing more and more on prescribing medicine and leaving therapy, and maybe even talking to patients, to everyone else. There are lots of reasons for this. Someday we'll talk about them. Not now.

"Second, although I do therapy with some patients and their families, I also prescribe medicine—when it's indicated, and after the child's parents and I have discussed it fully and they agree. As far as Rosie's concerned, nobody has mentioned medicine, and I don't know that we ever will, Mr. Parker.

"When I see patients, I usually prefer to do the therapy and be in charge of the medicine. I do write prescriptions for patients who are in therapy with psychologists and social workers I know. But more often I see the patient and do what I think needs to be done. If I think someone is more specialized in a particular type of therapy, I'll tell you so.

"For now, let's see if we can set up a behavior modification or point system to—"

Mrs. Parker jumped in, "Dr. Kalikow, we've done these before. They work for a while, then she doesn't care. Besides, I think Rosie is too far gone right now for sticker charts."

I knew that simply setting up a point system by which Rosie received a certain number of points if she made it to school without incident was too simplistic in a situation like this. Rosie was too intense, and there was too much emotional noise in the system. But I figured it would give the Parkers something to focus on, something to do, and I'd learn a lot about them by seeing what they did with the suggestion. I also knew that although many parents are initially successful using point systems, they often trip over the subtle details needed for continued success. I gave them an outline of how to implement a system by which Rosie received points for getting to school.

"Doc, I'm just not sure I agree with this. I never liked it before, either. Nobody gives me points to get up and go to work. I do it because it's my responsibility. I don't like the idea of paying Rosie to go to school."

"I appreciate your concern. Let's just use this briefly to see if we can break the cycle. I could argue that your customers reinforce you by paying you, but let's not get into that now."

"Talking about money, Doc, I like you, and I don't mind coming here to talk, but all these visits with Rosie, with us, we're talking some serious buckaroos." Mr. Parker was informal as always, but very serious. He was also correct.

I thought for a moment, then responded. "I know this is costly, Mr. Parker, but Rosie is certainly difficult, and if you continue down the road you are on, I'm not sure how it will end. Maybe she'll get easier as she gets older; maybe she won't. I think, though, that if we do some work now, to understand Rosie and help you and Mrs. Parker reduce the tension, you'll be giving Rosie and the whole family a better chance for now and in the long run."

"Listen, Doc, I'll do whatever it takes. You only go through life once, and what am I working for, if not my kids?"

CHAPTER 10

The next morning, another 7:55 A.M. phone call came in. I thought Mrs. Parker was learning my schedule and knew exactly when she might get me instead of my answering machine.

"Dr. Kalikow, this is Patti Parker. We did everything you told us. It was just one of those mornings. Rosie woke up with, you know, the look. I knew I was in for it. She ripped the point chart off the wall and tore it to shreds. She said she wasn't doing 'no f-ing chart,' if I can quote her exactly. I've had it, Dr. Kalikow. What are we going to do?"

The phone call is often a peephole into the reality of a family's life. It often makes palpable what parents have tried to describe in the office. I listened to Rosie screaming in the background.

"I can't stand you! You're a bitch! I don't give a damn about your f-ing star chart! I hate that school!" I heard a door slam.

I knew that for me the tirade would end when I hung up the phone, but that it would continue for Mrs. Parker.

"You can hear her, can't you, Dr. Kalikow? What are we going to do?"

"Why don't you get the other kids ready for school? Then after they leave, you can talk with Rosie."

"What will I say?"

"First, try to get her to sit down with you, so you can talk calmly. That might take a while. But if you stay calm and you don't chase her, I think you'll eventually be able to do it. Then tell her your expectations about going to school. Maybe it would be easier if you took her to school today and walked her to her classroom."

"I'll try, Dr. Kalikow."

CHAPTER 11

As the weeks rolled on, I received fewer frantic phone calls from Mrs. Parker. During that time, I tried seeing Rosie in the office. Sometimes Mrs. Parker could get her to come, and sometimes she couldn't. Sometimes Rosie was shy, then slowly warmed enough to tell me a joke, and sometimes she sat rolled up on a chair in the waiting room. Overall, she was slowly getting more comfortable with me.

I was also meeting periodically with Mr. and Mrs. Parker. We talked a lot about the particular incidents they faced with Rosie. Mrs. Parker was becoming a diligent note-taker. She would write down the details of the incident after it occurred, then take out her list of vignettes when she came in to see me.

The Parkers were clearly learning. The house was calmer. There was less yelling. Mr. Parker was less sarcastic and biting. The Parkers were more supportive of each other emotionally. And they stopped contradicting and undermining each other when they spoke to Rosie.

Rosie was also going to school—sometimes. Sometimes she went easily, sometimes screaming. Sometimes she feigned illness, and Mrs. Parker let herself be duped because she didn't have the strength to do otherwise. On those days, a guilt-ridden Mrs. Parker always called for my approval.

After Rosie had torn up the star chart, Mrs. Parker started walking Rosie to class. This helped a little. Then we added the star chart again. This helped a little, too. We planned for Mrs. Parker to gradually withdraw, as Rosie became more comfortable walking to class.

Often Rosie went willingly, though not happily, to class, and occasionally Willie, the gentle custodian, carried her under Mrs. Parker's supervision. Although Rosie made it to class, she frequently cursed through the first hour.

The school was terrific in supporting Mrs. Parker. Willie gave her physical support, and Mrs. Andrews, the school psychologist, gave her emotional support and tried to help Rosie's teacher appreciate the problem. The school even let Rosie stay in Mrs. Andrews's office each morning so she could slowly adapt to the day before heading off to class. There were many trials with many techniques of dealing with Rosie, and the school was with the Parkers every step of the way.

But as weeks passed, the school was running out of patience. Despite all the plans, Rosie would often yell and threaten as she adapted to the new day. Her teacher simply couldn't allow that behavior in class, but there didn't seem to be a consequence that would grab Rosie's attention. There was no reward, punishment, or principal powerful enough to dissuade her. She was faced with what seemed to be insurmountable anxiety every morning.

Mrs. Andrews called me one day to discuss Rosie. Actually, she had called to pass on the pressure she was getting from above. The school administration was suggesting that Rosie could not stay in this class. Even though the rest of the day was manageable, even though Rosie was one of the brighter children in the class, the mornings were simply too disruptive. And, although Rosie was getting to school fairly often, she had already missed 23 days of school.

Wanting Rosie to stay in this class, I pled my case.

"Mrs. Andrews, I don't know that Rosie will do any better if she gets pulled out of school. It might even set her back. Besides, she really needs the academic stimulation she gets from this class. She won't get that anywhere else."

"I know, Dr. Kalikow. I want to try to keep her here, but her teacher is at wits' end. Yesterday, Rosie told her she was a fat whore. I know Rosie feels terrible after she says it and she doesn't do that every day, but the teacher and the principal just don't know what to do. Sometimes she acts so impulsively. You don't think she has a little ADHD, do you?"

After working over the phone with Mrs. Andrews for a number of weeks, I had grown to respect her. She was perceptive and often had innovative and constructive comments about our behavioral management of Rosie. She cared. But what a powerful concept ADHD had become. When all else failed, you could raise it as a possibility. I yearned to swab a child's throat and arrive at an unequivocal diagnosis like strep.

"I don't think Rosie has ADHD," I answered. "Her impulsivity, which is really mostly in the morning, is due to anxiety. You can't be fooled by Rosie's tough facade. Underneath she's very anxious. Let me talk to her parents about keeping her in class. Then we'll talk some more."

CHAPTER 12

Mrs. Parker was taking her seat in my office. She looked glum.

"Patti, I think she's doing better," Mr. Parker offered. They had obviously been talking on the ride to my office.

"I know she is," admitted Mrs. Parker. "It's just that she's so tough. I'm exhausted, spent. I've given all I can give. I have to think about everything I say. I can never let down my guard. You just don't know how hard it is every morning. Even when she goes to school, I'm exhausted trying to get her there. Driving to the concert the other day, Rosie was tense and worried that I would hit a rabbit. Before we left for your cousin Mac's house, Rosie picked a fight with Chris. She wasn't angry at Chris. She was worried that Mac wouldn't remember that she only eats boiled hot dogs that aren't slit down the side and that there wouldn't be anything for her to eat. Everything's an issue. Everything's a battle. School is just the biggest right now."

"I spoke with Mrs. Andrews two days ago," I said. "She said that Rosie was continuing to improve, but she said the mornings are still impossible. I think she's getting pressure from above."

Mr. Parker was on alert. "What do you mean, Doc?"

"She was saying that every morning Rosie upsets the classroom for about an hour before she settles in. She implied that the school couldn't let it go on much longer."

"I'll tell you right now, Doc, no special schools. Rosie's too smart. She won't get what she needs from a class full of kids with problems."

"I understand your point, Mr. Parker, but I think the school is saying that, for whatever reason, Rosie right now has a problem with her behavior and that they can no longer deal with it."

"Doc, we've talked lots about how we should handle Rosie. But why is she doing this?"

As many times as a doctor explains something to a patient, it is always an ongoing process. I felt as if I had explained this at least a dozen times to the Parkers, but I guessed we would go over it again.

"Like we've said many times, beneath Rosie's misbehavior and irritability is anxiety," I offered.

"But you know, Dr. Kalikow," said Mrs. Parker, "you once said that Rosie has generalized anxiety disorder. I need to know if she is just anxious, or does she have a disorder?"

"Mrs. Parker, Rosie has a disorder. Her anxiety affects her functioning to a level that is clinically significant.

"Making a diagnosis is not just a matter of having a certain number of symptoms. It has to cause clinically significant dysfunction. Although that can be subjective, just being very anxious is not enough to get you a diagnosis of generalized anxiety disorder. Lots of children worry. They don't all have a disorder.

"But that diagnosis does not quite capture Rosie entirely. She also has elements of separation anxiety disorder and of social anxiety disorder. Those would account for her difficulty being away from you and her extreme shyness and fear of embarrassment. Not that she has those disorders. But if you recall our discussion of the slow-to-warm temperament, sometimes, as these children get older, their characteristics reach a level of disorder."

"So you're saying Rosie has three psychiatric disorders, Dr. Kalikow?" Mrs. Parker asked.

"No, Mrs. Parker. Rosie's worrying clearly affects her functioning. That's generalized anxiety disorder, and that's one disorder. But Rosie also has characteristics of separation anxiety disorder and of social anxiety disorder. When a child has one of these anxiety disorders they often have elements of the others."

Mr. Parker said, "But you talk about that opposition disorder sometimes, Doc, and that always sounds like Rosie to me."

"Oppositional defiant disorder. As we've talked about in the past, that's a diagnosis that captures the bald defiance of some children. It helps account for their anger. Seeing Rosie as ODD has also helped me guide you in your behavioral treatment of Rosie, and I think that's been at least a little successful."

Mrs. Parker gently turned her body away from Mr. Parker, but she kept him in her visual field.

"With everything evolving as you say it is, Dr. Kalikow, with all these diagnoses, how do you know when to use medicine?" Mrs. Parker asked.

Mr. Parker tensed as Mrs. Parker finished her question.

"Mrs. Parker, I'm happy to answer your question, but I think we have to acknowledge that Mr. Parker is uncomfortable with the idea of medicine. So I don't think that discussing it is the best use of our time."

"Thanks, Doc. Yeah, I'm uncomfortable with medicine," Mr. Parker said, as he sighed, running both his hands over his forehead and through his hair. "But I'll tell you, Doc, I'm feeling stretched. I look pretty opinionated, but don't think I haven't been thinking, and thinking hard, all these weeks.

"No, I don't like the idea of medicine. We don't know the long-term effects of this stuff. How is it going to affect her in 20 years? I don't want Rosie to be dependent on medicine, like my brother. The stuff scares me.

"But I see where Patti's going with this. I know that life is tough for Rosie. If there's something that can help her . . . "

"I appreciate what you've been going through, Mr. Parker. But we haven't even established that medicine would be a good idea for Rosie. Maybe I should answer Mrs. Parker's question about how we decide to use medicine."

CHAPTER 13

"Let me start with a question," I said. "What's the evidence that medicine can help Rosie?"

"Doc, let me start with a question," Mr. Parker chimed in. "What medicine are we talking about here?"

"Fair enough. If Rosie were to be on medicine, I would consider a family of medicines called the SSRIs, the selective serotonin reuptake inhibitors. You don't have to remember that, but this is the family of medicines that includes Prozac and others."

"Dr. Kalikow, isn't Prozac an antidepressant? You didn't say anything about depression," Mrs. Parker said.

"Prozac and the other SSRIs are mainly marketed as antidepressants. That doesn't mean they're helpful only in depression. Some of the SSRIs have also been found to be useful in other disorders, such as obsessive-compulsive disorder and social anxiety disorder.

"Sometimes a medication might be useful for a particular disorder, but the drug company decides not to seek FDA approval for the use of that drug in that disorder. That doesn't mean the medicine isn't useful, just that the FDA hasn't approved the medicine for that disorder. This off-label use is perfectly legal and ethical and is done every day by doctors across the country using a wide array of medicines, not just psychiatric medicines."

"So you're saying, Dr. Kalikow, that the SSRIs are approved for use in depression, but they're also useful in anxiety?" asked Mrs. Parker.

"That's right. Actually, some of the SSRIs are approved for use in adults with certain anxiety disorders, too."

"Doc, you seemed very careful about saying that the medicine is approved for adults. You didn't say anything about kids," said the ever-vigilant Mr. Parker.

"One of the difficulties in child psychiatry is that many of the medicines we use have never been FDA-approved for use in children. Some are approved for certain disorders in children of a certain age."

"So the SSRIs have been approved for use by the FDA in children with separation anxiety disorder and generalized anxiety disorder? Or is there just a lot of research that tells you this is going to help Rosie?" asked Mrs. Parker.

"What do you mean 'this is going to help Rosie'?" Mr. Parker blurted out, back on patrol. "Nobody said anything about Rosie. We're just talking. Right, Doc?"

"That's right, Mr. Parker."

"Okay," Mrs. Parker conceded.

"The evidence that an SSRI could help a child with these two anxiety disorders comes from a few sources. First, there are studies that show these medicines to be of help in adults with certain anxiety disorders.

"Next, there is some research to show that the SSRIs are helpful for some children with certain anxiety disorders. That research doesn't show that all children with a particular anxiety disorder are helped. But there are some studies that suggest that many children are helped.

"And, last, when we use SSRIs in children and adolescents with depression, we often note that their anxiety also is reduced."

"None of that seems real, real solid, Doc."

"Mr. Parker, it's fairly clear that these medicines can be helpful to children with anxiety disorders. Some well-done studies prove that these medicines lead to diminished anxiety in children with anxiety

261

disorders. Doctors are prescribing these medicines and discovering that they are often helpful with a minimum of risk.

"We use the time-honored formula of weighing risks versus potential benefits to decide if a particular medicine is worth trying."

"Kind of doing what works?" Mr. Parker asked.

"That's a good summary, Mr. Parker."

CHAPTER 14

A few weeks into January, Mr. and Mrs. Parker returned. This time it was Mr. Parker who looked demoralized and dejected.

"Doc, tell me again that Rosie's an anxious kid who doesn't mean any harm."

"What happened?" I asked.

Mrs. Parker let Mr. Parker explain.

"First of all, she was doing better. I mean, she was getting to school pretty much every day. Wouldn't you say, Patti?" Mrs. Parker nodded. "But a couple of weeks ago, after Christmas vacation ended . . . you were right, Doc, those vacations are killers. Getting her back to school was murder. I purposely stayed home that Monday morning to help Patti. I thought we were back to square one. The screaming and the running out of the house. We finally got her to school. I'll tell you, Doc, it was a pleasure to get to work.

"Anyway, she was getting to school a little easier by the end of the week. But she can be tough even when she's not in school. Some days she walks around the house like she's got a fly up her—you know.

"So Rosie's playing Nintendo. She just got it for Christmas. She must have been on it for an hour, and then she finishes. She leaves the playroom and goes into the kitchen. Meanwhile, her little brother, Matt, has been wanting to play the whole time. But he's been waiting patiently because he knows that if he asks Rosie at the wrong time she'll scream bloody murder. So when Rosie leaves, Matt decides to sit down and play.

"Well, when Rosie heard that music starting, she was in there like a bolt. 'Get off my Nintendo! I was playing! You didn't ask me!'"

Mr. Parker was imitating the grating, offensive, inflexible quality to Rosie's voice. He was very effective. I had to refrain from telling him to shut up and go to his room.

"So I tried to explain to Rosie that she had stopped using it and that we need to learn to share and that Matt had been waiting patiently. And I'm telling you, Doc, I was calm and collected. I mean, I was so angry inside. You had to see poor little Matt, who didn't mean to hurt anyone, stunned by the attack. Then, when Rosie stopped screaming for just a minute, Matt looks her right in the eye and says, like he really understands her, 'It's okay, Rosie. I know it's your Nintendo. Can you tell me when I can have a turn?' I mean who's the older sibling? You had to see the look on his face. But she didn't give an inch, not one inch.

"It's not just that she was completely unreasonable and inflexible, Doc. She just looked sour and unhappy. Not sad, but irritated. But later that day, we were going to see that new movie with those cartoon characters she loves, and she was as happy as a lark, Doc."

"I understand what you're saying, Mr. Parker. It isn't simply that Rosie has anxiety, she's also rigid, irritable, and intense. You originally came to see me because she wasn't going to school. But on a day-in, day-out basis I bet it's those personality characteristics that make you crazy."

"They dominate our life, Dr. Kalikow," said Mrs. Parker.

"She's right, Doc. Rosie just colors the whole house. She can be wonderful at times. But other times—"

"Would that get better if Rosie was on medicine, Dr. Kalikow?" Mrs. Parker asked directly. There was a loud silence from Mr. Parker.

"I don't know, Mrs. Parker. An incident like the one Mr. Parker just related demonstrates Rosie's irritability and rigidity. She doesn't fit your classic picture of depression. But medicine might make her more flexible by diminishing her anxiety."

Mrs. Parker turned to her husband and said with calm and certainty, "Pete, I think we have to consider using medicine."

"Patti, once we go down this road, I'm not sure where we'll end up. Look at Terry."

"Pete, we're not talking about your brother. We're talking about our daughter, Rosie. Terry has . . . Terry was mixed up with drugs . . . I don't know what Terry has. But Rosie is not Terry. We have a responsibility to do what we think is best for Rosie. Don't look at the next 20 years, Pete. Let's just focus on the next few weeks. Couldn't we simply try Rosie on medicine?" Mrs. Parker was not pleading, but she knew she would not proceed without Mr. Parker. Despite what she was saying, she was unsure about medicine herself and wanted Mr. Parker's support. I was moved by the intimacy of this couple trying to reconcile their deepest fears for the sake of their child.

Mr. Parker was silent. He nervously ran his hands over his head. He looked like the general who knew the war was over but could not concede.

"Patti, the medicine isn't magic. You're not going to know anything in a few weeks."

I interjected, "The fact is that these medicines can take a while to work. Sometimes a few weeks or even a few months. This can be real frustrating at times. If we try medicine, we should be committed to giving it a trial of a few months. There's also a chance that if one medicine doesn't work, another from the same family will."

I knew what Mr. Parker was thinking, so I added, "That doesn't mean we go from medicine to medicine until we try them all. It simply means that the rate of return after trying two medicines is probably better than trying only one."

Mr. Parker had his head in his hands. Mrs. Parker gently put a hand on his shoulder. "I don't know," he said.

"Pete, what are the risks of not using medicine? We could go on like this. She might not be able to stay in the school she belongs in. Our house is a battle zone. And most important, Rosie is not happy.

You see the other kids. If Rosie could be happy like that, why shouldn't she be? I'm afraid what she'll be like in 10 years if we don't give her medicine."

Mr. Parker picked his face up from out of his hands. He looked me in the eye and asked that most dreaded question.

"Doc, if Rosie was your daughter, what would you do?"

CHAPTER 15

"If I were Mr. Parker, what would I do?" I thought to myself. It's necessary—in fact, mandatory—that a doctor not overidentify with his or her patient. One needs to keep a healthy distance from one's emotions, so that one can think clearly about the risks and benefits of a potential treatment.

On the other hand, if a physician is too distant from his or her emotions and can't step briefly into the shoes of the patient, the doctor sacrifices one of the profession's most useful tools, empathy.

"What would I do?" I thought. My heart went out to Mr. and Mrs. Parker. They were nice people, hardworking people who cared about their children.

They shouldn't have to put their child on a medicine. On the other hand, their child shouldn't have to grow up with the chronic pain of irritability and anxiety, and they shouldn't have to live in a war zone. There was at least a fair chance the medicine would help considerably with a low probability of anything terrible happening. I had no idea what I would do, and I admired their courage in trying to tackle the decision, in risking change.

I was about to sidestep Mr. Parker's question and jump into outlining the risks and benefits of the medicine, when Mr. Parker blurted out, "Okay, let's do it." He had the "don't think twice" look of a high-wire artist who commits to the first step.

"Tell me the side effects, Doc. Let's go over everything. But as long as you tell me we're not etching this in stone, that we can always stop the medicine, and as long as you tell me that there probably won't be terrible side effects, I think we should do it. I don't think we should keep living the way we've been living."

Mrs. Parker looked relieved. She was willing to trade her family's painful present for whatever uncertainty the future had in store.

"Thanks, Pete. I think it's the best decision," she said.

I spent the next 30 minutes answering Mr. Parker's questions about the different families of medicine and the different medicines within the family I thought would be most appropriate for Rosie, the SSRIs. We chose a particular SSRI, Zoloft, because even though Rosie did not have obsessive-compulsive disorder, at least Zoloft was approved by the FDA to be used in children with OCD. Compared to Prozac, Zoloft also stayed in the body for a short time, which Mr. Parker appreciated. We reviewed side effects, dosages, and possible interactions with other medicines.

"So, Doc, you're telling me that this stuff can make Rosie more anxious or even like a manic depressive? You're saying there's a small chance that she becomes suicidal?" Mr. Parker was shaking his head slowly side to side. "I don't know, Patti. I don't know if I want to do this."

"Mr. Parker, I appreciate your concern. But realize that if we start at a low dose and increase it slowly, those side effects are very unlikely. And if they do happen, the worst-case scenario is that we lower the dose or stop the medicine completely, and within a few days you'll never know Rosie had those side effects. What I'm saying is that the side effects sound dramatic and they could be briefly uncomfortable. But I think that if we're careful and keep a close eye on Rosie, especially over the first month or two, she shouldn't have a problem."

Now it was Mrs. Parker's turn.

"Dr. Kalikow, I heard from my friend, Pam, that Zoloft causes ringing in the ears."

"I've never heard of that, Mrs. Parker. But I have to tell you a saying I have: Give me any medicine on earth, and I'll find someone in Iowa whose hair turned green from that medicine. There is risk involved with any medicine."

Mr. Parker was shaking his head again.

I continued. "So while I can't tell you that Rosie will not have ringing ears on Zoloft, I can tell you the probability of that is very, very low, just as the probability of your chair collapsing is very, very low. Before you take any medicine, you weigh the risks and the benefits. The risk of ringing in the ears doesn't weigh in very heavily. The possibility that Rosie's quality of life will improve does."

I gave the Parkers my best guess as to how long Rosie would probably stay on medicine.

"I have to reiterate one thing. All these medicines—that is, all the SSRIs—can work slowly. Every so often someone has a miraculous turnaround in 2 days. But more likely, it can take weeks to work, and that's after we reach an effective dose. And I don't know what an effective dose is for any particular child. So we increase the dose slowly and wait and then wait some more.

"What I'm saying is that this can be a frustrating process. And even though, Mr. Parker, you're feeling ambivalent about using medicine now, the time will come when you're frustrated and impatient and wanting it to work. And you're going to say to me, 'Doc, when is this stuff going to work?' And I'm going to tell you to sit back and be patient. I'm going to tell you not to overanalyze every little thing Rosie does to see if the medicine is working."

We finished by discussing what we would tell Rosie.

CHAPTER 16

Two days later, Rosie came in for an appointment. It was an inconvenient time for Mr. Parker, but he left his worksite to join us for a half hour. He wanted to be there when we presented the idea of medicine to Rosie.

Luckily, Rosie was relatively positive that day. We made a little small talk. I asked her how school was that week. School was good, she said, and she went on to tell me all about the dying bird her teacher, Mrs. Martin, had brought back to life. Mr. and Mrs. Parker sat, smiling, as Rosie went on about the details of Mrs. Martin's life-saving efforts.

"Rosie, tell Dr. Kalikow about how well you're getting to school," said Mrs. Parker, stretching the truth but trying to be encouraging and optimistic.

Rosie looked at the floor and was suddenly quiet. She was embarrassed and was not about to bring up her morning difficulties. I took the opportunity to jump in.

"Rosie, I know how hard it's been for you to go to school in the morning. Your mom and dad tell me how hard you try."

Rosie looked up at me with a sudden smile plastered across her face. "Do you know where the general kept his armies?" Rosie was engaged in one of her more mature defense modes, joke telling. She wasn't about to discuss getting to school, but at least she wasn't running down the street.

"No. Where?" I answered.

"In his sleevies, silly."

"That's a good one, Rosie." If I waited for Rosie to acknowledge her anxiety so that we could discuss the use of medicine, we'd never start the medicine. I decided to be direct.

"Rosie, I know that it's hard to talk about going to school. And your mom and dad and Mrs. Martin and Mrs. Andrews and I all know how hard you're trying every morning. What if I told you that there was a medicine that might make it easier for you in the morning? Do you think there could be such a medicine?"

"What did one wall say to the other?" Rosie asked, ignoring her anxiety and my attempts to bring her into the process.

"Rosie," said her mother, "listen to Dr. Kalikow."

"That's okay," I said, waving off Mrs. Parker's intervention on my behalf. "What?"

"I'll meet you at the corner." Another big smile.

"Rosie, your mom and dad and I talked about giving you a medicine that would make it a little easier for you to go to school in the morning.

You'd still have to try real hard, but this might make it easier. Do you have any questions, Rosie?"

"What did the carpet say to the floor?"

"That's not the kind of question I had in mind. And I think you know it," I said with a knowing grin. "But what did the carpet say to the floor?"

"Gotcha covered."

No, she wasn't the participant in the discussion I would have liked, but at least Rosie was talking to me. It was almost time to stop.

"Dr. Kalikow?" Rosie asked.

"Yes, Rosie?"

"Will I take the medicine with breakfast or at night?"

CHAPTER 17

Two days later, on Sunday morning, I received a message from Mrs. Parker.

"Hi, Dr. Kalikow. It's Patti Parker. We started the medicine, and Pete wanted me to ask you a question. Give me a call when you get a chance."

When I called, Mrs. Parker picked up the phone.

"Thanks for calling, Dr. Kalikow. We gave Rosie the medicine yesterday morning, and last night she had a headache. Pete just wanted me to call to ask you if you think it could be the medicine."

"Well, almost any medicine can cause a headache in some people. So it could be from the medicine. But how's Rosie feeling otherwise?"

"She's in bed this morning with a fever of 102°."

"I think the headache is probably from Rosie coming down with a virus. Let's continue the medicine. If the headache continues after she's better, we'll rethink our plan."

"Okay, Dr. Kalikow. That sounds right. I don't know why I didn't think of that. I won't keep you. Thanks again."

"No problem, Mrs. Parker. I'll talk to you soon."

Rosie continued on the medicine over the next 3 weeks. In deference to the medical maxim to "start low and go slow," we had started at a low dose. And although Rosie was not having side effects, she wasn't improving. But one of the hidden benefits of the medicine was that we had bought some time with the school staff, who were doing their best while we waited for the medicine to work. Rosie had been given a reprieve.

There was still pressure in the system, however. The school continued to deal often with a screaming Rosie in the morning. Mrs. Andrews was wonderfully supportive of Mrs. Martin, the classroom teacher, but Rosie was seeing to it that each was more than earning her salary.

After about 3 weeks, we increased the dose a notch, and a few weeks later, another notch.

At the next meeting with Mr. and Mrs. Parker, Mrs. Parker was clearly getting itchy.

"Dr. Kalikow, I was talking to my Aunt Marie about Rosie. She's a psychologist at a school for kids with problems. She said that the psychiatrist at her school often uses a cocktail—that's what she called it, a cocktail—of Zoloft and a medicine called Rispidilone or something."

"Risperdal?"

"Yeah, that's it. Risperdal. She says it calms them down pretty quickly. She says the Zoloft is good for the serotonin and the Risperdal is good for the dopamine."

Mr. Parker was shaking his head again, anxiously running his hands through his hair, which seemed to be thinning by the minute.

"A cocktail? What are you talking about, Patti? We're not mixing drinks at some dinner party. We're talking about medicine."

"Mrs. Parker," I said, "a couple of thoughts. First, as I mentioned to you before we started the Zoloft, these types of medicines can take a while to work. It can be very frustrating. We don't want to increase the dose of medicine too quickly, or we might pass the minimum dose necessary and reach a dose that is too high and gives Rosie side effects. So while I know how frustrating it must be, I think we should simply continue with the one medicine.

"Also, I need to caution you about seeing these medicines in simple terms, even though that's the way everybody talks about them. We can't reduce Rosie's difficulty to a little too much serotonin or not enough dopamine. We can't assume that any of these medicines works solely on one chemical in one part of the brain."

"I'm sorry. I guess I just really want something to make a difference already. The other day Chris spread out the sports page on the table, and it touched Rosie's book. She had a fit. Of course, Chris apologized, shook his head, and went to his room. The whole house revolves around that child."

"I know how difficult it is for you all," I said, "but let's continue with the medicine as we had planned."

"Not a problem, Doc," said Mr. Parker, "Let me take care of Aunt Marie."

CHAPTER 18

A month later, Mr. and Mrs. Parker were in the office telling me about Rosie's progress. At this point, I was seeing Rosie or her parents every 2 weeks. She had been on the same dose of medicine for about 4 weeks.

"I don't know, Dr. Kalikow, I think we're turning a corner. Lately, she seems easier. She doesn't get frustrated as quickly. She goes with the flow. I mean, she's still Rosie. She still takes on the worries of the world. But I don't know—the house is just quieter. What do you think, hon?"

I wasn't sure about Rosie, but there was certainly a warmth between Mr. and Mrs. Parker of which I only had glimpses previously.

"Patti's right, Doc. Rosie's still Rosie, but she's a toned-down Rosie. She's not a zombie or anything. She's just easier to live with."

"She definitely does better the mornings that Pete is home. He's been trying to go to work a little later on Mondays. But there's no more running away. Some days she still begs me to stay home from school, almost like it's a habit. I'm always trying to distract her, give her a quick answer, then move on.

"And she's less angry than before. When I'm driving her in the car, she doesn't kick the back of my seat when she's angry at me.

"But she's still anxious. She says she won't return to ballet. But that's okay. I can deal with that. She's always got to be thinking about something, anticipating, worrying."

"Like at night, Doc. She still wants to be near us. We don't let her sleep in our bed anymore, but the night before last, I woke up and found her sleeping on the floor right outside our door. I almost started to cry."

Mrs. Parker took over. "Life seems so easy for Chris and Matt. They go to soccer. They do well in school. They get along with everyone. I know Rosie is jealous of them. She almost comes right out and says it."

"It does seem like the medicine is helping," I said. "Over the next few weeks and even months, hopefully her anxiety will continue to diminish. But there's no magic. You'll have to keep trying to figure out ways of dealing with her anxiety, her rigidity, her intensity. But you're doing a terrific job."

CHAPTER 19

"Dr. Kalikow, this was different. This was not Rosie. In the past, even though she would have had a tantrum in public and not given a hoot that she was making a fool of herself, there were certain behaviors she just would have been too embarrassed to do in public."

I maintain a healthy skepticism about some things parents tell me, but I also strongly respect some parents' certainty about the subtleties of their child's behavior. Whatever had happened, Mrs. Parker was sure this was not typical Rosie.

"What happened?" I asked with more than a hint of curiosity.

"One of Pete's customers gave us tickets to the ballgame. The boys were in heaven. Rosie was, you know, *mezza mezza* about the whole thing, but she went without a fuss. Anyway, we're sitting in these front-row seats. Not front row right on the field, but one level up.

"Anyway, we're sitting in these seats, and everyone stands for the national anthem, and Rosie goes up to the rail in front of these seats and leans over the rail . . . "

My brain was telling me that Mr. and Mrs. Parker would not have been so calm if anything terrible had happened, but my heart was saying, "Oh, no. Don't tell me she . . . "

Mrs. Parker went on, ". . . she leans over the rail and squirts some soda through her teeth onto the people below. At first, I couldn't believe my eyes. Ordinarily, Rosie would have been mortified at the embarrassment of doing something like that.

"So I said to her—I mean, I was so shocked I almost yelled during the national anthem and sent the poor child flying over the railing—I said to her, 'Rosie, what are you doing?' And she looks at me like 'Mom, what's the problem?' and she says, 'I was just trying to see what they'd do.'"

"It was a little weird, Doc," said Mr. Parker.

"What do you make of it?" I asked.

Mrs. Parker answered, "Lately, Rosie has this kind of a 'whatever' attitude. If you didn't know her, you might not think anything of it. But there's a difference. She's a little more, I don't know, brassy. She has a kind of 'who cares?' attitude. I don't know if I'm explaining this the right way, but there's a difference."

"You're doing fine, Mrs. Parker. Some observations are difficult to capture in words. I'm glad you brought up your concerns because there's a possibility that this is a side effect of the medicine."

"Doc, don't tell me that spitting soda over a rail is a side effect listed in one of those fat books you've got there," a grinning Mr. Parker gestured toward my bookshelf. I thought Mr. Parker was actually beginning to like a less rigid Rosie and that he was afraid to acknowledge that this could be a side effect.

"Well, Mr. Parker, sometimes with the SSRIs people can develop a slightly uninhibited quality. For example, I once had a very anxious, timid teenager who began to tell off the school bully. His anxiety decreased a little too much. People need a bit of anxiety to prevent them from acting dangerously. I had another teenager who shoplifted a few DVDs. He knew it was wrong, but he just figured, 'Whatever, I probably won't get caught.'"

"What if we changed SSRIs?" offered an always-prepared Mrs. Parker.

"There's no reason to think she wouldn't have the same response from another SSRI. She might not, but she might," I answered. "Lowering the dose is probably the most prudent course to take. We'll go back down a notch and see how she does."

"One second, Doc. If this medicine can make Rosie so 'whatever,' how do we know what it's doing to her personality? I know Rosie's doing well, but I'm worried that we're changing her brain."

I needed to respond candidly to maintain the Parkers' trust yet help Mr. Parker keep his concern in perspective, even though I wasn't sure what the proper perspective was. I started slowly, to allow myself to prepare a cogent response.

"Mr. Parker, Rosie is doing better on the medicine. She's getting to school. She's doing better with the other kids. She's doing well with her schoolwork. Your house is quieter, with less tension between you and your wife and between Rosie and everyone else.

"But the fact is that we are changing Rosie's brain chemistry. That's how these medicines work. We have an idea how they work, but I've always said to you that we are only beginning to understand how brain chemistry correlates with behavior. We've got miles and miles to go.

"So ultimately, we need to weigh the risks of using the medicine against the benefits. The immediate benefits are pretty clear. There might be long-term benefits as Rosie matures without some of her former difficulties.

"Some of the risks are clear. Like these short-term side effects. The longer-run side effects are hazier. We haven't studied children who have taken these medicines for a prolonged time and are now in their 30s. The medicine simply hasn't been around that long.

"But we do have research on generations of other mammals that does not indicate a problem. And we don't have a particular reason to think that this should be a problem, especially if we try not to keep Rosie on the medicine for too long.

"So here's what I suggest. Rosie is unquestionably benefiting from the medicine. Let's deal with the short-term side effect, this change in attitude, by lowering the dose. Whether she'll have long-term side effects is unknown. We have no crystal ball. But our best guess is that she won't.

"So we have a clear benefit versus a hopefully unlikely risk. I think it would be best for Rosie to stay on the medicine for the near term. And we'll try to stop the medicine after a reasonable time period. But as always, you and Mrs. Parker have the final say."

I was waiting for Mr. Parker to nervously run his hands through his hair, but he didn't.

"I understand what you're saying, Doc. And I guess I agree. I don't want to give up what I've seen. Patti, I say we lower the dose, like Doc here says. And we'll see what happens."

A less than certain Mrs. Parker agreed, "Okay, Pete, I think you're right."

CHAPTER 20

When I opened my office door, Rosie was standing in the waiting room. She had obviously been waiting for me to open the door. Her parents were seated. Mr. Parker held a gift box on his lap.

"Dr. Kalikow, why did the man kiss—"

An embarrassed Mr. Parker quickly interrupted. "Rosie, why don't you tell Dr. Kalikow the one about, you know, catching flies?"

"Oh, Dad. Dr. Kalikow doesn't care if it's about—"

"I think it would be better, Rosie."

"Okay. What has 18 legs and catches flies?"

"Uh, I give up. What has 18 legs and catches flies?"

"A baseball team."

"You got me, Rosie. Why don't you come in, and in a little while, I'll see your mom and dad?"

Rosie entered the office eagerly. She seemed to have lots to tell. Not about medicine or anxiety or temperament. Jokes. That's what she wanted to talk about. Was she avoiding the difficult topics? Perhaps. But she was also doing much better.

We were approaching the end of the school year. A changed Rosie was nearing this year's academic finish line. She was a more relaxed Rosie. She smiled more easily and was having fewer meltdowns. Over the course of the year, she had started learning to recognize when her anxiety level was rising and what she could do about it.

Rosie did not say much about the medicine. Once she said she was glad she took it because it gave her better control of her temper, but I wasn't sure those were Rosie's words. She actually seemed oblivious to taking medicine. She took it because her parents gave it to her. Once she started taking it without objection, I figured we would remain in the clear.

After a little while, Rosie went into the waiting room, and her parents came into the office.

Mr. Parker handed me the gift box. He seemed a bit self-conscious as he looked down at the floor.

"We brought you a little something so you and your wife could celebrate the end of the school year. We're finished the school year. She can have you back."

Mrs. Parker added, "I guess we're going to make it, Dr. Kalikow. We really appreciate everything you've done over this year. We know everything's not all better. She's still Rosie. But we just wanted to say thank you." Mrs. Parker was finally beginning to look more at ease. There are few thank you's as satisfying as those from a grateful parent.

"I'll be honest with you, Doc. I still hate the medicine. I can't get used to the idea that my kid needs to take medicine, even though I now see what you're talking about when you say Rosie's biologically different from the boys. I know the medicine is helping, but I still worry. What can I tell you, Doc? I'm a father. I've got to worry about this stuff."

"You have every right to worry, Mr. Parker. Rosie's your daughter. Parenting is filled with lots of tough decisions. Using medicine is only one of them."

"Isn't it the truth, Dr. Kalikow? We still struggle every day with parenting Rosie," said Mrs. Parker.

"And we struggle every day with the idea that she's taking medicine," added Mr. Parker.

"And, that's okay, Mr. Parker, that's okay."

For the Parkers, the hard work is far from over. As Rosie changes, so too might her treatment, and the Parkers will continue to reevaluate their decision.

Every child and every family is unique. Let's review the principles that guided the Parkers; this will help you in your own decision of whether your child should use medicine.

CHAPTER 19

The Time Is Now

||||||||||||||||||||||||||||||||||||||||||||||||||||||||||||||||||

Crunch time. Medicine, or not? The time to decide is now. Wait too long, and your child is older, and the decision has been made.

But how to decide?

First, evaluate the benefits and risks of medicine. This is subjective, as different parents will value different outcomes and fear different risks. You will need a talking relationship with your child's doctor so that you feel comfortable enough to share your concerns and have enough time to ask your questions.

Don't feel rushed. Most decisions about psychiatric medicine are not emergency decisions. Although the patient's safety must be assured, even suicidal depression is not a *pharmacological* emergency, given the few weeks' lag in the time antidepressants take to work.

Next, though a parent's most dreaded fear is to make the wrong decision, remember that you can change your mind. You can start medicine, then stop it, although you should not do so without discussing it with your physician. Medicine can be given a trial. If it is ineffective or your child suffers an uncomfortable side effect, the medicine can be stopped. For most psychiatric medicines, there is minimal risk of dangerous side effects in the short run. If there is a positive response, then you'll have to decide whether to continue medicine, but at least you'll do so with more information.

Keep your emotions in check and your expectations modest. Don't allow your hopes to turn into visions of unrealistic and unlikely benefits, or your fears to turn into imagined side effects.

Use these questions as a guide:

Benefits

1. Which specific symptoms will improve by taking medicine?
2. What is the likelihood that these symptoms will improve?
3. How will you monitor these symptoms for improvement?
4. Will the benefit be limited to a particular time and place, such as school or homework time? Is that okay?
5. How much more functional will your child be?
6. Can this benefit be accomplished without medicine? If so, how?
7. Who else will benefit from your child taking medicine?
8. Will their benefit come around to benefit your child?
9. Is the medicine being used for an FDA-approved indication, or is this an off-label use of medicine?
10. If off-label, how commonly is the medicine used for this purpose?

Risks

1. What are the side effects of the medicine?
2. How common are they?
3. Are the side effects nuisance-level, or are they truly dangerous—life-threatening, irreversible, or very painful?
4. When might the side effects begin?
5. Can your child benefit from medicine, then discontinue it before the side effects begin?
6. If you stop the medicine, how quickly will the side effects reverse—within hours, days, or months?
7. How does the medicine interact with other medicines being taken?

The Grid

Now force your assessment into the following grid (Figure 19.1). Rate the potential benefit of using medicine as high or low. Rate the potential risk as high or low. Think about the concrete benefits and risks to your child, temporarily putting aside consideration of the subtle and amorphous consequences medicine has on society. Don't disregard them, but for now, focus on the concrete.

Figure 19.1 Rating Potential Benefits and Risks

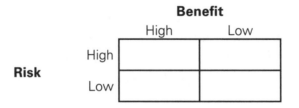

Be slightly callous in making your assessments. Helping a child in school is of *relatively* low benefit compared to treating a suicidal depression. Side effects that are reversible or not life-threatening are of *relatively* low risk compared to irreversible or life-threatening side effects.

Here are examples of each type of situation:

Low Benefit, Low Risk

Sonny is 14 years old. He has a long history of mild ADHD and mild learning disabilities and was treated with Ritalin during elementary school. He is now in ninth grade and has found his stride. Because he can focus through most of his classes, he does not want to take medicine for the school day. With high school's greater demand on reading and writing, however, focusing on homework continues to be a burden. Despite attempts to manage homework in a manner suitable to his ADHD, Sonny continues to have difficulty completing it. This is much improved when Sonny takes Ritalin after school.

Sonny clearly benefits from taking Ritalin, but the benefit is relatively low. If medicine were not available, perhaps Sonny would have some academic difficulties, and maybe his self-esteem would take a small though transient hit. But one has the sense that Sonny would go on his merry way to college and eventually find his niche in life. Sonny is otherwise happy and has good prospects for the future. The benefit of Ritalin to Sonny is relatively low, but so is the risk. He is taking a medicine that has been used for decades, and if it is taken responsibly, there is no reason to believe the medicine will cause irreversible damage. Although there is always risk, for Sonny we would have to rate the risk as low.

High Benefit, Low Risk

Callie is 9 and is stuck in a morass of compulsions that dominate her life. She has obsessive-compulsive disorder, manifested by her illogically dividing the world into permissible "clean" areas and forbidden "dirty" areas. Her home is clean, and her school is dirty. Therefore Callie refuses to go to school for fear of bringing home dirt that would then pollute her home. By October, she has missed 3 weeks of school. In the bathroom she goes through an elaborate hour-long ritual to clean herself for fear of bringing "dirt" into the rest of the house. Cognitive-behavioral therapy has been tried, but Callie's parents are too easily frustrated to assist her. No therapist is available to come to Callie's house.

Callie will be started on the SSRI fluvoxamine for OCD. The potential benefit is great. If the medicine helps, Callie will be able to do some of the basics of life, such as toileting and going to school, in a far less laborious manner. She will be able to go to a friend's house after school and to a movie on the weekend. The risk is low. Fluvoxamine is FDA-approved for use in children with OCD. Fatal and other irreversible side effects are essentially nonexistent. Potential side effects will need to be monitored, but there is no reason to believe that they would be permanent if fluvoxamine is discontinued.

This decision is straightforward. Medicine can return a child to being functional without significant risk.

Low Benefit, High Risk

Maury is 5 years old. Though he was a fairly easygoing 3-year-old, for the past year he has been rambunctious and oppositional. He curses at his parents, who are in the throes of a contentious divorce. They simply don't know what to do with Maury. The frustrated pediatrician has tried unsuccessfully to treat Maury with Adderall and Concerta. He refers Maury to a pediatric specialist for evaluation. The specialist examines Maury and finds no evidence of physical dysfunction, but she feels pressured by Maury's distraught mother to prescribe something to try to solve this problem. Maury's mother tells the doctor that her husband's attorney is driving her crazy, threatening to change custody arrangements, and she simply cannot deal with the divorce and an ever-screaming Maury, who is about to get booted out of kindergarten. The physician writes a prescription for Risperdal. She'd like to see Maury for follow-up in 3 months.

Maury's mother has her hands full, but there is little chance Risperdal will help. It's likely that Maury is responding to the turmoil within his family. The preferred treatment would be to help Maury and his family through their difficult times. This will not be easy, but it makes sense. Risperdal is not approved for use in 5-year-olds and has not been sufficiently studied in that age group. It is being used without a clear diagnosis having been made. The proper diagnosis, adjustment disorder, would not be an indication for the use of Risperdal. The medicine also comes with the risk of reversible weight gain, diabetes, and, less likely, a potentially irreversible movement disorder. Even if Maury benefits from taking the medicine, a 3-month follow-up is entirely too long.

One can appreciate the busy specialist's desire to help but be alarmed by the low potential benefit for the risk.

High Benefit, High Risk

Kayla is 15 years old. After having been an irritable, impulsive elementary-school student with learning disabilities, for the past 3 years she has been plagued with more severe psychiatric symptoms. Kayla is morose and sometimes suicidal. Often she sits alone in her room slicing her forearm with a kitchen knife. She does not talk to her parents, aside from screaming at them to leave her alone and threatening to run away from home, which she has tried twice. After school, Kayla regularly eats a pint of ice cream and a box of donuts, then immediately vomits them up. Kayla has episodes of high energy during which she doesn't go to sleep until 3 A.M. She has been caught stealing laxatives from the local drug store and has had a host of sexual liaisons with boys she barely knows from neighboring schools. Kayla also has a long history of tics. Her paternal grandfather had been hospitalized for manic depression (bipolar disorder) and eventually committed suicide.

Kayla has been in therapy for years and has been tried on a number of different medicines. Currently, she takes Depakote, Seroquel, and Paxil each day. At bedtime, she can only fall asleep by taking Catapres.

Kayla has a very serious psychiatric problem that fits the criteria of a few psychiatric disorders. There are no studies of adolescents taking this regimen of medicines. In fact, there are only a few studies of adolescents taking these medicines individually, and studies proving that they help are even harder to find. If these medicines work for Kayla, however, there is a high benefit, possibly lifesaving. Though theoretically these medicines should not interact, because of the lack of information, the risk is also relatively high. However, the risk of not prescribing medicine to Kayla is that she continues on her current road. Although she might turn herself around without medicine, there is a good chance she would be headed for a lifetime of serious problems.

The Four Pitfalls
of Evaluating Risks and Benefits

In deciding where your child is on the grid, beware of four major pitfalls.

Underestimating the Benefit of Medicine

Psychiatric disorders are not inevitable stages of life. They are painful and carry significant risk. When you evaluate the benefit of medicine, do not underestimate the long-term deleterious effect of untreated psychiatric disorders and the potential benefit of ameliorating them. Although definitive research proving the long-term benefit of medicine is not yet available, many children with psychiatric disorders grow up to be adults with these disorders and are prone to debilitating outcomes. The potential benefit of medicine should not be underestimated.

Do not underestimate the positive effect of medicine on the entire family. Sometimes children with psychiatric disorders can initiate a cascade of anger that ripples through the entire house. Siblings are affected, and marital tension rises. Likewise, do not underestimate the extent to which medicine can help relationships with peers or teachers. Getting along with peers is an important goal of childhood. Being labeled the class "troublemaker" is a risk in itself. If your child's teacher is better able to teach him or her, your child benefits.

Overestimating the Benefit of Medicine

Medicine can be seen as a panacea, the all-powerful intervention that will eliminate all your child's problems. No medicine is so powerful. Although the effects of medicine can be dramatic, do not expect them to be. Children with psychiatric disorders are prone to having difficulties in a variety of spheres. Medicine does not necessarily address them all. By overestimating the benefit of medicine, the role of the environment is underestimated. The powerful effect of parents and teachers should not be overlooked. Children also mature and shed some difficulties as they get older, whether through learning or the maturation of neurons.

Underestimating the Risk of Medicine

Today's medicines can be so easy to use that we risk forgetting that we are living on the frontier, often prescribing medicines for which we have only a modest amount of information. Rare side effects do happen, and they are usually impossible to predict. The newer the medicine or the more complicated the combination of medicines, the lower our certainty about side effects. Although medicines like Ritalin have been around for decades and prescribed for thousands and thousands of children, many of the medicines we prescribe are not well studied in children. The knowledge we extrapolate from studies in adults is only sometimes accurate for children. One should never be cavalier.

Overestimating the Risk of Medicine

Although there is much to be learned, we have extensive experience with some medicines. We can weigh the likelihood of most side effects, the overwhelming majority of which are reversible and not dangerous. Parents sometimes worry excessively about side effects that are unwanted but not dangerous. Being overly cautious can be as detrimental as being cavalier.

Communicating With Your Child

After you've evaluated the more obvious risks and benefits of medicine, consider its more subtle effects. When medicine is virtually mandatory, these considerations carry less weight. However, when the benefit is relatively low, these subtleties are more important.

Try to imagine the hidden messages your child receives by taking medicine. These will, in part, be a function of how the decision to use medicine is communicated to your child. Children expect their parents to make decisions about them, so it is not necessary to give your child a vote in the decision to take medicine, though asking for his or her thoughts is certainly respectful. If your words or tone of voice imply that the goal of medicine is to control his or her bad behavior, your child will be understandably offended.

Your child will more readily accept an explanation that implies that medicine will help him or her deal with the underlying biological style that serves the child well in some circumstances but not in others. For example, a child who understands that his impulsivity is the foundation of his spontaneity, but that he needs help controlling this characteristic in school, will see the medicine as an aid. It is not the enemy whose existence proves his guilt.

Sometimes explaining the medicine as treatment for an underlying disorder is important. Children often manage the idea of having a disorder if it is explained properly. Your doctor can be of help in explaining symptoms, diagnosis, and medicine to your child, but parents should decide what is appropriate for the child to know.

Your child should see the medicine as helping him or her to be who he or she is capable of being, not as a means to control his or her faults. Your child should not see the medicine as implying that he or she is bad, crazy, or dumb. Your child's view of himself or herself, in other words, should not be compromised.

Adolescents, on the other hand, often like to have a say in elective matters. They require the same style of explanation in age-appropriate terms. But after you've put forth your best explanation, some older adolescents then vote down your plan. When an adolescent feels strongly about elective medicine, it is often prudent to give him or her the final say. Some adolescents decline medicine, then request it a few years later.

Regardless of your child's age, consider the attitude you are communicating about managing life's adversities. Does your attitude convey that life's solutions are found in a pill, or that when necessary people can use medicine as a tool to help them adapt?

Ultimately, communicate your unconditional acceptance to your child. Although your child is responsible for the behavior he or she can control, the goal of taking medicine is to help the child manage what is beyond his or her control. Your child should not feel that you are a discontented parent trying to change the essence of who he or she is.

The Ten Commandments of Medicine

Some parents will decide fairly readily that medicine is the proper next step for their child. Other parents will struggle with the decision after weighing its risks and benefits against those of other treatments, including the possibility of not treating. However, the following rules are relevant to all.

1. Have your child appropriately evaluated by a trusted professional.* Be guided by your doctor's clinical judgment, not your own reading of *DSM-IV*. Don't be disappointed if your child does not fit neatly into a specific diagnosis. Instead, accept the use of comorbid, or coexisting, diagnoses or "not otherwise specified" (NOS) diagnoses, and spend your effort assessing your child's functional difficulties.

2. Before jumping to medicine as the answer, ask whether changing your child's environment would be helpful. Sometimes this takes time, patience, and a willingness to change your parenting style. Other times it means changing the teacher's

---

*A psychiatric evaluation tries to fit the child into the symptom profile of a particular psychiatric disorder. However, it also tries to understand the child's fit within his or her family, the stresses the child endures, the nature of the child's temperament, and the depth of the child's psychological conflicts. A good evaluation examines medical history, social history, and academic history. The psychiatric history and medication history of family members are also relevant. Sometimes a child is referred for further evaluation to a psychologist, learning specialist, language therapist, occupational therapist, or other specialist. A good evaluation takes longer than a half hour.

expectations or trying to minimize a life stress. Understand whether psychotherapy would be helpful and how.

3. Never use a medicine based simply on your neighbor's response to that medicine. Everyone is different. However, if closely related biological family members have responded to a specific medicine, inform your physician. Sharing similar genes might indicate a greater chance of success or side effects.

4. A diagnosis is not an excuse. Medicine is a tool to help treat a diagnosed biological disorder or symptom. Your child should not fear medicine changing his or her personality and should understand that he or she is still responsible for his or her behavior.

5. Know what you're treating. Know whether you're treating a disorder or a symptom and if the medicine is FDA-approved to treat the disorder or if it's being used off-label. Know the probability of the medicine being effective and the estimated time your child will be taking medicine.

6. Give the medicine time to work. Don't bail out early, fleeing before the medicine has time to act or at the first sign of side effects. Many side effects are mild, not severe or dangerous, and will disappear in time. Beware of polypharmacy (taking multiple psychiatric medicines), especially the adding on of medicine after medicine, having lost sight of the original symptoms. Multiple medicines should be used only under your physician's careful supervision.

7. Medicine must be monitored. Don't avoid your doctor. Make follow-up appointments. You can't expect your doctor to truly know a child he or she rarely sees.* The decision to discontinue medicine should be made with your physician, but if you

---

*Your doctor must see your child to monitor the medicine's effectiveness and side effects as well as to monitor the social, academic, and behavioral difficulties to which children with psychiatric disorders are prone. Parents also need an opportunity to talk about the challenges of parenting.

decide to discontinue medicine, inform your physician so he or she can tell you how to do so safely.*

8. Avoid the medicine "rut"—the use of medicine year after year without reexamining your decision. The decision to continue to use medicine should be an ongoing, dynamic process, based on periodic follow-up discussions between parent and doctor. If you are given a choice of treatments, which treatment you choose is often less important than the need to follow up with your physician and adjust the decision as needed.

9. Parents should present a unified stance about medicine. At the very least, they should not contradict each other. The opinions of disagreeing teachers, grandparents, and housekeepers should be kept in check.

10. Know when to quit your search for the medicine solution. Medicine is not the solution for every problem.

Final Thoughts

Your child is in pain, vulnerable, exposed, at risk. You think of tired, old Dr. Brown saying, "I'm sorry. There's nothing more we can do." No longer. Today we can do. But now that we can help, should we? Are we potentially hurting by helping?

There is no definitive answer to the question of whether a particular child should take any medicine. Parenting is all about using one's best judgment to decide what is in the child's best interest. The decisions are difficult, and the decision-making process is entirely imperfect. Parents will feel the push of benefits and the pull of risks. They will each value different benefits and fear different risks. And then, with their child in the balance, they will decide.

---

* Some medicines must be discontinued gradually to lower the risk of withdrawal side effects and the risk of a return of the disorder. Therefore, always consult your physician before discontinuing medicine.

Are You Wise
If You Try an SSRI?

||||||||||||||||||||||||||||||||||||||||||||||||||||||||||||

When the first edition of this book was published in 2006, the SSRIs had been plastered on the covers of countless newspapers and magazines, accused of causing adolescent suicide. In 2004, the FDA issued an advisory about the use of SSRIs in youth, which was followed by a decline in the number of prescriptions for SSRIs. These events continue to cast a shadow over many parents' decision of whether to allow their child to take an anti-depressant. Let's examine the facts and try to bring some reason to this heated debate.

Just a Little History

As we've already seen, before the 1970s, children were thought to be too young to experience depression, and adolescents seemed capable only of acting out anger against their parents in so-called masked depression. By the 1980s, however, new research showed that depression was not limited to adulthood. Unfortunately, there was no research proving any treatment to be effective in children. The tricyclic antidepressants, which had been proven effective in adult depression, were used in children and teens for lack of a reasonable alternative, but over the years a growing body of research demonstrated that they were no more effective than placebo and carried the risk of side effects, some of which were serious.

In 1988, Prozac was introduced; other SSRIs followed soon thereafter. They seemed to cause fewer side effects than the tricyclics and were not a significant danger if taken in an overdose attempt. Nevertheless, they were new and prescribed without the benefit of accumulated experience. With data from adults and for lack of an alternative, doctors used the medicines to treat young people with depression. Were they effective? Some people improved, but as we've seen, that's not good enough. That's not science. Our friend, Dr. Kaplan from Missouri, would not have been impressed.

Over the past decade, double-blind, placebo-controlled studies showed that some of the SSRIs were effective in treating children and adolescents with depression, obsessive-compulsive disorder, and anxiety disorders. However, a few problems surfaced as well. It came to light that other research with less convincing results was not open to review by physicians or the public. Pharmaceutical companies were accused of showing only the positive results, which would certainly skew a doctor's opinion regarding potential benefits. Medical journals tended to publish studies with positive findings more frequently than those with negative findings. This would also skew opinions unfairly.

Despite these difficulties, after reviewing all the research, the FDA was sufficiently impressed to approve Prozac for the treatment of child and adolescent depression, Lexapro for treatment of adolescent depression, and Luvox, Zoloft, and Prozac for treatment of OCD. The benefits seemed to outweigh the risks. None of these medicines have been FDA-approved for use in children with anxiety disorders, probably because the drug companies have not applied for the approval for treatment of these disorders. Nevertheless, in looking at all the research on the use of the SSRIs in youth, Bridge and colleagues (2007) reported that the SSRIs exert a more powerful effect on youth with anxiety disorders than on those with depression or OCD.

Even before FDA approval, because of the research done in adults and many clinicians' individual experiences with children, the SSRIs had increased in popularity through the 1990s and into the new millenium. They were used for their FDA-indicated purposes—and then some. Concomitant with the increased popularity of SSRIs, the teen suicide rate in the United States diminished by about 25% from 1992 to 2001 (Lubell, Swahn, Crosby, & Kegler, 2004). Some hypothesized that this was, in part, due to the widespread use of the SSRIs.

However, another problem arose. Had the risks of the SSRIs been properly evaluated? As physicians used more of these medicines over a longer period of time, it seemed clear that they were medically safer than their predecessors. Blood pressure was stable. Heart function was unperturbed. The bone marrow kept churning out blood cells as it was supposed to. With more experience, however, psychiatrists noted some unusual behavioral side effects, such as a "who cares?" kind of apathy in a minority of children and an agitated, disinhibited, high-energy excitement, possibly more likely when the dose was increased too quickly. An increase in suicidal thoughts was another possible side effect, perhaps related to the apathy or agitation.

Unfortunately, deciding what constitutes a suicidal thought or act is more difficult than one might think. For example, is a child banging his head against the wall a suicide attempt? Is an angry child yelling "I wish I was dead" a statement of suicidal intent? A varying threshold for what was labeled "suicidality" would change the risk assessment dramatically.

All of these issues eventually came to a head. There were a lot of accusations and attempts to clarify, but, for our purposes, let's use the known data to answer the frequently asked questions about the SSRIs.

A Primer on the Danger of SSRIs

Do children and adolescents benefit from the SSRIs? Yes. Even though there are negative findings, sufficient short-term studies have demonstrated that some of these medicines are more effective than placebo in some disorders in children and adolescents. All the SSRIs are not effective in all disorders, although for some disorders, such as anxiety disorders, a number of different SSRIs have proven useful. For other disorders, such as depression, some feel that only Prozac and Lexapro have been sufficiently proven to be effective. Moreover, not all youth respond. For some disorders, such as depression, the evidence is clearer for adolescents than children. But the FDA findings of efficacy stand. Further research will bring greater knowledge about which medicines are effective for which disorders.

Are there risks associated with the SSRIs? Yes. Like any medicine, the SSRIs have side effects. The overwhelming majority of these side effects, however, are reversible, are not acutely dangerous, and occur in a minority of patients.

Are all the side effects known? No. There is always more information that we would like. These medicines have been around for about 20 years and used in treating children for only part of that time. Knowledge of side effects, particularly rare side effects, will increase as more children and adolescents use the medicine. In addition, the known behavioral side effects can be vague and sometimes difficult to distinguish from the patient's symptoms of anxiety or depression.

Are the side effects nuisance-level, or are they lethal, irreversible, or very painful? Although the overwhelming majority of side effects are at the nuisance level, the possibility of new suicidal thoughts or behaviors certainly raises the question of lethality. Of note, when researchers reviewed the accumulated data from all the research studies, which included approximately 4,400 children and adolescents who took SSRIs and other antidepressants, there were occurrences of new suicidal thoughts and behaviors but no completed suicides.

Parents of children who have committed suicide have blamed the SSRIs. But just as the single child or small group of children who respond positively to medicine does not prove its efficacy, the single child or small group of children who commit suicide does not prove the medicine's guilt. That is not to diminish the devastating pain suffered by the child and family, but it does not prove causality. It is possible that a completed suicide is so rare that, even if caused by the medicine, more than 4,400 patients would have to be studied before one would discover a patient whose SSRI use had caused suicide.

What is the probability of new suicidal thoughts or behaviors? Remember, knowing possibility without probability is virtually useless information. Researchers found that approximately 1% to 2% of children taking placebo experienced new suicidal thoughts or acts and that about 3% to 4% of the group of children taking antidepressants experienced new suicidal thoughts or acts, though there was some variability in the probability among the different antidepressants, and Bridge and colleagues (2007) found the relative suicide risk of taking medicine even lower. That means the risk of this side effect for those taking medicine is about twice that for those taking placebo. It also means that of 100 depressed or anxious children and adolescents, approximately 1 or 2 of them will experience new suicidal thoughts or make some suicidal act *because* of the medicine (as half of the 3% to 4% would have experienced new suicidal thoughts or made some suicidal act even if taking placebo). Given that there were no completed suicides, the chances of the medicine causing a completed suicide act seem to be significantly smaller than that.

Do these children need to be followed closely? Absolutely. These children need to be followed because they have a dangerous psychiatric disorder that puts them at risk for suicide. They also need to be followed because they are on a psychiatric medicine that, like all psychiatric medicines, is not completely understood. This is why one needs an ongoing, working relationship with one's physician.

Where does all this leave the individual parent and society as a whole? It is clear to most physicians that the observable successes by a significant handful of well-done studies prove the benefit of SSRIs for some patients with some disorders. With suicide as the third leading cause of death in older adolescents, the majority of whom have depression or an anxiety disorder (Shaffer et al., 1996), most physicians see the SSRIs as a godsend. If the SSRIs are even in part responsible for the decreased suicide rate, many lives have been saved because of these medicines. The help they have given some patients with obsessive-compulsive disorder and other anxiety disorders has been life-altering. Overall, most physicians believe the benefits of SSRIs clearly outweigh the risks.

It is also clear to most physicians that the SSRIs can affect some patients in ways that are more difficult to assess. These include the apathy and agitation noted earlier. The factors determining these side effects need to be better understood. Some patients seem to become more anxious or agitated if the medicine is used at too high a dose or if the dose is increased too quickly. Others seem to experience a side effect like apathy only after months of being on the medicine. And a better understanding of side effects is not confined to the behavioral or psychological. For example, one group of researchers reported growth problems in four children taking SSRIs (Weintrob, Cohen, Klipper-Aurbach, Zadik, & Dickerman, 2002). If this turns out to be caused by the medicine, we will need a thorough understanding of this consequence, including how rare a side effect this is. There is much more to be learned.

The SSRIs need to remain a part of our collection of tools for treating children and adolescents until better treatments come along. These medicines, like all medicines, need to be treated seriously and used only when necessary. Parents need to evaluate the risks and benefits and the probability of each for their child. Physicians need to evaluate their patients carefully before prescribing and follow them diligently during treatment.

Brand Names and Generic Names of Medicines Used in this Book

||||||||||||||||||||||||||||||||||||||||||||||||||||||||||||||||||||||

ADHD Medicines

Brand Names	Generic Names
Ritalin	methylphenidate
Focalin	dexmethylphenidate
Concerta	methylphenidate
Adderall	mixed amphetamine salts
Dexedrine	d-amphetamine
Vyvanse	lisdexamfetamine
Strattera	atomoxetine
Catapres	clonidine
Kapvay	clonidine
Tenex	guanfacine
Intuniv	guanfacine

Anti-depressant/anti-anxiety medicines

Brand Names	Generic Names
Prozac	fluoxetine
Zoloft	sertraline
Paxil	paroxetine

Luvox	fluvoxamine
Lexapro	escitalopram
Wellbutrin	bupropion
Effexor	venlafaxine
Tofranil	imipramine
Norpramin	desipramine
Parnate	tranylcypromine

Anti-psychotic Medicines

Brand Names	Generic Names
Risperdal	risperidone
Zyprexa	olanzapine
Seroquel	quetiapine
Abilify	aripiprazole
Haldol	haloperidol
Orap	pimozide

Mood Stabilizers

Brand Names	Generic Names
Depakote	valproate
Tegretol	carbamazepine
Lamictal	lamotrigine
Topomax	topiramate
Trileptal	oxcarbazepine

Anti-anxiety Medicines

Brand Names	Generic Names
Xanax	alprazolam
Klonopin	clonazepam
Valium	diazepam

Recommended Reading

||||||||||||||||||||||||||||||||||||||||||||||||||||||||||||||||

There are many books about diagnosing and treating the psychiatric disorders of children. The following is not a comprehensive list. Rather, this is an array of books, written by reliable authors, that capture child psychiatry today.

American Academy of Child and Adolescent Psychiatry. Pruitt, D. B. (Ed.). (1998). *Your child: Emotional, behavioral, and cognitive development from birth through preadolescence.* New York: HarperCollins.

American Academy of Child and Adolescent Psychiatry. Pruitt, D. B. (Ed.). (1999). *Your adolescent: Emotional, behavioral, and cognitive development from early adolescence through the teen years.* New York: HarperCollins.

Birmaher, B. (2004). *New hope for children and teens with bipolar disorder.* New York: Three Rivers.

Carey, W. B. (1997). *Understanding your child's temperament.* New York: Macmillan.

Diller, L. H. (1998). *Running on Ritalin: A physician reflects on children, society, and performance in a pill.* New York: Bantam.

Haerle, T. (Ed.). (1992). *Children with Tourette syndrome: A parents' guide.* Rockville, MD: Woodbine House.

Hallowell, E. M., & Ratey, J. J. (1994). *Driven to distraction: Recognizing and coping with attention deficit disorder.* New York: Simon & Schuster.

Kalikow, K. T. (2011). *Kids on meds: Up-to-date information about the most commonly prescribed psychiatric medications.* New York: Norton.

Koplewicz, H. S. (1996). *It's nobody's fault: New hope and help for difficult children and their parents.* New York: Times Books.

Koplewicz, H. S. (2002). *More than moody: Recognizing and treating adolescent depression.* New York: Perigree Books.

March, J. S., & Mulle, K. (1998). *OCD in children and adolescents: A cognitive-behavioral treatment manual.* New York: Guilford.

Owens, J. A., & Mindell, J. A. (2005). *Take charge of your child's sleep: The all-in-one resource for solving sleep problems in kids and teens.* New York: Marlowe.

Rapoport, J. L. (1989). *The boy who couldn't stop washing: The experience and treatment of obsessive compulsive disorder.* New York: Dutton.

REFERENCES

‖‖‖

Abikoff, H., Hechtman, L., Klein, R. G., Weiss, G., Fleiss, K., Etcovitch, J., et al. (2004). Symptomatic improvement in children with ADHD treated with long-term methylphenidate and multimodal psychosocial treatment. *Journal of the American Academy of Child and Adolescent Psychiatry, 43*, 802–11.

Althoff, R. R., Verhulst, F. C., Rettew, D. C., Hudziak, J. J., & van der Ende, J. (2010). Adult outcomes of childhood dysregulation: A 14-year follow-up study. *Journal of the American Academy of Child and Adolescent Psychiatry, 49*, 1105–1116.

Ambrosini, P. J., Wagner, K. D., Biederman, J., Glick, I., Tan, C., Elia, J., et al. (1999). Multicenter open-label sertraline study in adolescent outpatients with major depression. *Journal of the American Academy of Child and Adolescent Psychiatry, 38*, 566–72.

American Psychiatric Association. (1968). *Diagnostic and statistical manual of mental disorders* (2nd ed.). Washington, DC: Author.

American Psychiatric Association. (1980). *Diagnostic and statistical manual of mental disorders* (3rd ed.). Washington, DC: Author.

American Psychiatric Association. (1987). *Diagnostic and statistical manual of mental disorders* (3rd ed., Rev.). Washington, DC: Author.

American Psychiatric Association. (1994). *Diagnostic and statistical manual of mental disorders* (4th ed.). Washington, DC: Author.

Angold, A., Erkanli, A., Egger, H. L., & Costello, E. J. (2000). Stimulant treatment for children: A community perspective. *Journal of the American Academy of Child and Adolescent Psychiatry, 39*, 975–84.

References

Aylward, E. H., Richards, T. L., Berninger, V. W., Nagy, W. E., Field, K. M., Grimme, A. C., et al. (2003). Instructional treatment associated with changes in brain activation in children with dyslexia. *Neurology, 61,* 212–19.

Baxter, L. R., Schwartz, J. M., Bergman, K. S., Szuba, M. P., Guze, B. H., Mazziotta, J. C., et al. (1992). Caudate glucose metabolic rate changes with both drug and behavior therapy for obsessive-compulsive disorder. *Archives of General Psychiatry, 49,* 681–89.

Berard, R., Fong, R., Carpenter, D., Thomason, C., Wilkinson, C. (2006) An international, multicenter, placebo-controlled trial of paroxetine in adolescents with major depressive disorder. *Journal of Child and Adolescent Psychopharmacology, 16, 59-75.*

Birmaher, B., Ryan, N. D., Williamson, D. E., Brent, D. A., Kaufman, J., Dahl, R. E., et al. (1996). Childhood and adolescent depression: A review of the past 10 years; part I. *Journal of the American Academy of Child and Adolescent Psychiatry, 35,* 1427–39.

Bridge, J. A., Iyengar, S., Salary, C. B., Barbe, R. P., Birmaher, B., Pincus, H. A., et al. (2007). Clinical response and risk for reported suicidal ideation and suicide attempts in pediatric antidepressant treatment. *Journal of the American Medical Association, 297,* 1683–96.

Brotman, M. A., Kassem, L., Reising, M. M., Guyer, A. E., Dickstein, D. P., Rich, B. A., et al. (2007). Parental diagnoses in youth with narrow phenotype bipolar disorder or severe mood dysregulation. *American Journal of Psychiatry, 164,* 1238–1241.

Conners, C. K., Casat, C. D., Gualtieri, C. T., Weller, E., Reader, M., Reiss, A., et al. (1996). Bupropion hydrochloride in attention deficit disorder with hyperactivity. *Journal of the American Academy of Child and Adolescent Psychiatry, 35,* 1314–21.

Connor, D. F., Fletcher, K. E., & Swanson, J. M. (1999). A meta-analysis of clonidine for symptoms of attention-deficit hyperactivity disorder. *Journal of the American Academy of Child and Adolescent Psychiatry, 38,* 1551–59.

Curry, J., Silva, S., Rohde, P., Ginsburg, G., Kratochvil, C., Simons, A., et al. (2011). Recovery and recurrence following treatment for adolescent major depression. *Archives of General Psychiatry, 68,* 263–70.

Dailey, L. F., Townsend, S. W., Dysken, M. W., & Kuskowski, M. A. (2005). Recidivism in medication-noncompliant serious juvenile offenders with bipolar disorder. *Journal of Clinical Psychiatry, 66,* 477–84.

DiScala, C., Lescohier, I., Barthel, M., & Li, G. (1998). Injuries to children with attention deficit hyperactivity disorder. *Pediatrics, 102,* 1415–21.

...eis, S., Zito, J. M., Safer, D. J., Gardner, J. F., Puccia, K. B., & Owens, L. (2005). Multiple psychotropic medication use for youths: A two-state comparison. *Journal of Child and Adolescent Psychopharmacology, 15,* 68–77.

Duffy, F. F., Narrow, W. E., Rae, D. S., West, J. C., Zarin, D. A., Rubio-Stipec, M., et al. (2005). Concomitant pharmacotherapy among youths treated in routine psychiatric practice. *Journal of Child and Adolescent Psycho-pharmacology, 15,* 12–25.

Elia, J., Ambrosini, P. J., & Rapoport, J. L. (1999). Drug therapy: Treatment of attention-deficit-hyperactivity disorder. *New England Journal of Medicine, 340,* 780–88.

Emslie, G. J., Heiligenstein, J. H., Hoog, S. L., Wagner, K. D., Findling, R. L., McCracken, J. T., et al. (2004). Fluoxetine treatment for prevention of relapse of depression in children and adolescents: A double-blind, placebo-controlled study. *Journal of the American Academy of Child and Adolescent Psychiatry, 43,* 1397–1405.

Emslie, G. J., Rush, A. J., Weinberg, W. A., Kowatch, R. A., Hughes, C. W., Carmody, T., et al. (1997). A double-blind, randomized, placebo-controlled trial of fluoxetine in children and adolescents with depression. *Archives of General Psychiatry, 54,* 1031–37.

Ferro, T., Carlson, G. A., Grayson, P., & Klein, D. N. (1994). Depressive disorders: Distinctions in children. *Journal of the American Academy of Child and Adolescent Psychiatry, 33,* 664–70.

Findling, R. L., McNamara, N. K., Youngstrom, E. A., Branicky, L. A., Demeter, C. A., & Schulz, S. C. (2003). A prospective, open-label trial of olanzapine in adolescents with schizophrenia. *Journal of the American Academy of Child and Adolescent Psychiatry, 42,* 170–75.

Fleming, J. E., Boyle, M. H., & Offord, D. R. (1993). The outcome of adolescent depression in the Ontario Child Health Study follow-up. *Journal of the American Academy of Child and Adolescent Psychiatry, 32,* 28–33.

Froehlich, T. E., Lanphear, B. P., Epstein, J. N., Barbaresi, W. J., Katusic, S. K., & Kahn, R. S. (2007). Prevalence, recognition, and treatment of attention-deficit/hyperactiviey disorder in a national sample of US children. *Archives of Pediatric and Adolescent Medicine, 161,* 857–64.

Garber, J., Kriss, M. R., Koch, M., & Lindholm, L. (1988). Recurrent depression in adolescents: A follow-up study. *Journal of the American Academy of Child and Adolescent Psychiatry, 27,* 49–54.

Geller, D. A., Hoog, S. L., Heiligenstein, J. H., Ricardi, R. K., Tamura, R.,

Kluszynski, S., et al. (2001). Fluoxetine treatment for obsessive-compulsive disorder in children and adolescents: A placebo-controlled clinical trial. *Journal of the American Academy of Child and Adolescent Psychiatry, 40*, 773–79.

Gibbons, R. D., Hur, K., Bhaumik, D. K., & Mann, J. J. (2005). The relationship between antidepressant medication use and rate of suicide. *Archives of General Psychiatry, 62*, 165–72.

Harrington, R., Fudge, H., Rutter, M., Pickles, A., & Hill, J. (1990). Adult outcomes of childhood and adolescent depression. *Archives of General Psychiatry, 47*, 465–73.

Hechtman, L. (2004). Long-term stimulant effects in children with attention deficit hyperactivity disorder (ADHD). *Child and Adolescent Psychopharmacology News, 9*(1), 1–6.

Hechtman, L., Weiss, G., & Perlman, T. (1984). Young adult outcome of hyperactive children who received long-term stimulant treatment. *Journal of the American Academy of Child Psychiatry, 23*, 261–69.

Hunkeler, E. M., Fireman, B., Lee, J., Diamond, R., Hamilton, J., He, C. X., et al. (2005). Trends in use of antidepressants, lithium, and anticonvulsants in Kaiser Permanente–insured youths, 1994–2003. *Journal of Child and Adolescent Psychopharmacology, 15*, 26–37.

Jensen, P., Kettle, L., Roper, M. T., Sloan, M. T., Dulcan, M. K., Hoven, C. et al. (1999). Are stimulants overprescribed? Treatment of ADHD in four US communities. *Journal of the American Academy of Child and Adolescent Psychiatry, 38*, 797–804.

Keller, M. B., Ryan, N. D., Strober, M., Klein, R. G., Kutcher, S. P., Birmaher, B., et al. (2001). Efficacy of paroxetine in the treatment of adolescent major depression: A randomized, controlled trial. *Journal of the American Academy of Child and Adolescent Psychiatry, 40*, 762–72.

Kovacs, M., Akiskal, H. S., Gatsonis, C., & Parrone, P. L. (1994). Childhood-onset dysthymic disorder: Clinical features and prospective naturalistic outcome. *Archives of General Psychiatry, 51*, 365–74.

Kovacs, M., Feinberg, T. L., Crouse-Novak, M. A., Paulauskas, S. L., & Finkelstein, R. (1984). Depressive disorders in childhood: I. A longitudinal prospective study of characteristics and recovery. *Archives of General Psychiatry, 41*, 229–37.

Kovacs, M., Feinberg, T. L., Crouse-Novak, M. A., Paulauskas, S. L., Pollack, M., & Finkelstein, R. (1984). Depressive disorders in childhood: II. A longitudinal study of the risk for a subsequent major depression. *Archives of General Psychiatry, 41*, 643–49.

Kovacs, M., Goldston, D., & Gatsonis, C. (1993). Suicidal behaviors and childhood-onset depressive disorders: A longitudinal investigation. *Journal of the American Academy of Child and Adolescent Psychiatry, 32*, 8–20.

Kumra, S., Frazier, J. A., Jacobsen, L. K., McKenna, K., Gordon, C. T., Lenane, M. C., et al. (1996). Childhood-onset schizophrenia: A double-blind clozapine-haloperidol comparison. *Archives of General Psychiatry, 53*, 1090–97.

Lasser, K. E., Allen, P. D., Woolhandler, S. J., Himmelstein, D. U., Wolfe, S. M., & Bor, D. H. (2002). Timing of new black box warnings and withdrawals for prescription medications. *Journal of the American Medical Association, 287*, 2215–20.

Leibson, C. L., Katusic, S. K., Barbaresi, W. J., Ransom, B. S., & O'Brien, P. C. (2001). Use and costs of medical care for children and adolescents with and without attention-deficit/hyperactivity disorder. *Journal of the American Medical Association, 285*, 60–66.

Levin, A. (June 5, 2009). Early experiences change DNA and thus gene expression. *Psychiatric News, 11*, 18.

Lewinsohn, P. M., Clarke, G. N., Seeley, J. R., & Rohde, P. (1994). Major depression in community adolescents: Age at onset, episode duration, and time to recurrence. *Journal of the American Academy of Child and Adolescent Psychiatry, 33*, 809–18.

Lubell, K. M., Swahn, M. H., Crosby, A. E., & Kegler, S. R. (2004). Methods of suicide among persons aged 10–19 years—United States, 1992–2001. *Centers for Disease Control and Prevention Morbidity and Mortality Weekly Report, 53*, 471–73.

March, J. S., Biederman, J., Wolkow, R., Safferman, A., Mardekian, J., Cook, E. H., et al. (1998). Sertraline in children and adolescents with obsessive-compulsive disorder. *Journal of the American Medical Association, 280*, 1752–56.

March, J., Silva, S., Petrycki, S., Curry, J., Wells, K., Fairbank, J., et al. (2004). Fluoxetine, cognitive-behavioral therapy, and their combination for adolescents with depression. *Journal of the American Medical Association, 292*, 807–20.

March, J. S., Silva, S., Petrycki, S., Curry, J., Wells, K., Fairbank, J., et al. (2007). The Treatment for Adolescents with Depression Study (TADS): Long-term effectiveness and safety outcomes. *Archives of General Psychiatry, 64*, 1132–1143.

McCracken, J. T., McGough, J., Shah, B., Cronin, P., Hong, D., Aman, M. G., et al. (2002). Risperidone in children with autism and serious behavioral problems. *New England Journal of Medicine, 347*, 314–21.

McDougle, C. J., Scahill, L., Aman, M. G., McCracken, J. T., Tierney, E., Davies, M., et al. (2005). Risperidone for the core symptom domains of autism: Results from the Study by the Autism Network of the Research Units on Pediatric Psychopharmacology. *American Journal of Psychiatry, 162*, 1142–48.

McKenzie, I., & Wurr, C. (2004). Diagnosing and treating attentional difficulties: A nationwide survey. *Archives of Disease in Childhood, 89*, 913–16.

Meier, B. (2004, June 3). Medicine's data gap: Selective disclosure; Two studies, two results, and a debate over a drug. *The New York Times*.

Metzl, J. D., Small, E., Levine, S. R., & Gershel, J. C. (2001). Creatine use among young athletes. *Pediatrics, 108*, 421–25.

Molina, B. S. G., Hinshaw, S. P., Swanson, J. M., Arnold, L. E., Vitiello, B., Jensen, P. S., et al. (2009). The MTA at 8 years: Prospective follow-up of children treated for combined-type ADHD in a multisite study. *Journal of the American Academy of Child and Adolescent Psychiatry, 48*, 484–500.

The MTA Cooperative Group. (1999). A fourteen-month randomized clinical trial of treatment strategies for attention-deficit/hyperactivity disorder. *Archives of General Psychiatry, 56*, 1073–86.

Guthrie, D. (1990). The history of medicine and surgery: Medicine and surgery before 1800-The roots of western medicine. In The new encyclopaedia britannica, Vol. 23, pp. 888-894[KK2][KK3],.[CR4]

Olfson, M., Blanco, C., Liu, L., Moreno, C., & Laje, G. (2006). National trends in the outpatient treatment of children and adolescents with antipsychotic drugs. *Archives of General Psychiatry, 63*, 679–85.

Olfson, M., Gameroff, M. J., Marcus, S. C., & Waslick, B. D. (2003). Outpatient treatment of child and adolescent depression in the United States. *Archives of General Psychiatry, 60*, 1236–42.

Olfson, M., Marcus, S. C., Weissman, M. M., & Jensen, P. S. (2002). National trends in the use of psychotropic medications by children. *Journal of the American Academy of Child and Adolescent Psychiatry, 41*, 514–21.

Olfson, M., Shaffer, D., Marcus, S. C., & Greenberg, T. (2003). Relationship between antidepressant medication treatment and suicide in adolescents. *Archives of General Psychiatry, 60*, 978–82.

Patel, N. C., Crimson, M. L., Hoagwood, K., Johnsrud, M. T., Rascati, K. L., Wilson, J. P., et al. (2005). Trends in the use of typical and atypical antipsychotics in children and adolescents. *Journal of the American Academy of Child and Adolescent Psychiatry, 44*, 548–56.

Pediatric OCD Treatment Study (POTS) Team. (2004). Cognitive-behavior therapy, sertraline, and their combination for children and adolescents with obsessive-compulsive disorder: The Pediatric OCD Treatment Study (POTS) Randomized Controlled Trial. *Journal of the American Medical Association, 292,* 1969–76.

Pine, D. S., Cohen, P., Gurley, D., Brook, J., & Ma, Y. (1998). The risk for early-adulthood anxiety and depressive disorders in adolescents with anxiety and depressive disorders. *Archives of General Psychiatry, 55,* 56–64.

Rapoport, J. L., Buchsbaum, M. S., Weingartner, H., Zahn, T. P., Ludlow, C., & Mikkelsen, E. J. (1980). Dextroamphetamine: Its cognitive and behavioral effects in normal and hyperactive boys and normal men. *Archives of General Psychiatry, 37,* 933–43.

Reich, W., Huang, H., & Todd, R. D. (2006). ADHD medication use in a population-based sample of twins. *Journal of the American Academy of Child and Adolescent Psychiatry, 45,* 801–07.

Ressler, K. J., Rothbaum, B. O., Tannenbaum, L., Anderson, P., Graap, K., Zimand, E., et al. (2004). Cognitive enhancers as adjuncts to psychotherapy. *Archives of General Psychiatry, 61,* 1136–44.

Riddle, M. A., Reeve, E. A., Yaryura-Tobias, J. A., Yang, H. M., Claghorn, J. L., Gaffney, G., et al. (2001). Fluvoxamine for children and adolescents with obsessive-compulsive disorder: A randomized, controlled, multicenter trial. *Journal of the American Academy of Child and Adolescent Psychiatry, 40,* 222–29.

Roth, T. L., Lubin, F. D., Funk, A. J., & Sweatt, J. D. (2009). Lasting epigenetic influence of early-life adversity on the BDNF gene. *Biological Psychiatry, 65,* 760–69.

Rowe, R., Maughan, B., & Goodman, R. (2004). Childhood psychiatric disorder and unintentional injury: Findings from a national cohort study. *Journal of Pediatric Psychology, 29,* 119–30.

Rushton, J. L., & Whitmire, J. T. (2001). Pediatric stimulant and selective serotonin reuptake inhibitor prescription trends: 1992 to 1998. *Archives of Pediatrics and Adolescent Medicine, 155,* 560–65.

Rynn, M. A., Siqueland, L., & Rickels, K. (2001). Placebo-controlled trial of sertraline in the treatment of children with generalized anxiety disorder." *American Journal of Psychiatry, 158,* 2008–14.

Shaffer, D., Gould, M. S., Fisher, P., Trautman, P., Moreau, D., Kleinman, M., et al. (1996). Psychiatric diagnosis in child and adolescent suicide. *Archives of General Psychiatry, 53,* 339–48.

Shaw, P., Gilliam, M., Liverpool, M., Weddle, C., Malek, M., Sharp, W., Green-stein, D., Evans, A., Rapoport, J., Giedd, J. (2011). Cortical development in typically developing children with symptoms of hyperactivity and impulsivity: support for a dimensional view of attention deficit hyperactivity disorder. *American Journal of Psychiatry, 168, 143-151.*

Spencer, T., Biederman, J., Wilens, T., Harding, M., O'Donnell, D., & Griffin, S. (1996). Pharmacotherapy of attention-deficit hyperactivity disorder across the life cycle. *Journal of the American Academy of Child and Adolescent Psychiatry, 35,* 409–32.

Staller, J. A., Wade, M. J., & Baker, M. (2005). Current prescribing patterns in outpatient child and adolescent psychiatric practice in Central New York. *Journal of Child and Adolescent Psychopharmacology, 15,* 57–61.

Visser, S. N., Lesesne, C. A., & Perou, R. (2007). National estimates and factors associated with medication treatment for childhood attention-deficit/hyperactivity disorder. *Pediatrics, 119*(Suppl. 1), S99–S106.

Vitiello, B., Zuvekas, S. H., & Norquist, G. S. (2006). National estimates of antidepressant medication use among US children: 1997–2002. *Journal of the American Academy of Child and Adolescent Psychiatry, 45,* 271–79.

Wagner, K. D., Berard, R., Stein, M. B., Wetherhold, E., Carpenter, D. J., Perera, P., et al. (2004). A multicenter, randomized, double-blind, placebo-controlled trial of paroxetine in children and adolescents with social anxiety disorder. *Archives of General Psychiatry, 61,* 1153–62.

Walkup, J. T., Albano, A. M., Piacentini, J., Birmaher, B., Compton, S. N., Sherrill, J. T., et al. (2008). Cognitive behavioral therapy, sertraline, or a combination in childhood anxiety. *New England Journal of Medicine, 359,* 2753–2766.

Walkup, J. T., Labellarte, M. J., Riddle, M. A., Pine, D. S., Greenhill, L., Klein, R., et al. (2001). Fluvoxamine for the treatment of anxiety disorders in children and adolescents. *New England Journal of Medicine, 344,* 1279–85.

Weintrob, N., Cohen, D., Klipper-Aurbach, Y., Zadik, Z., & Dickerman, Z. (2002). Decreased growth during therapy with selective serotonin reuptake inhibitors. *Archives of Pediatrics and Adolescent Medicine, 156,* 696–701.

Wilens, T. E., & Biederman, J. (1992). The stimulants. *Psychiatric Clinics of North America, 15*(1), 191–222.

Wilens, T. E., Faraone, S. V., Biederman, J., & Gunawardene, S. (2003). Does stimulant therapy of attention-deficit/hyperactivity disorder beget later substance abuse? A meta-analytic review of the literature. *Pediatrics, 111*, 179–85.

Zito, J. M., Safer, D. J., dosReis, S., Gardner, J. F., Boles, M., & Lynch, F. (2000). Trends in the prescribing of psychotropic medications to pre-schoolers. *Journal of the American Medical Association, 283*, 1025–30.

Zito, J. M., Safer, D. J., dosReis, S., Gardner, J. F., Soeken, K., Boles, M., et al. (2002). Rising prevalence of antidepressants among US youths. *Pediatrics, 109*, 721–27.

INDEX